About the Author

Liam Thomas is a former undercover detective for the Metropolitan Police, where he worked for nearly two decades. In 2018 he was the subject of a documentary for Vice about his life as a detective. He is now an actor, playwright, and screenwriter; he recently produced and appeared in the award-winning short film *The Tide* (which he also wrote), funded by the BFI, a story of place, unravelling identity and mental health within a community fighting for its very existence. He is currently developing a feature-length screenplay.

THE
BUYER

LIAM
THOMAS

1

Ebury Press, an imprint of Ebury Publishing,
20 Vauxhall Bridge Road,
London SW1V 2SA

Ebury Press is part of the Penguin Random House group of companies
whose addresses can be found at global.penguinrandomhouse.com

Penguin
Random House
UK

First published by Ebury Press in 2023
This edition published by Ebury Press in 2024

www.penguin.co.uk

A CIP catalogue record for this book is available from the British Library

ISBN 9781529107685

Printed and bound in Great Britain by Clays Ltd, Elcograf S.p.A.

The authorised representative in the EEA is Penguin Random House Ireland,
Morrison Chambers, 32 Nassau Street, Dublin D02 YH68

Penguin Random House is committed to a sustainable future
for our business, our readers and our planet. This book is made
from Forest Stewardship Council® certified paper.

'Far from being the basis of good society, the family, with its narrow privacy and tawdry secrets, is the source of all our discontents'

Edmund Leach

Prologue: Deployment

The sound of a tape whirrs softly in my head like a lullaby for the damned. A voice, distant, interrupts my concentration; I can't make out who or what it is exactly they are saying, but one word jars. 'Walking?' I try and focus – still I can't quite make out this word. You can suffocate with words in my world, flail in the turbulent froth, because every word is important, the key to your success and survival. An intercept, a tapped phone line, a probe or any form of intelligence 'product' in the covert world, the satellite world of the undercover detective, is important – I learned this early on. Understand . . . Every . . . Single . . . Word . . . One word can change everything. It could potentially fuck everything, fuck you.

But I'm good at this, gathering product, reading, interpreting product. Understanding the game. And yet here I am. Struggling to understand. 'You need to walk, David.'

Who is David? Not one of my names. I had an Uncle David, a tragedy, the death of his firstborn sent him to America, but I never, ever, use family when building a covert identity, known as a legend. What am I doing, what is the job, the commodity?

Throw the words up in the air, decipher and organise, understand the context. It's not always possible to get this right. It is not an exact science, a precise world, but this is my world nevertheless. And it is imprecise, a shadowland, amorphous. Like me. An amorphous man in an ill-defined world. Still the tape whirrs in the quiet fella's head.

'Quiet fella', whispered words uttered by northern mafia, picked up on a surveillance probe and repeated to me by an ops team member with a smile: 'What do you think about him, the quiet fella?', talking about me. What did they think? Did they believe me? I suppose we had to wait and see; you always have to wait. Bide one's time. But this conversation now, I can't quite make it out. Why am I going again, back into the ring? I feel anxious, like there's not enough time, there was never enough time. Not in 'the job'.

I hear him too. *Him*, I do know. *'Focus, you cunt. Focus!'* Always there, my invisible friend, Marv. He's the voice in my head, my invisible voluble friend since childhood – we all have one, right? Marv is mine, at times relentless, but he's right. Best focus on the job, whatever it is, and come back to the words later. I'm anxious because I have to get back to the office, where the job always begins and ends. But I don't have my ID, my warrant card. I'm a detective back from a 'bit of work' – only an idiot takes a warrant card on a bit of work, a dope. Because if they search you, and sometimes they will, then any number of outcomes are possible. I walk quickly, over carbolic washed floors of an anonymous police station. My shoes paradiddle a rhythm to the beat. Who wears Blakey's these days? . . . All the while, these fucking words, in my head, I wish . . .

'Here he is! Just the man we're looking for. Got a job for

you . . .' I recognise him immediately. Not seen him for years but I do know him – his colleague, no – but him, he's . . . *'He's a cunt.'*

'You don't know that.'

'I fuckin' do, he's the one who kicked—' I silence him, Marv. Push Marv and the memory to the back of my mind.

'I'm a bit busy right now, I . . .' I stop mid-sentence. I stop out of curiosity, which as you probably know, has a habit of favouring or damning. 'What is it?'

'Theft. A painting,' he explains. 'One in the pokey. He hasn't coughed, and we've no hands on the painting. It's a still life. Nice tickle for you.' 'Pokey' means an arrest, a man now in the cells. 'Nice tickle' means a plum job, so I fumble for the ID I don't have, smile at the vocabulary favoured by those more keen to swagger with jargon rather than walking among the action.

'Why has he gone all Sweeney, when he's a posho apparatchik?' Marv can't help himself sometimes.

The other guy suddenly opens the security door and gestures me through. Result!

'What's it called? The painting?' I ask.

He looks down at a Manila docket. Haven't seen one of those in years either. *'Serendipity.'*

I step through the open door and smile as it slams shut. It's my favourite word, serendipity. As I try to figure out what I should do next, a distant voice on tape there again, in the background, but now I think I understand . . .

'Are you awake . . . Dada?'

Finally. That one word brings relief, Dada. It is their name for me. I open my eyes. There they stand, brother behind sister. Where the sun rises and sets in an altogether different world.

'Yes, I was dreaming.'

'What about?' asks my son.

'Oh, the past.'

'When you were a policeman, a detective?'

'Mm.'

'Was it a bad dream?' asks my daughter.

'No,' I say. 'No, I had a friend with me.'

She smiles. 'What were you doing?'

'I was . . . looking for something.'

I want to say more, but I don't. Because an undercover detective is recruited in childhood. It just took me some time to understand that.

Mill Town

The back garden of a plain semi-detached house in Failsworth. It is a bone-cold winter's day and I have visited the first house I remember. Standing in the street now, the house still unloved, locked in time and then some, I'm eyed suspiciously as I stare and remember. The iron gates I fell from, breaking an arm, are long gone. If there is love here now, it is probably still thinly spread. Once it was one of a pair of grace-and-favour police houses for rank-and-file police officers, full of cold rooms and linoleum, coal fires and little laughter. I travel back in time and there I am: standing with one of my two brothers, three boys who will always share the one name, 'our kid'. A northern term of endearment. Me and Our Kid are by a bonfire watching our mother, Grace, Ma. She is dancing, happily alone in her thoughts, the Manchester Lewis's cosmetics girl, striking, glamorous, flirtatious. Popular with men, less so with women, Ma sways, a drink in hand, the beat from a record player helping to create the vibe. She has a look on her face that says, don't interrupt this. You come to understand the masks your parents wear. They pass them on – the question is, will you wear them yourself in time, or

will you create your own? Ma moves to the beat as others watch –
she knows she is the centre of attention and doesn't care.

It's bonfire night in Failsworth, and a mixed group of off-duty
cops and neighbours are gathered by the fire. Across the garden
my father Derek, Pa, also stands outside the group, tapped out of
the banter, sipping his drink, observing, as alone with his thoughts
as Ma. He watches her gyrate, crimson lit by the fire. Pa is a dog
handler with the Manchester police at a time when male officers
are recruited for the size of their feet, smile and knuckles. They
are all polished buckles and trilbies, and they are both judge and
jury. Cut and dried.

Police family gathered together, as they always have done –
some things don't change. The banter is fuelled by drink, stoked
with laughter. Me and Our Kid watch the glowing embers rise
into the night sky as we chew on sticks of treacle toffee, a treat,
tray-baked by Pa's mother. Our grandma, the indomitable Florence, has come to visit her latest grandson, come to see her boy,
come to protect the family reputation. As the fire sizzles and
snaps, the adults rich with booze sing and whoop as two effigies
burn on the fire. It is a special celebration, not that we know it, as
we slurp at our toffee, thinking ourselves lucky to have two Guy
Fawkes burning on the fire and wondering why one of them
wears a dress.

Pa's thoughts may be concealed by a smile, but I know that
look, its meaning. Menace. He stands shoulders side on, weight
evenly distributed, set and balanced like the middleweight boxer
he was. The hard man takes a draw on his drink, all the while
wearing that half-smile, the glance, the look. I'm standing next to
Timmy, one of his two German shepherd police dogs. Known

for his nose, able to 'smell an angel's breath in flight'. Pa's other dog, Mac, sits in the pen, his one eye fixed on the gathering. A car crash took the other. Pa had been taking a drunk senior officer home from a councillor's Christmas party in his dog van when it happened. He thanked Pa for keeping *that* out of his accident report but was less impressed with Mac, who bit him on the arse when freed from the wreckage as the officer vomited by a ditch. Mac's ability to 'calm' aggressive suspects saved him following the crash. 'Skin eels with his gob, that dog.'

Timmy's nose had recovered some exhibits in the Moors murders investigation. The Bonfire Night party is celebrating the anniversary of the arrest of Ian Brady and Myra Hindley. Held every year until we leave the fog of Manchester that hides family secrets. In the late autumn chill, Failsworth cheers as the effigies burn and Ma and Pa each wonder what the other knows. Barely settled into their twenties, they don't share in the laughter echoing through the street – they have other things on their mind. The newest addition to the family, my other our kid whom I will call Bruv, sleeps in his cot. Grandma is by his side, also alone with her thoughts, watching down on us from the window, contemplating recent events; we're good *observers* in this family – we say little. There was a knock at the door earlier in the week, an unwelcome visitor, curtly and quickly shooed away from the front door by Grandma before she returned to her ironing. I watched him walk away.

'Who was that man, Grandma?'

'Don't know, chicky, he knocked on the wrong door.'

But I think she does know, and I think the whispers have brought her over the Pennines tonight. A stout, strong, unyielding presence to iron out creases in Pa's police shirts and his relationship. She watches from a window as the adults play their games of bonhomie – she has seen it all before: treacle toffee, sparklers and the odd firework.

My toffee slips from my hand and falls into the fire's edge as the big people sup and sing. I look down, thinking if I reach in quickly and snatch it, it will be fine. Our Kid says nothing – he's the tough one. Nails. He pushes out his hand, offers me his own toffee. I decline. Brothers even then too proud and stupid to accept a kindness. Soon the family will up sticks, move from grey city to grey sea. Overland to Trawler Town, a place of crisp fresh air and occasional fun in the streets, alleyways and beachfronts where I'll always know where Our Kid is, even when we go our own way, separated by the antics of Ma and Pa. He watches in silence, words as always scarce, unnecessary to him, burdened even then by his thoughts. Adults, well-oiled and oblivious to my problem, bop heads as the music energises. Our Kid's look suggests I roll my sleeves up, so as not to mess my coat and avoid a leathering. It's okay, Grandma is here, so we're safe from excessive discipline. All is good.

Aged twelve, Grandma began working in a Lancashire mill. She is stoic, practical, always a calm hand at the tiller, full of love. Along with Ma's sister, Aunt Kath, who is another source of respite and warmth, she offers protection from the worst aspects of difficult times – Ma and Pa's endless battle with each other, both blind to the casualties caught up in their hostilities. Aunt Kath and Grandma possess protective, maternal instincts not present in Ma. They understand the importance to children of nurturing love within the home. There is always laughter within their protective walls. Grandpa, Billy, his entire working life spent on the railways in various capacities, comes home at the end of each week and places his wages on the kitchen table. Never a complaint, happy to let Florence make all key family decisions. Because she really holds everything together. She has raised their three children, sent her daughter to university, first of the family (far smarter than her two boys), and is always willing to offer, insofar as able, financial support she's never known herself. By middle age she owns three small two-up two-down Accrington brick terraced houses, rented out to supplement the family income.

Once, hearing a local builder was planning to build a small terrace of similar houses, she was all for putting down a deposit to buy the whole row. But Grandpa disagreed, the only time in their marriage he refused to take up her idea. She regrets it for the rest of her life and is proved right over time, though never once chides Billy, who has long come to accept her strength: 'See now, Florrie has the vision.' The vision diminishes as her houses are sold off to help her family over the years. She will see out her days in the last of the Accringtons. From her my love of film is born and nurtured. Initially we watch old movies on the TV, Grandma offering a running commentary on stars she first saw at the 'flicks'. Eventually we migrate to the local cinema, the Rialto, a little subterfuge often required to get past the owner whose zealous conviction to a film's age certification is matched only by Grandma's determination to get me in.

'He's a bit on the short side for this, Florrie?'

'He's had a big tea, Mr Barrett. Weighed his knees down.'

'Oh, right . . . One and a half it is then?'

At the end of a screening Mr Barrett always insisted on playing the national anthem, though by the seventies few were inclined to be upstanding. Not Grandma: up she'd shoot, and as I tried to sink into the velour seat, I'd feel a gentle grip on my collar, helping me to rise in unison. It was the same parting words from Mr Barrett for years as we left: 'Night, Florrie . . . How's his knees?'

Her house is an oasis of calm and tranquillity for Our Kid and me, infused with glorious smells from the small bakery next door. We play football in the alley or help Grandpa fight his losing battle with the slugs that attack his vegetable garden. 'That's it, I'm gonna balley marmalise them with salt!' He never did, too gentle to hurt even garden pests. At night I'm tucked in tight under cotton sheets to tales of cotton mills and fall asleep to the chime of their old German Kienzle mantel clock downstairs. Its tick is the first thing I check for on arriving at the house. The soothing metronomic beat signalling all is well while also providing Grandpa with the odd absurd line, 'Bombed us to balley bits, but they know how to fettle a clock, eh?'

'Who?'

'Hitler.'

'Hitler made clocks, Grandpa?'

'No, he made socks, love . . . For marching in.'

Here was the best of sleeps, the best of food, the best of times. When I leave for home, they're always together at the front gate waving, him with a white hankie flapping enthusiastically high in the air until I'm out I'm of sight. Even when I'm older and I cycle over to see them, I can't resist looking over my shoulder to check, and without fail there they are, Grandpa's arm raised, hankie fluttering on the breeze. An innate understanding on his part that all children really want for is security.

Aunt Kath's house in the shadow of the Lancashire coalpits is another sanctuary in the early years. I'm dispatched alone, an 80-minute bus ride towards Wigan – tucked in at the back with a book, the time soon passes. Kath waiting at the bus stop, always dressed the same, hat and coat, rain or shine. Her small end-of-terrace in Bryn Road, the centre of an area known as Little Wales founded in the heart of Lancashire by migrating miners in search of work and full of love. A huge Victorian cooking range and fire dominates the small front room. When I arrive, it's the regular greeting – 'Now, let's have a look at you' – followed by a squeeze of the cheek, a kiss on the top of the head and a quick scan for marks. This began after I travelled with my arm in plaster one time, a genuine accident, but somehow she knows that my bumps and bruises are not always innocently obtained. I'm never sent to Grandma's with a bruise – no hiding the truth there. But here in Little Wales I am a prince. Early mornings are spent accompanying her on her cleaning rounds around central Wigan. Seated in the green leather chairs of the local high and mighty, I read as she sweeps, polishes and sings hymns to me in Welsh. Then it's back home for an Oxo cube in hot water and several slices of bread . . . 'pit broth'. For years I thought it was beef soup. There is Chapel on Sundays, a deafening gusto underpinning the hymns as a competitive edge either side of the aisle, men and women separated, giving full voice to whatever is on their minds. The congregation always appears to me to be in trouble, castigated the moment the minister arrives in the pulpit.

'Why's the vicar angry, Auntie Kath?'

'He's not angry, lovely. It's his tight shoes – feet are unforgiving souls,' she said.

The chapel closed in the nineties, the mines and the congregation long gone, the minister, defiant to the end, insisting on conducting every service in Welsh to the dwindling few. His licence to preach was eventually removed because of this refusal to conduct his service in English. The building now sells carpets and furniture to all, regardless of denomination.

There is also Kath's sister, my Aunt Ceridwen and her Liverpudlian husband Alan, a 'bread man'. We take trips to Goodison Park to watch his football team, Everton. I ride shotgun in his bread van on early morning deliveries. He saunters to and fro, pulling down an imaginary Stetson with the words, 'Okay, kiddah. Let's you and me head out west.'

I love spending time with them, but all is not as it seems. Later, I'll discover we are not in fact related. Over the years, Ma's relationship with her Welsh relatives falters, partly driven by memories of her own unhappy childhood, which she speaks of in mysterious terms. When I learn more about her family, I come to understand her better. Kath, it transpires, is not her sister but the daughter of a friend of Ma's own mother, the grandmother I never meet, having been told that she died years before I was born. In fact, as I run free along the back alleys of Little Wales, she is very much alive, incarcerated a few miles away. The grandmother I am told died before I was born is in fact a bus ride away in Rainhill Hospital, for many years known as the County Lunatic Asylum, Lancashire. The name changed in the 1920s to the County Mental Hospital. It had quietly hidden the mentally unwell by incarceration since the nineteenth century.

Sectioned on dubious grounds over an incident involving a broken window in her twenties, most likely suffering from untreated postnatal depression, she remained detained in the institution for the rest of her life. Ma was sent to live with Aunt Kath's family, in an adoption of sorts. A small weekly and irregular payment was made for board and lodgings. It was a better start in life than being taken into state care, the fate that befell her brothers, but one that scarred her. Her children, in time, would themselves feel the fear and rage that consumed her. If Pa was a man afraid of his vulnerability, Ma was on the run from the ghosts of her past, memories of her own mother, haunted by the fear her family history might repeat itself.

But for now, back in Greaves Avenue, Failsworth, there is hope, because this surely is a new beginning. It's earlier in the day, before the bonfire, and I'm sat by a lamppost opposite the house, late afternoon, waiting for Ma to come home from work as I often do. I'm excited about the promised special Bonfire Night, happy that Grandma is here with us and making treacle toffee. It's an otherwise grey day, nothing good to say for itself, but the evening promises far better. I play with lolly sticks in the gutter and look up every few minutes, hoping to spot her walking up the road. And there she is, jauntily swinging her handbag, the glamorous counter girl, the epitome of carefree. She doesn't beckon to me and I don't run to her – I never do – but there is the smile. The look that says, I see you, I see you there.

I walk back to the house holding her hand, silent and proud. Later, I catch Ma's eye through the flames as she dances. She raises her glass to me. I smile back at her and reach for the fallen sweet treacle to prove just how brave I am, very much the good son. Timmy's bark alerts the adults to my cries. Now we're in the kitchen, Grandma appearing in a flash, rubbing butter into the burn. Doesn't work, of course, but those were different times. I still bear a reminder of the night Greaves Avenue burned the killers and danced – a tiny scar. Grandma wipes away my tears and whispers that there is exciting news. The big move to be nearer to Grandma, a fresh start in Trawler Town. Cleansing sea air to blow away the city fug and grime, that's bad for Our Kid's asthma, so the story goes, but also bad for the young couple burdened by temptation and rumour. Their marriage is already in trouble, the love they possibly once had for each departing as silently as the embers floating up into the night sky.

Trawler Town

Decimus Burton, the nineteenth-century architect and urban designer, founding fellow of Royal Institute of British Architects, arrived in Fleetwood charged with producing a townscape to rival the majestic lines of Bath. But he left long before he could finish his work. It was such a short sojourn it remains a small entry in most accounts of his life. The man who commissioned him ran out of money and that was it. He packed up his straight edges, French curves and compasses, leaving behind few notable buildings and two extraordinary lighthouses, both of which continue to function today long after the fishing fleets they guided home were made obsolete. Trawler towns have a history bound in failed promises, so it was probably the perfect place for Ma and Pa to make a fresh start.

We are parked under the shadow of one of Burton's lighthouses, waiting to collect the keys to our new house, another grim police semi skirting a large council estate in the town. We arrive a dog short: Mac doesn't make the journey with us – the officer whose arse and pride he had punctured finally got his revenge, and Mac was put down. Most first memories of any trawler town in their pomp are ships, sharp suits and a pungent smell. It's a smell so overpowering and noxious that when we arrive at the house, Ma sends Pa in to check for vermin. Our new neighbour, a police sergeant, greets us, explaining the smell is from Isaac Spencer's, a nearby fish-processing plant. We'll get used to it, he says. We don't. No one does, but you do come to see it as a point of pride.

We have travelled in hope, a new adventure that Ma and Pa have set about with vigour. We have a garden, smaller than in Failsworth, a garage and a pen not just for the police dog but also a smaller one for rabbits, and the sea is just a spit away. A good start, if only that smell would go away.

For Pa, Trawler Town might have represented an opportunity to not only rekindle his relationship but also to develop his career. Sounded out as a CID recruit in Manchester, he declined the offer for reasons unknown and does so again when approached by his new constabulary. The riddle of Pa: what was it that the middleweight champion was afraid of? Avenues of opportunity viewed by him as dead ends, hurdles to be avoided. He'd fluttered across various departments in the police since joining from the army. Last of the line of young men conscripted into National Service, he'd served with the military police in the Middle East. An apprentice butcher prior to National Service he'd hoped to carry on with it, but on his return he'd discovered the butcher had taken on a replacement apprentice, something he'd often lament throughout his life. In the process of looking to leave the Manchester police, as he did every now and then, he contemplated becoming a pig farmer, but it came to nothing, and I wouldn't discover the possible answer to the riddle of the reluctant policeman for a long time.

In this new setting, my parents muddle on, never able to reach agreement on what's best for them or us. Neither possesses sufficient emotional maturity to temper the more damaging elements of their relationship. He believes himself eroded by Ma's reluctance to align her desires with the demands of a young family. And as always with Pa, from the root to the fruit, his frustration often manifests in anger, easy for a man who is never shy of confrontation, a significant component of Pa's DNA, as an incident that takes place shortly into his new post demonstrates.

It is a midweek night shift during his first winter in Trawler Town. Bleak weather, early hours, he's parked up, peering out of the steamed windows of a Black Maria over the dock basin. Pa is sat with the dock authority police sergeant, ports having their own constabulary at the time. He's giving Pa the lowdown on the trials and tribulations of working for the dock authority when my father notices a young deckie being dragged out from behind a fish train and on the wrong side of a beating by a much larger man.

'Nah . . . Leave well alone, Derek, it's Piggy. Biggest money-lender on the dock, in more ways than one. You don't want to mess with him.' But Pa's already left the van and is across the road.

'Had enough, wouldn't you say?' Pa asks.

Piggy gives him the eye and keeps a grip of the deckie.

'I'll be the judge of that. You're not dock plod. Fuck off, or I'll straighten yer nose.'

Pa's nose has a lazy kink from his days in the boxing ring – it causes him no problems, so he figures leave it be, unlike Piggy, on whom he unleashes a ferocious torrent of 'sharpeners', driving

Piggy back so swiftly he loses his footing and falls headfirst off the dock wall, disappearing with a roar. The drop, determined by tide, is of no concern to Pa; however, drowning the local moneylender is of grave concern to the dock sergeant and not something he envisioned when offering to give Pa a tour of the fish dock. Together they haul Piggy up from the filth and slime, chugging up his guts and not by any stretch inclined to let things lie: 'You fuckin' bastard, I'll do you, I will.'

Piggy rears and squares up to Pa, who utters the line I will hear repeated often by others over the years: 'You're not the sheriff, I am.' And with that he bops Piggy full square on the nose, sending him straight back down into the fish dock.

'Changed man afterwards, Piggy. Near death can do that. Your dad was out of the van so quick for the big fella, think his blood were up, like.'

The paradox of Pa: saint or sinner? The answer solely dependent on where his blood was at.

Over the years more of his exploits as sheriff of Trawler Town come to light. The day the 'leccy man' called the police, wanting help to evict the family of a fisherman behind on his utility bills but instead finding himself greeted by Pa, who tells him, 'You. Get in there, have a civil conversation, or feel my boot up your arse,' before marching him through the front door, locking it and standing guard outside while some form of mediation takes place.

His meeting with Piggy is followed by his continual badgering of the trawler companies to allow an advance on wages, a policy eventually adopted and which puts a stop to a variety of pernicious moneylending practices that cause havoc to families struggling with the vagaries of the fishing industry. A man who struggled with committing time to his own sons' sporting activities would buy football boots for the kids of deprived or problem families, confident a game of football with their mates meant less chance of trouble with the police. Throughout his life he found it far easier to help a stranger in need than spend time with his family. It is as if the notion of sustained commitment was troublesome to him, and if something wasn't easy, Pa is on his way.

We'd set about a variety of activities, embarked upon with fulsome gusto, creating the belief that a close and meaningful father–son relationship would be the inevitable result, only to be thwarted by lack of investment from him in time and effort. Line fishing on windswept beaches, utterly frozen in clothing not fit for purpose, but providing happy memories of walking with him at low tide to check the lines and see if we'd hooked any fish. A famous day trip out to sea on an old 'prawner' with her completely mad skipper, a steam-powered drunk of the old order from eastern Europe, a man scarier than Pa who was known locally as Ivan the Terrible. He had an accent so heavy as to be barely understandable, yet the two men were good friends. Ivan got steadily pissed as the day progressed, roaring with laughter as Pa took to a bunk floored by chronic seasickness. 'Derek, I peese bigger vaves.' Ivan got me to gut the few fish we caught and rubbed the blood in my face, shouting down to Pa, 'Your keed, I tell you, he make a feesherman, Derek! Ha, ha! I peese bigger sea.' I couldn't sleep that night from the adventure, while Pa vowed never to set foot on a boat again.

I am nine when Pa determines it is time his boys learn how

to defend themselves. As Trawler Town fisticuffs are not viewed as unusual in either street or playground, he decides we ought to have a degree of ability should the need arise. Off to the gym we go, a damp-walled bruise and blister academy located in a redundant industrial building. It's run by an acquaintance of his, Tommy, a slick-quiffed hard man with an engaging smile. Tommy smells permanently of Brylcreem and warm slapped liniment, and shouts every sentence like a gunnery sergeant. Our Kid and I are lined up and formally introduced to Tommy, who barks, 'Keep your hands up and your ears open!' and, with that, Pa's off out of the door. He had promised to stay with us for the first few training sessions, but clearly he has other plans. Tommy proves himself to be another random stranger with whom you wish your parent shared some qualities. We throw ourselves into the training, convinced this will build a closer relationship with Pa. Tommy informs him I have natural footwork and fast hands while Our Kid has a strength that belies his age.

Pa doesn't have much interest in our training: he is busy with other things. He has become involved with the Police Federation. He'd always had a lack of confidence in police management, and this had been stoked by personal knowledge of a couple of divisional incidents in which senior officers had, he said, scapegoated junior colleagues when their operational decisions were questioned and seemed likely to impede career advancement. Ironic, given his own tendency towards actual violence, but to him this was workplace bullying and the incidents rattled him enough to act. He begins to advise the officers and in time is elected as local representative on the national Police Federation. He throws himself wholeheartedly into the business of the union. Eventually he becomes northern treasurer, where his willingness to assist union members (up to the rank of chief inspector) ultimately extends way beyond basic advocacy – but let's leave that rabbit hole for later.

As for Ma, well, she is always busy being Ma. On my tenth birthday, the day arrives when for whatever reason things will be different, better. Today both of them have promised they will watch me play football, standing with the other parents in the wind and rain. It's a cup game, high stakes. When the game kicks off they are yet to arrive but I know they will – we live opposite the park. They will be here because we have just had the best Christmas ever, a sign things are getting better. I don't start the game well – maybe it's just as well they're late – then I spot the rolling shoulders of the sheriff of Trawler Town, that ambling walk. No Ma, but at least he is here – it's a start. My game improves. With increased effort I chase every ball; my sliding tackles, an art form yet to be outlawed, have never been better. I break up opposition play, I harry, race the line, whipping balls in with precision. Then the moment in a game every child hopes for when their parent stands watching. The opposition gifts me the ball, I bring it under control with ease, side of the boot, and my feet barely touch the ground as I drive forward. Now I am better, now I am good. Space opens up as I charge forward, wind in my hair, a boy full of guts and purpose. I jink out towards the touchline, perhaps for him, knowing he's there. Bazzer races with me and cuts in towards the box. I look up before releasing the ball cross field, across all the sharp words, the slaps and blows, across all our past, and in that moment, as the ball takes flight, I know that this is the best of times, the best of me. I hear him shout,

'What a bloody ball!' Parents whoop encouragement. I run towards the goal as the ball lands with pinpoint precision at the feet of Bazzer, who hammers it home, and Trawler Town memorial park erupts as the wind and rain bears down. I just about hear him again above the din. 'Mag-bloody-nificent!' I smile and turn to him. Mr Bond, 'Bondy', my schoolteacher, grins and raises his hands to applaud. And Pa? Pa is long gone, some business having called him away.

I begin to navigate home life a bit better thanks to a simple discovery: the written word as a means of escape. Energised by my trips to the library, I subscribe to the same method to entertain and distract my brothers when Ma and Pa's fights distress them. 'Plughole Pirates' and 'Uncle Stan's Pigeon' are popular narratives. Any old text will do: books, well-thumbed magazines, comics, newspapers destined for firelighters. At one parents' evening Mr Bond suggests to my parents that they might encourage my interest in reading beyond the school curriculum. In that brief sweet spot of marital harmony over Christmas, *the* Christmas, there are several books by the tree. *Devil in the Fog*, the *Shoot!* football annual, a book on world aircraft and one on the life of Buffalo Bill, obviously. It is an eclectic mix entirely suited to the generally bonkers atmosphere of joy felt that particular Christmas. Laughter, a roaring fire, playing out in the cold, joyous mirth keeping the cold at bay. Ask my brothers to name the best Christmas we ever had as kids, they would give the same answer. Because there was only ever one Christmas, *the* best Christmas. I don't know why but for the first time there is an abundance of love, effort and all the gravy. Grandma and Grandpa make the day complete. Eating dinner, Grandma asks Our Kid what he intends to do when he grows up. He thinks carefully before replying . . . 'Eat a whole chicken.'

The laughter around the table echoed, all the more special because it happened just once. By some strange deliverance we had pulled ourselves up to a position we thought was the beginning of what was surely always planned. But we were wrong. It was the highpoint – we had reached our summit.

Grandma first took me to the library, a magnificent building in the shadow of the docks, where all but the occasional breath was forbidden. To me it was a vast and comforting haven of peace and tranquillity. By enormous Victorian windows I read, daydream and watch the coloured funnels of deep-water trawlers head off to Icelandic waters. Our Kid watches them depart too, knowing that one day he will be on board, if not to escape Trawler Town, then at least a step closer to eating a whole chicken. We occasionally meet at the library. He's not particularly interested in reading, often finding himself glared at by a member of staff, this being a period when northern librarians were cautioned against treating children with respect. But he is always happy to sit and wait for me, content in his own world until it's time to head back home, where he will wonder out loud what's for tea. One day at the library he did pick up a book. Kept coming back to it over several weeks, a huge reference book on the constellations, a subject that will occupy his mind for the rest of his life.

This love of reading and the response to Bondy's teaching means that soon, when I take the eleven-plus entrance exam, I pass. Ma suggests a new set of clothes to celebrate the occasion, her treat. I can choose myself, Ma promises – she will only offer advice. And whatever else, she has style, panache. The following Saturday morning is spent in Trawler Town's best boutique – not the duds of a deckie, a firm no to white socks and drainpipes, a big yes to leather Chelsea boots and two-tone and penny round collar finesse. Laughter while we shop. She compliments me on my choices and coordination, and a long interest in choosing the correct duds for the occasion is born. But my first year at grammar school does not go well, and the ease at which I pass the eleven-plus is not replicated in my first term. There's a little snobbery against the kids from Trawler Town, with our flatter vowels and snotty noses. The teachers have neither the wit nor warmth of my primary-school teacher Mr Bond, nor his appetite to inspire.

My tiredness caused by early starts to get the bus to school is exacerbated by Pa and Ma's rows late into the night, often several times a week. One night, during my first term, the fighting is so vicious that my brothers ask me to make them stop. We sit on the landing listening for a while until I build up the confidence to go downstairs. When I open the door slowly Ma and Pa are entwined on the sofa. For a split second I might be forgiven for mistaking closeness for intimacy, save for the fact Ma has a large knife in her hand, the carving knife last seen at the best Christmas *ever* a few months earlier. Ivory handled, it's part of a wedding set from Uncle Stan. The open fire behind them casts shadows onto the ceiling. I say nothing, and keep quite still, finding it easier to watch their shadows. They don't see me standing in the doorway until I find my voice and ask what they're doing and say that we can't sleep. They freeze in a pose of sculpted malevolence, smiling and telling me not to worry before politely asking me to close the door and go back to bed. As I join my brothers, the fight resumes. So we take a blanket off the bed and head into the bathroom and climb into the bath. I try to forget about the knife, huddle in with my brothers and continue the story about a boy, the sea, a bathtub and the Plughole Pirates.

We fall asleep wishing we could sail away ourselves. When hostilities cease, Pa finds us asleep under the blanket. Our Kid tells him we were trying to get down the plughole to a magic island. I wait for the violence but there is none, no harsh words, just an embarrassed smile. Ma doesn't come upstairs to check on us, which is no surprise, but as always it upsets Our Kid and Bruv. The sense of abandonment that will haunt both forever has already begun. We hear the door slam as Ma leaves the house. Next morning, though, we are all reunited, no mention of the night before during another silent breakfast prior to running for the bus. A weather pattern is established: storms rage until spent, followed by exhaustion and calm, all underpinned by the sure knowledge that at some point the weather will again turn dark in Trawler Town. Their barnstorming bust-ups carry on well into the autumn and as the leaves fall so does any belief that our situation will improve.

My first end-of-term school report at grammar school reflects my poor start. A note from the headteacher indicating disappointment, given the high expectations on my arrival, adds an unhelpful zip to it. One thing is certain: his dismay will be nothing compared to Ma and Pa's. I'm riddled with guilt. How could I do this? Why have I let them down and not done my bit by working hard, helping to make the next Christmas something special again? I know the die is cast insofar as the problematic school report is concerned. I also know I can't take it home. I will have to sign it myself. Show them next term's report when I've improved, when things are better, because hope is the only safety net between you and despair when you're a child. In the following months my term reports, like the prevailing mood at home, show no improvement. I also discover to my horror that, having signed the first report, the previous report is explicitly referred to in the second, and so on.

So I continue to sign on their behalf. Ma and Pa have two wholly different signatures. The first report I sign as Ma, a small, tightly bound signature, rage in every letter. Pa's is surprisingly expansive, a flourish in the first and last letter. I practise signatures in the same notebook I use to write stories for my brothers. The front pages filled with stories of Uncle Stan, the ruddy-faced builder and his motley crew of racing pigeons, and in the back pages, evidence of a capital offence. What could possibly go wrong?

I wish I could go back to Mr Bond's class and start again. One day I kick ciggie stubs near my old primary school on the pretence of waiting for Our Kid, whose school is over the road, secretly hoping to bump into Bondy because he would know what to do. When I do bump into him it is with Ma and I'm monosyllabic while he tells her how proud he is of me. I can't wait to get away. I wish Ma and Pa could start again. In class I daydream, take myself elsewhere. The year pushes slowly towards spring, that first breath of warmth in the air, the sky somehow a better blue. The clouds are something else to me – hieroglyphical scripts, fantastic beasts running wild. I want to climb up and up and join them, pelting across the sky on their backs. Sometimes my invisible friend, my inner voice, the one I now know as Marv, is increasingly loud, the teacher's voice increasingly muted.

*

I'd better tell you a bit more about Marv, because he's going to be around a lot. Let's briefly fast-forward. Some years later, I'm in my twenties working as a detective in London. You'll see more of this world. Manor Park, east London, an early summer evening, I'm fishing. Not the watery type, though it's a good comparison. Exploring an opportunity to develop an informant.

It comes to nothing. Heading home, at the back of my local video store I find myself speaking to a former soldier. In the early evening light, at the back of a row of shops, he is fixing a car's entertainment system. We are both ex-services and like me he is a boxer, only off-the-scale better, a different league and on the cusp of turning professional. Nigel Benn will go on to become middleweight champion of the world. We chew the cud as he fiddles and tweaks with the sound system on an old saloon. *'He's a proper fuckin' fighter.'* He, Marv, is right. My inner voice is apt to express his opinion whenever the mood takes him. Benn and I get to talking about the fight game. I mention Pa's habit of waking me up to watch Muhammad Ali when I was kid.

'Marvellous for me, mate. Duran, Leonard obviously . . . but Hagler, he just keeps on . . .'

'Relentless'

'Isn't he?'

Marvellous Marvin Hagler. A lightbulb flashes. That's it, that's him I realise, the name of my silent partner, the voice in my head, as relentless at closing down space as the undisputed middle-weight champion of the world. And he needs a name. From that moment my binary bro becomes Marv. I wish Nigel all the best. Our paths never cross again. He was one hell of a fighter, and he helped me christen another one.

Back to the Trawler Town of my childhood. Spring has finally arrived, and everything changes. One day the smell from Spencer's, the fish-processing plant, has a sweeter syrupy smell to it. It's the kind of day that convinces you something good will happen, despite all the raggedy-arse uncertainties and barely concealed rage. When I step off the school bus and walk the along the road that leads to home I'm feeling positive, full of renewed confidence. When I see Pa in the distance, I run, shouting out to him, 'Pa!' He doesn't hear me. I call him again and again. 'Pa? . . . PA!' Eventually he stops, turning slowly, the easy roll of the shoulders. I smile and wave, start running again. He looks at me, that hard stare. I stop, smile and wave again, a little less enthusiastically this time. Nothing. He turns away and carries on towards the house. I stop, exhale slowly, a nervous laugh, take a look behind me. I suddenly don't want anyone else to see this moment.

'He knows.' I . . . 'He knows.' Shut up! I don't want to hear Marv's thoughts . . . 'He knows. Don't go home. Go to the park, hide by the pond. Go now.' I can't . . . I have to go home. 'Why? HE KNOWS!' The wind picks up, straight off the sea. Maybe spring isn't coming after all. Takes me a while to walk the last few hundred metres. I peer in through the kitchen window as I head to the back door . . . 'Don't go in.' But I do. Our Kid is in the corner, subdued, sensing the tension. Ma shoos him out and returns.

They both stand over me saying nothing until Pa quietly reminds me of the time he asked if the school issued an end-of-term report and I said not. Ma sits at the small kitchen table, impassive. I say I can't remember. My gym bag, all ready for Tommy's, is in the corner. I should be having my tea now – I'll be late. Tommy is a stickler for punctuality. I can hear breathing other than my own inside my head. It's Marv – he's scared too. Pa repeats the question, steps in closer, closing in on me. I won't be going to Tommy's tonight. Because this, this is my lesson. This will be the ring, the lonely place. 'No hiding place in the ring, lad,' according to Tommy. Pa takes another step closer. I see now how his eyes change. It's like the furrow of his brow casts a shadow over his eyes, warning of trouble. Our Kid peeks through the hallway door unsure of what to do, certain we've been here before. Ma shoos him away again and takes her seat, ringside, as always. There's no subtlety to Pa's interrogation. He would never have made a detective, on reflection – too restricted. Too much of a 'let me brace him' type of cop.

He asks me again, each time more quietly, softly. I look up at him: there is so much I want to say, but he interrupts. 'Do not lie to me, BOY!' I hear a mate who lives a few doors along cycle past, pinging the bell on his Raleigh Chopper bike, letting us know he's out playing. It's a great bell. His dad bought it from a second-hand shop. It rings again. My Lords, Ladies and Gentlemen . . . LET'S GET READY TO STUMBLLLLLLE!

In the grammar-school mud-brown uniform and weighing in at the below the average percentile weight of a thirteen-year-old, fighting out of Trawler Town instinct and fear, introducing the undisputed Accuuuuused . . . BOOOOOYYYYYYYYYY! In the blue uniform of authority and weighing in with little in the way of parental insight, fighting out of fear of being made to feel a right cunt in front of a middle-class headteacher, the former middleweight champeeeeeaan of the combined services and still

29

the undissssspuuuted misunderstood bully in the boy's wooorlllld . . .
PAAAAAAAA!

The bell rings for round one and here we go! Boy immediately on the back
foot, Pa trying to get to Boy with that long reach advantage. Boy, dancing,
good movement, clearly remembering Tommy's tuition – never leave yourself
unprotected, keep moving – but Pa gets off a good combination there, opening
up on Boy. Whoah! A good right by Pa. Boy, weaving, dancing, as Ma,
Trawler Town's very own Harry Carpenter in a cheesecloth blouse, sits as
always, watching the action . . . Boy backing off, looking to use the ring, Pa
relentless, Boy holding on. Whoah! A tremendous combination from Pa but
Boy refuses to go down – clearly thinks he'll gain respect and maybe . . . love.
He changes feet but he's tiring now, taking more punishment, if only he could
punch back . . . A left–right combination as the ref looks on, impassive,
letting the contest continue. Boy no longer dancing – he seems to have forgot-
ten Tommy's words, looks distressed, his legs have gone, surely the ref will
step in now. Pa, moving forward, catches him with a left and, WHOAH!,
a hard right and he is down! Boy hits the canvas, round one! Head bounced
on the concrete step there. He won't get up from that. No count required in
this one – it's over, it is definitely over . . . Boy still down, in some distress . . .
And if you ask me, I think the referee should have stepped in much
sooner . . .

But whenever we stumbled, she never did. Ma and Pa are
united in defeat and destined to repeat. But something changed
this time, if not in them certainly in me. I was distressed, and not
because of the pain. At some point I pissed myself – my school
trousers are soaked. When my head bounced on the concrete step
it opened a cut in the corner of my eye. I lie on the floor feeling
woozy, a trickle of blood running from my eye into my mouth. I
also landed awkwardly on my wrist, but curled up on the floor it is

not the pain but the shame that hurts, the fact I pissed myself. Ma doesn't notice and Pa is already quiet, silenced by the onset of his own shame. When I stand up I see Our Kid peering through a gap he's opened in the doorway. He raises his hand. Pa leaves to speak to Our Kid. He doesn't look back. He never did. Still dizzy, I hear Marv whisper, *'I told you.'* Good friend that he is, he doesn't mention my shame. A taxi to A&E reveals no broken bones, just a bad sprain to my wrist. It's put into a splint but my eye needs a few stitches.

I'm a trainee detective at West End Central police station in London a little over a decade later when I ask Ma (who has arrived unannounced, having by then been AWOL for several years) about the incident over tea in a café in Piccadilly. She claims to remember little about it, the *stumble* in the jungle. 'Just one of those things,' she says before changing the subject to the real purpose of her visit: Pa.

But it isn't just one of those things. It was, however, my last time in the ring. He never raised his hand to me again. Ma, on the other hand, was well into her stride with her own form of psychological pugilism. When reason was required to explain a break, bruise or stitch, her adroitness at coming up with an alibi served primarily to protect her reputation as much as Pa's, but a child needs a voice too. Perhaps that's why my secret friend knocked when he did and the voice became stronger. He was someone to watch over me – a separate voice but also my inner voice. At first I worry about the erratic, dissonant voice living inside my head, convincing myself something is wrong. The 'clips around the ear' have scrambled my senses. I'm sure he will fade, this voice, as I get older, but he gets louder, more assertive. He moves in.

That night, everything changes for me. When I get home from the hospital, I take off my damp trousers and leave them on the bed. On a layer of condensation on my bedroom window I write in underscored capital letters, 'I HATE MY DAD'. The words are visible for days until somebody cleans the window. Our Kid peers round the door before coming in carrying his Etch A Sketch. He sits on the bed. There's no conversation. I'm not really in the mood for company. Eventually he points to his pad – he has sketched a sad face. He puts his pad down and places his hand on top of mine. We sit in silence.

Bigger House, Smaller Dreams

We move again, this time to a larger police house, and despite the endless snarking, the eroded confidence, we again buy into the promise of better times ahead. Grandma and Grandpa hope this will be a defining moment, the point we turn a corner as a family, but the rows continue, the doors slam, voices raised and spirits low. I take to leaving the house even earlier in the morning, preferring to wait at the bus stop than be among it. There's no improvement in my performance at school. I'd bumped into my head of year in the corridor after the stumble in the jungle, black-eyed and splinted. He'd looked at me sheepishly and asked what happened. *'Tell him to fuck off,'* suggests Marv. 'I fell, sir,' I say.

At the first sign of summer in Trawler Town, warmer temperatures push the smell from the fish-processing plant further afield while the fuggy output from the local ICI plant stunts the growth of the local population, or so we all believe. 'Why is everyone a short arse in Trawler Town?' The question is being debated by the shortest boy of a group of friends standing on a street corner as I amble past one summer evening. One is about to become my lifelong pal, until death do us part. Born into a long line of fishermen who have colonised this particular street, he challenges me to a fight when I accidentally wander into their territory, demarcated with the words 'FUCK OFF GRIMSBY YOUR SHIT' scrawled on the outside of a red BT phone box. I'm not from Grimsby, but it is an early sign of the absurdist humour popular with this gang. Perhaps sensing I have had several weeks of Tommy's gym tuition, the contest will now be a wrestling match. Whoever pins his opponent 'to the deck' will be declared the winner.

Bud, my blond-haired adversary, squares up and the contest begins. Midway through the bout, which I am clearly losing, a young woman steps over us as we roll over the pavement and enquires after another boy's sister as she enters the phone box. Bud, who has now pinned me to the ground in an arm lock, pauses to ask if from my vantage point I can see what colour her knickers are. A question I struggle to answer, given my restricted movement, though it serves to confirm the passage from childhood to teenage summers is not too far from this street corner. Having established he is stronger than me, and as I am unable to assist in identifying the colour of said knickers, Bud offers to release me if I accept defeat. We stand, shake hands and I am formally introduced to the group. And so begins our lifelong friendship. It becomes ever-more important as war on the home front continues unabated. We are two boys who in adulthood will find themselves as detectives at opposite ends of the country and in very different worlds.

We become inseparable, hanging out at the local youth club and surrounding streets in all weathers. It is hard not to notice that Bud's house and those of his extended family have a greater warmth and sense of purpose to them. It is still a time of plenty for the fishing industry, reflected to a degree in the homes, but there is also something else that I can't quite identify. In every sense, Bud and most of the Trawler Town Bash Street Kids I am now a part of, appear, at least to me, to be the manifestation of what a *real* family looks like on the inside. No doubt they have their own issues but from where I was standing, Bud's house always guaranteed a warm welcome and a sense of home. The way his ma put a plate of food down without request and with a smile. The dry humour his pa shared with all and sundry whenever he was back from sea. It was the shape of family.

I never share what I see with my brothers, as inevitably our new home goes the way of our others. My first bike, a gift from my grandparents, becomes my trusty steed on which I charge through Trawler Town at the gallop, daydreaming, in search of something else. The marriage limps on for a few more months and then one day, Ma is off, taking one of my brothers with her.

As I head for the school bus one morning, Our Kid asks to walk with me as far as the bus stop, the conversation urgent. Where is she? Why didn't she take all of us? It was later I knew why, why she only took one. I found a letter that laid bare the deceit. In it, Ma wrote to a lover explaining how she had passed off my youngest brother as Pa's. There was tenderness in the letter that my years didn't allow me to understand and rage that personal experience did. It took a lifetime to even begin to understand that letter, and the unwarranted guilt it made me feel, and in that moment I doubted every thread of what I had known or what I believed to be true. I put the letter back in the trunk where I found it secreted, consumed by the idea that in some way this was my fault, that my inquisitive mind was to blame and sooner or later another beating would follow.

After school that night, as Pa goes out to buy a chippy tea, I join Our Kid in his bedroom. He's playing with his Etch A Sketch, which by now has become more coping mechanism than toy. I ask him if he can keep a secret. He answers by writing a loopy *Yes* on his pad. I outline the semblance of a plan to find out what is happening and maybe even a solution. Updates from Pa are limited to 'There's nothing for you to worry about', which, given we live in a constant state of anxiety with only the level varying, is not reassuring.

I don't know why, but Grandpa becomes key to my plan to reunite the family. Despite his known commitment to never making a fuss, always making do, he possesses a calm serenity I know could fix the crisis. We were due to go over to see our grandparents at the weekend, but Pa tells me we have to rearrange. Grandma had planned to take us up to see Grandpa working his signal box – a huge treat. I'd been a couple times but it would have been Our Kid's first trip. Hard to imagine now but at a set time we would have walked the short distance along the railway bank from the station platform and up to the old Victorian wooden signal box. There would have been tea and cake or, if very lucky, eggs cooked on the stove. Honoured guests seated on the well-worn leather armchair, watching in pride as he fixed the huge wood and steel levers into position with a satisfying clunk. Then, waiting, hearts racing, for the tell-tale sound of the metal lines flexing under the weight of an approaching train.

My plan was to carry on as arranged anyway and head straight to the signal box to ask for Grandpa's help in fixing the situation at home. Pa is easier in his parents' presence, more relaxed. My wages are settled every Saturday morning after I finished my paper round, and I had a few weeks' banked. With another week's money I knew it would be enough to execute the plan. This was a scrawny Trawler Town boy's reconnaissance mission in a rapidly changing situation, a covert operation to make a 'buy'. What I was trying to *buy* was time. Because underpinning all the uncertainty was the belief that I was in some way responsible. Ma never tired of telling us of the sacrifices she had made for us, and of our lack of appreciation or understanding. So, my first covert deployment would salvage something positive from the chaos to which we had contributed and Grandpa was going to be my cover man.

He is a gentle soul, at the time in the final chapter of 50 years working on the railways. Messenger boy, steward, fireman and, finally, signalman. The kindest man I know. Perhaps not as savvy as Grandma but just as full of love and warmth, decency and dignity. He will have the wherewithal to mend a broken home. Saturday morning arrives and, with still no sight nor sound of Ma, it is time to act. The day before, I asked Pa if Our Kid and I could spend the afternoon at the pier. He agreed. Saturday afternoons for him, if not working, were often focused on the horses. So, on Saturday I finish my paper round, collect my wages and race back home on the trusty charger. Not owning a watch, I spend the morning clock-watching until Pa is ready to head off into town. We don't own a car, so the three of us sit on the bus – Our Kid's jaw set rigid; me, petrified that he will give the game away before it begins. Pa, subdued since Ma left though not exactly morose, the air of a man who is also working on a brilliant idea himself, one yet to be revealed – we are yet to realise Pa never has a plan.

With paper-round money pocketed and money box emptied I've worked out we have enough to get a taxi to the train station seven miles away and the bus fare home. This will allow time to present the plan to Grandpa and still arrive home well before Pa. A cotton canvas rucksack, a gift from my grandparents for passing the eleven-plus, is fully provisioned for the operation with a bottle of Vimto and two banana sandwiches, but its real purpose is to carry a key component of the plan: a large Grimes's meat and potato pie, Trawler Town's finest purveyor of all things pie. The mighty meat and potato is Grandpa's favourite: 'A pie to put hairs on your chest.'

We double back from the bus stop as soon as Pa turns the corner. I've many years to wait before training in the art of countersurveillance, so for two wee Trawler Town runts the walk to the taxi office is a fraught affair taking us as it does in an opposite direction to the pier. Our Kid's nerves are calmed by the thought that at some point a slice of pie will be his if all goes well.

We wait at the taxi rank. It's barely midday but shoreside fishermen are already putting the hard yards in, supporting Trawler Town's many pubs. Three-day millionaires on a mission to get bladdered as quickly as possible. We wait for our taxi and pray Pa doesn't turn back. Taxis, like the pubs, are plentiful in Trawler Town, more for functionality than comfort. No adult walks anywhere in Trawler Town – even if it would be quicker to walk the few yards to the next pub, you take a taxi. A three-day millionaire spreads the love, oils the local economy, so in order to service this high demand there are more taxi companies in a thriving fishing port than elsewhere in the UK. That said, what actually passes for a serviceable taxi is open for debate – four wheels and you are pretty much good to go. So it proves with our ride out of town.

This is before seatbelts are compulsory. Sat in the back of the taxi as I explain the essence of my plan, we fast approach a notorious roundabout with several exits. It's near a popular pub as you head out of town, and the time-honoured tradition is to approach it at great speed, psyching other approaching drivers into braking while softly uttering 'knobhead' under your breath as you gun your vehicle through the chicane. As we fly around the roundabout, wheels screeching, the rear door opens; I instinctively grab Our Kid as the driver, without stopping, explains that it often does that and suggests I give it a good tug to close it. The remainder of the journey is conducted in uneasy silence. Years later, on a night out as adults, a little worse for wear and with two of Our Kid's friends squeezed in with us, the same tactical approach by the driver produces a similar result, only this time, as the door opens, my brother's pal barrel rolls out of the vehicle. It may well have been the same taxi. It was the drink that saved him.

We arrive at the train station intact. I peer over the station wall along the tracks to see if I can see Grandpa in his signal box, but I can't. Our Kid, excited by the prospect of actually getting inside the signal box, feels we should push on with the plan, whatever it is. I begin to have doubts, my plan has a simplicity – that is its strength. The problem is, I am now less confident. I clamber up the station wall again. This time I think I can see Grandpa on his feet inside the signal box. As we've come this far and without actually telling my brother the fine details, we walk into the station, down the long platform that leads to the embankment and on towards Grandpa carrying a pie and a plan to fix a broken home. Our Kid focuses on the pie. We clamber down to the embankment, and while I'm not sure if my re-found confidence is misplaced, we push on down the slope to the gravel bank and start walking the couple of hundred metres or so to the signal box. I keep Our Kid on my inside and tell him we have to listen out for trains.

Twenty-five metres. This plan, it's really just a suggestion. Fifty metres. Because surely it's better to live together in a broken house than be a broken family. One hundred metres. Our Kid is falling behind. I grab his hand, tell him to keep up. I see him now, smoke rising from his favourite pipe, a Half-Bent Billiard. He thinks Grandma doesn't know he enjoys a smoke at work or on his daily walk but of course she does. One hundred and fifty metres. I know if we speak to Grandpa, who now turns in our direction – he must be able to see us now – he will know what to do. The ground beneath my feet begins to vibrate, the track lines flexing. Grandpa throws open the signal box and stands at the top of the stairs shouting, his arms frantically summoning us through a cloud of smoke. We run the last few metres as the lines groan under the weight of the approaching train and in the last few seconds I forget the plan.

Why are we here? We bolt up the wooden stairs and into the box as if being chased by the train. We're panting, Grandpa bemused. No time to speak. He looks out of the window and waves to the driver of a lumbering goods train as it trundles and clanks past. Our Kid is transfixed. He watches intently as Grandpa steps behind the huge levers, takes a cloth from his belt and uses it to grip then heave the levers back and forth before turning to face us.

'Thought you were poorly, couldn't come over?'

Pa must have told him that. I don't reply because I can't bring myself to tell him why we are here. Our Kid tells him we've brought him a pie as I stand mute, trying to remember why I thought this was a good idea. My brother takes the pie from the rucksack, presents it with pride: a meat and potato from Grimes's! Grandpa smiles, not a whiff of anger. 'You know you should have come with Grandma. Anyway, what's wrong?' I don't know where to begin, what to say. Our Kid will grow up to be a man of few words, tortured by his own voices, never known for verbosity on any subject, but this day, you can't shut him up.

As the signal box clock ticks and I stand wondering why on earth I've dragged him here, Our Kid tells gentle Billy that Ma has run off with our brother, that Pa won't tell us what's happening, that Pa often took out his anger on me, gave me the still livid scar above my eye because I wasn't doing well at school, how I read him stories at night to stop him listening to the fights, made up stories of magic that helped him sleep and that maybe he and Grandma could help Ma and Pa with some sort of story. 'You could help them, Grandpa, like Our Kid helps me.'

Neither Grandpa nor I have spoken a word. A bell in the signal box breaks the silence. He takes out the faded cloth tucked under his belt again, gently manoeuvres us over to an old armchair in the corner. As he leans in and grips the heavy metal levers, which thunk into place, I remember the plan: 'Like you do here, making sure the trains go in the right direction. You could do that for us – help us go in the right direction, Grandpa?'

When he's finished adjusting the signals he holds on to a lever and polishes the brass plates with his cloth as a passenger train passes the box. Our Kid rushes to the window and waves. Grandpa now diligently wipes down the lever, making a half-cough as if trying to clear his throat. As Our Kid waves at the passing train and I wait for Grandpa to say something I spot a tear, just one, in the corner of his eye. The first I've ever seen on a grown-up. It hangs like fresh-blown glass. He turns away from me but I see it, straining under the weight. He coughs again and deftly catches it with the lever cloth before turning to us, the famous smile returned.

'Well, let's have a think now. But eh, let's eat first. Meat and potato, you say?'

A few weeks later Ma was back in our life, along with Bruv. There is no explanation as to where she has been, just a brief announcement that all is back to normal aside from the fact she has a new home in Trawler Town now, and that one or two of us will move into this house with her at some point soon. This, they say, will be better for everybody, though they never quite explain why. Instead, Ma begins to canvass for our vote as the parent we wish to live with. Pa may be active in the Police Federation but he underestimates Ma's political nous when it comes to gerrymandering an emotionally scarred electorate. She sets out by listing Pa's obvious faults to me on a daily basis. Ma's campaign is based on claiming maternal capabilities on a par with Mother Teresa while vilifying Pa at every opportunity. It's relentless. The primary focus of her efforts is me and I have no idea why. At all hours of the day she recounts chapter and verse Pa's lacking, his beating on me, sidestepping her own role in often promoting the event and always managing the post-bout PR.

Both Our Kid and Bruv assume they will be living with Ma going forward; I am the floating voter who doesn't know what to do for the best. I certainly have no idea why Ma is so determined to outline Pa's shortcomings, but one thing is for sure, it begins to have an impact. I find the only way to avoid the diatribe is to agree with her. Ma moves into her new house, a run-down, small two-bedroom terrace with a yard. We alternate between Ma's and Pa's. In a way, it's no different from how it's always been.

One morning Ma tells me I need to stay home, as we have an important meeting with someone who needs to 'sort out the paperwork for the divorce'. There follows a three-way meeting with a social worker. Bushy beard and little else. Ma, Pa and me. A summit of sorrow. Pa full uniform. Ma full bonhomie. Boy, full of regret. I stare at gas fire flames, as the grown-ups stare at the wreckage. By the end of the afternoon my future is confirmed: from now on, I'll be living full time with Ma.

A few weeks later, I am introduced to Bill over tea. Ma's next husband, he is a merchant sailor ready to step ashore and settle down. Tall, prematurely grey, his face has the look and shape of a family tent that's had its main beam removed. He moves in within a few weeks of our meeting and soon he too wears the glazed look of a school kid who hasn't understood the question. Bill never finishes a sentence. 'I'm off to . . .' 'Your mother is a woman of . . .' I soon feel sorry for Bill, who Pa nicknames 'Barnacle', though he demonstrates no such stickability when confronted with the harsh reality of Ma's plans. Hoping for a simple life in his middle years, he is shocked to find himself in trouble within a few months of marriage, clueless as to how the weather turned so quickly and with such ferocity. He takes shelter in the lee of the small kitchen, endlessly polishing his boots, his shoulders rolling from side to side, giving him the look of a distressed elephant.

Eventually, realising any form of defence against Ma's tongue is pointless and lacerated to the point of no return, that is exactly what he does. The tired old mariner signs on again and sails off in search of calmer waters, his polished boots left to gather dust in the corner. I come home from school and find them outside in the back yard, a sign as authoritative as papal smoke that Ma has moved on. The marriage lasted barely a year. Ma tells everyone he was weak, 'not up to the task'. We don't ask what the task was, and free of chivvying Barnacle along Ma sets about identifying his replacement. Candidates are whittled through in short order. In preparation for one such interview I'm waiting at the bus stop with Ma when a short exchange occurs that was possibly the only time she was motivated to do something selfless for me.

Out of the blue and into the silence she asks me if I'd be interested in joining a drama group, though not in Trawler Town where art is viewed suspiciously. Why, I wonder, does she want me out of the house? At the same time, I'm also thinking, actually, yes, I would like that. I love the stories in my books, and this might be just the same. She knows a drama teacher, she says, that she thinks I'd get on with. Ma looks me over. 'And it would give you something to do . . . with . . . you know . . . those voices of yours.'

'What voices?' I ask defensively.

'I don't know . . . when you're with your brothers.'

I explain that's just playing about, just me telling stories.

'Well exactly . . . She'll teach you how to do it properly.'

When I get home that evening I'm pleased to find no

immediate replacement for Barnacle and that Ma has arranged for me to meet Rose the following week. Our meeting is not a success – in fact, it's excruciating. The shy sullen boy from Trawler Town stands in the bright and airy house of the drama teacher who starts by walking over to a piano and suggesting we begin with a song. My range extends only as far as the occasional football chant and I'm awkward in this type of house. It's disorientating, all family photographs, house plants, art on the walls, cats and coffee. Nobody drinks coffee in Trawler Town, and if they did, I know what they'd be called: a knobhead. I'm still not quite sure what the derogatory term means but *he*, Marv, is convinced that is exactly what I will be known as if I stay much longer with Rose. In Trawler Town you cannot be a knobhead and expect to fit in.

Trawler Town's list of knobhead offences is extensive. Not eating most meals with gravy. Inability to create perfect smoke rings within three feet of the opposite sex. Not possessing sufficient linguistic ability to use 'fuck' as noun, verb and adjective within one sentence, preferably while undertaking any of the above.

Scarred by my introduction to Gilbert and Sullivan, I wait for the bus certain of one thing: I'm not going back. By the time I get off the bus I have changed my mind. One more go because, as I left, Rose had made a suggestion.

'Next week, if you come back' – she is clearly an expert on body language too – 'we'll read a book together, bring it to life.'

'Err . . .' – awkward silence, as she waits for a reply – 'What book?'

'Any – you choose. Bring it with you.'

Ma asks how it went. I mumble and disappear off to find my book of choice. *Oliver Twist*. Drama lessons with Rose continue. I love visits to her house, and the sullen boy I had become post-social worker emerges from his shell. Her idea of bringing text to life is a revelation. We undertake a wide variety of readings, sometimes with other students. It is the house of calm. If the meat-and-potato-pie adventure provided the first fledgling signs of abstract thinking to solve a problem, this is the foundation of building an undercover 'legend', acting out a cover story. I don't simply read the text: I try to become who or what it depicts. Dickens is devoured and then some. I don't know why, but I don't want my friends to know that I have a drama teacher.

I ask Ma not to say anything to them. Busy with the hunt for Barnacle's replacement, she laughs at the suggestion, but I insist and make her promise not to tell anyone. Bud and I are by now the best of mates, and while he and I share every detail of our lives there is something about my weekly trip out of Trawler Town that I want to keep secret. Ma agrees and thereafter rarely enquires how things are progressing. The evening develops into an opportunity for her to go to the cinema with her latest love interest, a fishmonger from the next town.

Pa is now settled with a new wife, and eventually, unable to deal with Ma's rages, we find ourselves migrating towards him and Stepmother. But three boys are too many for Stepmother, and Ma loves to fight, using her sons as weapons, which leaves us bloodied and everyone tired. One day, Ma hits the road again before returning to buy a different house and taking the son she hopes will be easier to cage. She chooses Bruv, Our Kid rejected. As for me, for some reason, I'm allowed to choose. I move in with Pa. Ma doesn't speak to me for two years after that – letters and cards returned unopened. The game continues.

Life with Pa and Stepmother is certainly different, while school is the same: a disaster. I play truant, sit out school days on the promenade staring out to sea knowing I will leave at the first opportunity. It's not Trawler Town. I have salt in the blood, but I need to run away. I finish school with one O level in English. 'Big surprise that, mate. No one speaks it here,' says Bud in support. My history master, the only teacher ever to show an interest in me, urges me to resit the exams – others are more keen to wave goodbye. Pa and Stepmother think if you're only going to leave with one, it's not a bad one to have but I see the unexpressed disappointment in Pa. Bud and I work on a holiday camp during that last summer and think about the future. As it draws to a close, I'm sure the sea holds the answer. Trawler Town: one road in, many boats out. I try fishing with Ivan the Terrible, but it's a miracle we return. Fishing, I conclude, is not for me. While Bud knows exactly what he wants to do – join the police – I have no firm ideas regarding a career beyond escape. A career is something to be considered when I have figured out more pressing concerns, such as why exactly it is that everyone I know seems to have a plan and I do not. The police have not registered on my radar save for one abiding image: the occasional night when detectives visited Pa to play with a deck of cards. There is something alluring about that brief memory that I do not yet understand. There is a combination of sadness and cynicism, of power and vulnerability.

Instead, I trawl military recruitment centres and consider the army. I'm drawn to the excitement and maybe a desire to prove something to my father – he was in the army after all. At this Pa wakes from his usual inertia. He doesn't want to see me posted to Northern Ireland, refuses to sign the authority required as I'm under 18. Stepmother, on the other hand, suggests the army has a 'lotta perks, love'. All the recruitment officers suggest I go back to grammar school and resit my exams, make things easier on myself. One afternoon I meet Rose in town. She asks after Ma, but when Ma disappears, she's gone. I waffle on embarrassed, and when I tell her of my plans, she is at least honest. I am making a terrible mistake, I really should go back to school, resit my exams, stay in education. But I need to leave and Charles Dickens seems a long way from where I need to be.

Pa figures there's not much chance of a boy being shot over the water if he's in the Royal Navy and signs the papers. A travel warrant and joining papers arrive, and my bag is packed. In late November I leave Trawler Town for good. Stepmother believes it will make a man of me and sets about redecorating. Pa struggles to find words, now he is on the verge of losing his sons. When the day arrives, he drives me to the train station, the same platform I walked along a few years earlier carrying a meat-and-potato pie. We watch the station clock tick goodbye.

He kicks a dog end off the platform edge, takes a breath.

'You don't have to do this. It's not too late to change your mind.' We both know that it is. My turn to push at a cigarette stub with my shoe.

As the train pulls in, he lunges forward and hugs me, catching me by surprise. As if the sudden movement jogs his memory, he tells me to watch out for Grandpa's signal box as the train leaves. I know he's embarrassed by the show of emotion. We shake hands, a firm grip. A 'proper handshake', the unwritten law of the north, and I board the train. The big man clamps his jaw as the train pulls away and, despite his efforts to hide it, the glass-blower's pipe has fashioned another tear.

I lose sight of him as the train skirts the bend and sit down waiting to see the signal box, a few hundred metres outside of the station. I'm greeted by Grandpa, arms like windmill blades at full tilt, flailing two white hankies. While the rest of the carriage wonders if the old boy's gone mad, I rush to the carriage door and pull down the window. As I wave back, he shouts something, but his words are lost in the wind and then he too is gone. I sit down, a little lost, neither man nor boy, reflecting on my last moments with Pa. I think every family has a glassblower in heaven or somewhere, each crystal-blown tear filled with mem-ories of what is and what might have been. Perhaps somewhere they wait to pick up the blowpipe for me. But not for a time yet. I am off to wander the world, march through time and place and feel the sun on my back, while the glassblower watches, and waits.

Navy Days

The cold, bleak weather that hung over me as I boarded the train and waved goodbye to childhood persists as I arrive in Ipswich. It's a dark, gloomy night. I await military transport with several other recruits, to begin the transformation from teenagers to teenagers in uniform. We nod at one another, but there is little conversation as we travel the short distance to the base and within the hour begin an immediate immersion into military life. Scratchy twill-weave clothing of every description is issued, all of it guaranteed to irritate teenage acne. The next three months disprove the concept that marching everywhere is the preserve of the army. For some, basic training proves too much too soon and we lose several recruits within the first few weeks, including one who asks the gunnery petty officer (PO), responsible for all matters of discipline (and marching), if he might be excused from wearing the winter jumper as it irritates a skin condition that runs in his family but which he chose not to mention at the recruitment office.

Like Grandpa's goodbye, the PO's reply is lost in the freezing gale whipping across the parade ground, but so apoplectic is he with rage that it seems to consist mainly of a series of unintelligible and incoherent screams, although we do establish that this recruit will henceforth be known as Cabbage. We stand frozen to attention as the PO carries on regardless: 'Ahhhh heeeee hoo futt ard heee you, Cabbaaaage! Aaaaafft the double!' To his credit, Cabbage at least understands the order and immediately begins running around the perimeter of the parade ground. It is a brutal and hilarious spectator sport so long as you are not on the receiving end. Gunnery staff poke and prowl, scanning for what at the time is perceived as weakness, their task to build a chain whereby each link is as strong as the next. Fragile metal is discarded before the next blow of the hammer.

Some recruits stand out, and make basic training look so easy it's a wonder the Royal Navy managed to persuade them to join. For them no cruel and ironic words of encouragement, while for the rest of us, it's a question of keeping your head down and avoiding incoming. The class is whittled down, and most remaining recruits are from a similar background and class. We bond easily and laugh loudly at the often surreal absurdity that basic training puts our barely formed young minds through. To some extent, I am unwittingly being shaped for later employment in the police. If nothing else, military training teaches you that in order to survive, you must never stand out from the crowd. Never disturb the environment, the basic tenet of the undercover detective's deployment. On we rattle, at a steady lick through the early weeks of basic training as Cabbage continues to test the patience of the gunnery staff.

Part of our drill training involves each recruit taking charge of the class while on the parade ground, issuing commands as we march left, right and about turn. Cabbage and another recruit are so softly spoken that we repeatedly fail to hear their orders to deviate, frequently marching off the parade ground and into the distance, demonstrating we have at least grasped the basic principle of not thinking independently. Our instructor, unable to take any more, his face puce with incoherent rage, screams, 'Arhhh ouuu Cabbbggge! Aft ooo ift aaah ooo farrkkin imbiceeel!' Cabbage finds himself standing on an upturned box at the end of the parade ground reciting the Lord's Prayer as we march to and fro. It's clear he does not know all the words to the invocation. As foul weather and incessant shouting from the instructor increase in volume, two officers casually stroll past, causing the instructor to stop berating Cabbage, bolt to attention and snap a clean salute before returning to his task, all while the softly spoken prayer from Cabbage gently plays out.

'Our father whose art is in heaven . . . Harold Beethe is thy name . . .' Our gunnery instructor is now on the verge of a seizure, as I nearly draw blood biting hard on my lip to stifle laughter.

Cabbage is gone by the end of the month, an empty bunk signalling his departure.

One particular recruit is a machine. He eats up basic training, top in every module by such margins that we think he must be the son of Poseidon. Built like a prop forward, he is fazed by nothing, aloof but pleasant enough. Understandably he is made class captain. We know this boy, Cools, will not be long among the lower ranks. The rest of us muddle on, each day bringing a new challenge and sharp contrast to our previous lives. But, shoulders to the task, we feel the changes within, less connected to the kids we were.

The time comes for us to prepare for an exercise in fire and damage limitation training. I know it will be practical, rigged to be as authentic as possible, but have no idea what else to expect. A nervous excitement runs through the class. Wearing full heat-retardant clothing and breathing apparatus it involves us crawling individually through a compartment set aflame and filled with dense smoke. It is claustrophobic, the temperature intense. It might be an exercise but I have never encountered anything like it. That evening in the mess as we eat our scran (quickly adopting naval slang), Cools is full of his prowess on the day as he explains how he mastered belly crawling through searing heat. Marv thinks different: *'I think it spooked him.'* It certainly spooked the rest of us. I was shitting myself.

Weeks and weeks of drills, classroom teaching and practical exercises culminate in one final exercise. We are marched to what looks like a large metal box. In some perverse way I want this to be shocking. I want to prove something to Pa, to Trawler Town, to myself. But I have no idea what exactly – that I am indestructible, unbreakable?

'Open the fuckin' hatch. I am ready for this bastard!' Marv is full of bravado, and it helps calm my nerves and the worry I will be found wanting. An NCO opens a hatch, considers the spotty-faced initiates standing to attention and asks if we are all ready. No loud shouts of 'Yes, sir!' But nods, nervous laughter and a little gallows humour in a variety of accents suggest that we are, more or less. But this is a spade in the ground for me, a first foundation. Not that I know it then, but this is why I will be invited, in the distant future, to be part of SO10 – the department in the Metropolitan Police that was at one point the UK lead in covert

policing. This is now the official start of that journey. It begins at barely 17 years old with teenage spots and an overwhelming urge to do something worthwhile, to stand out, to make Ma and Pa notice, as if born of guilt. The instructor tells us the next hour or so will decide if we are ready.

We file towards what turns out to be a mock-up of a compartment within a warship. Instructors usher us inside, where we are split into smaller groups. It looks like an engine room, and we are told in no uncertain terms to react to whatever events take place. All the equipment and tools we are likely to need are to be found within the compartment. But what about within ourselves? Cools bounces on his toes. It's infectious – we all start to do the same, waiting, smiling. We've got this. There is nothing more powerful than youth.

We are on our toes and BANG! All lights in the compartment suddenly fail. Total darkness, silence. What the fuck do we do? We haven't done the lesson on what to do when the lights go out. BOOM! Jesus that was loud. Then, after the explosion, through the darkness comes a raging torrent of ice-cold water. An authoritative voice informs us the ship has been hit by enemy fire and we are working to restore power. BOOM! The compartment appears to shake. I lose my footing as some lighting returns. In the half-light we take stock of the situation and find the primitive tools in the damage control kits that have repaired ships in distress for over a hundred years: wooden mallets, wedges and cones of soft wood to be battered into fractured bulkheads.

We set to it. I'm getting the hang of it, starting to enjoy it – bring it on. BOOM! BOOM! What the fuck? Surely they're not using actual explosives in a confined space. My ears feel like they are bleeding under the assault. Silence. I look over at Cools – no bounce now. Then comes a fourth explosion – BOOM! And we know what is next. We don't see it because the lights have failed again but we feel it. It freezes breath to lung. Thousands of gallons of ice-cold seawater are pumping into the compartment: it's January, and the water is being pumped straight from the sea. Marched in as children, in the rapidly rising seawater we must quickly become adults. A second blast of water hits me in the back with such ferocity I fall. It is so cold it renders me temporarily mute. We huddle together as instructors scream and cajole, but such is the shock at the floodwater coming in we have little capability beyond shivering.

Eventually emergency lighting kicks back in – now we must stop the flood of water flowing in unabated at an alarming rate. I ask Cools what the fuck we are supposed to do, my mind a blank. The water, fast reaching our genitals, feels close to zero. I slosh over to him, shouting out the question. An instructor singles me out: 'Don't fucking stand there, soppy. Get on with it or you'll fucking drown!' I try to remember exactly what I'm supposed to do. I see a lad reaching for a bag of shoring tools, my brain slowly unfreezing, I get the bag, and we repair the two holes in the bulkheads through which thousands of gallons of water are pouring in. I've gone from sloshing to wading over to the damaged bulkhead, collecting shoring wedges en route. It's so fucking cold. With another recruit, I batter chunks of wood into a gaping hole. I can't feel my hands. Slowly the flow rate reduces but still the water comes.

The emergency lighting flickers on and off, ensuring the task remains as difficult as possible. I'm doing a good impression of turning hypothermic. 'Exercise'? It doesn't feel like it. Maybe this is how they whittle numbers down further – by drowning us.

I once found four kittens drowned in a tank in Trawler Town, I suddenly remember. I didn't say anything at the time, guilty that I hadn't saved them. *'Fuck off, get the fuck away, focus!'* Marv slaps me awake.

I shout again at Cools: 'Wake up!' He hasn't moved a muscle. He's rooted to the deck and takes no part – he can't. The water, fast reaching our shoulders, has left his strength dead in the water. I need the large spanner behind him. Teeth rattling, I shout again and again. He doesn't respond. I howl louder as the water roars and squeals, adding to the chaos.

I can't vote yet, take a pint. I was playing keepy-uppy with mates in the playground a couple of months ago just before – when was that?

BOOM! A dull cracking noise. We've shored the main hole, reduced the flow to a trickle but now . . . You bastards, you fucking bastards! Another gaping hole appears on the opposite bulkhead through which yet another torrent rages in, screaming its way into the compartment, a shrieking angry bastard. It shatters the spirits of the entire class, but instructors are having none of it. They've seen it all before and respond the same way: 'Stop fucking gawping and get on or you'll all fucking drown.' It doesn't work for Cools or another boy who withdraws, shaking, to a corner of the compartment as the instructors continue to spit expletive-laden encouragement at us. I float across the compartment, shouting, pointing to the spanner fixed behind Cools, but he's somewhere else – he's left this madness. He stares through me and out to a place where none of this is happening. 'Leave him, fix the fucking damage! Yes, you, you fucking moron!' We're all just boys, shouldn't that mean something?

Cools unclips the spanner, reaches out. Our arms flap around in the cold wind like spinnakers and the spanner drops through his numb fingers and sinks to the bottom of the compartment. Now only our heads are above the freezing water. I laugh at the absurdity of it. I laugh at the fact that if this is how my plan to leave Trawler Town is working out, drowning in a metal box, I could have saved the Ministry of Defence the rail fare. In this moment of liberation I do something I first began at school swimming lessons when feeling stressed about the other stuff, the 'stumbles' – I drop under the water and sink.

I sit on the compartment floor, let the water hold me in a brief moment of peace. Squinting at the kicking legs dancing in the madness, I fan out my arms and find the spanner. I rise triumphant, howling banshee encouragement. Yes, yes, YES!

When it is finally over, we sodden, trembling initiates gather to hear the verdict of our instructors. It's positive – we completed the task. But Cools's swagger drained away with the seawater, and it doesn't return. Off we squelch at the double, warm clothing, hot drinks, encouragement from our class instructor, the bookish bard, waiting with his usual dour observations. He examines his boys, owl-like over the top of his glasses: 'Brassic in there, boys? We had to do it in shorts in my day. My Johnson was traumatised for days.'

Basic training over, the next stage of my instruction will follow at HMS *Collingwood*, an onshore military training school in Hampshire. I am to be a weapons electrical mechanic. Seamanship would have been a far better choice looking back, but I am adrift – I go with the flow to see where it takes me. Collecting additional kit on arrival, I chat to someone who becomes a great friend for the rest of training. Clive, a big lad marshalled by a gentle innocent love of all matters food, he'd never survive Trawler Town, but I like him immediately. A couple of years older than me, you'd never guess it from his demeanour and unique observations on military life.

'I joined coz me feet aren't made for marching but it's the only thing I've done so far . . . They're killing me.'

'Your feet?'

'What? No, the navy. What is it with the marching? By the time I've soaked me feet there's no time to eat.'

Clive loves his food and is as innocent as a newborn, with a wild-eyed wonderment at life's inclination to surprise. His views on the world are articulated through a face that appears to be moulded from timber putty.

'You been to the barbers yet? I asked them not to cut mine short but they don't listen. You been?'

I'm near bald, so I know exactly what he's talking about. If he survives the next stage of training it will be a miracle.

'Thought I'd be a stoker. Least I'll always be warm.'

He struggles with turning out correctly dressed and has a habit of wandering around with his hands in his pockets, a capital offence in the eyes of gunnery instructors or the master-at-arms, who must be addressed as 'Master', giving him a *Doctor Who*-style villainous status. Once, after guard duty, walking across the parade ground in full uniform, we spot the master heading towards us. Clive, on a bad run of minor infractions, is today turned out, quite literally, as smart as a guardsman. He beams at the master, willing him to notice the shine on his boots. He stops and asks where we are going. Clive says the NAAFI, which the master explains is perfect as we are about to volunteer to join the rugby team, which is short of numbers and is currently recruiting in the NAAFI. I hope simply barking 'Yes, Master' will allow us to quietly disappear, but Clive has other ideas. He seizes the opportunity to explain the issue of his feet. Fascinated by Clive's podiatry travails he accompanies us to the canteen where we are paraded in front of a group of NCOs tasked with signing up 'volunteers' for a variety of sporting activities. As Clive offers to remove his boots to prove his point, a petty officer asks, 'Are they for rugby or football' to which the master replies, with comic timing that has the staff in uproar, 'What, with their feet?' The canteen collapses in laughter. Clive and I have no idea why, but when the laughter subsides we are signed up as 'volunteers' for the boxing team. The joke drops years later when I'm watching re-runs of the comedy *Porridge*. The protagonist Fletcher is undergoing a prison medical, moaning about the state of his feet. When asked if he has ever been a practising homosexual he replies, 'What, with these feet?'

We prepare for a life at sea with more marching, training in weapons electrics and now boxing. While I have some experience from Tommy's gym, Clive, despite his size, is clearly not a natural. Our trainer, a petty officer in the last stretch of his service, is a ferocious Welshman with a squint. He describes Clive's main strength as being a sizeable target for any opponent. Clive's style is to throw haymakers until exhausted before switching, not without some success, to wrestling his opponent to the ground.

Despite being less than enthusiastic 'volunteers' for the

boxing team, Clive and I enjoy the routine, and our fitness levels improve. We enjoy the craic and are even allowed to call our trainer Taff, whose squint aggressively accentuates whenever Clive steps into the ring.

In a competitive bout arranged against a civilian club, one of Clive's haymakers actually connects, flooring his opponent. Before the referee can begin a count Clive drops to one knee and apologises to his dazed opponent, igniting Taff, who fires a volley of incoherent shouts as Clive sulkily wanders off to a neutral corner. Henceforth known as Slugger, Clive remains convinced the sport is not for him. 'Can't move my hands as fast as you . . . then there's me feet.'

One bonus, however, is we are given vouchers for the NAAFI and additional time off. I use it to take driving lessons, learning to drive in a 1970s mint condition Fiat 500 (two-door saloon Azzurro Chiaro Blue. Nice). I pluck a name at random from the Yellow Pages, which it transpires belongs to the only female driving instructor in the area. She is available the following week and turns out to be a force to be reckoned with.

Brenda, a baker, traveller and sage, is large of presence in every respect, forthright in opinion, with a strong maternal instinct. 'Are you eating enough, young man?' Each session begins or ends (the choice is mine) with a slice of homemade cake and a drink from a Thermos. At the end of my first lesson, while slicing a piece of Battenberg with a penknife, she informs me with unquestionable confidence that I have made the right choice in instructor and will pass my test at the first attempt, adding, as a grammar-school boy, I should be continuing my educational journey, not 'faffing around with sailors'. She is a magnificent Miriam Margolyes-esque matador of the road. I get lessons on everything: the navy, politics, family and life in general. We take to the road like Wallace and Gromit. As promised, I pass my driving test first time and am prepped in part for my onward journey in the navy.

Boxing and part-two training continue apace. I don't particularly enjoy the technical element, the feeling I should have opted for seamanship only growing stronger, as I'm clearly more interested in the workings of a ship and basic seamanship. I might be on the run from Trawler Town, but I have salt in the blood, and I love to be by or on the water to this day. When I broach the subject, suggesting I may have become a weapons technician by mistake, I receive the same level of incoherent screams and profanities as Cabbage heard on the parade ground. It continues to be a slog to find interest in the subject of rewiring lethal military ordinance and associated launchpads.

Though I remain sanguine regarding the looming combined services boxing tournament, I work hard in training and, no doubt influenced by Clive's healthy outlook on life, aired frequently, come to appreciate the routine. During two rounds of a preliminary bout, Clive, utterly convinced the sport is not for him, mutters as such as he is pursued around the ring by his opponent on the wrong end of a beating. In the final seconds of the last round, somehow he finds the beast deep within and unleashes a tremendous right hook that silences the hall. Sadly, it completely misses his opponent, landing with tremendous precision on the chin of the referee, knocking him clean out.

As an exhausted Clive looks to Taff for advice, our instructor has only two words for him: 'Jesus Christ.' An officer observing at ringside suggests that as the referee is the local vicar, come the main competition we might not be able to count on the support of the Almighty. But Taff is now struggling to mask his delight, his squint going into overdrive at the thought of Slugger's devastating new weapon.

Mulling over events in the canteen, Clive finally asks why I joined the mob, as the Royal Navy is sometimes called. For him it was a simple decision: tootling around the world for the next 20 years or so appealed to him, providing there was no actual conflict. He senses my motivation is different and asks what I am rushing to or from. It's the first time I have been asked why I was so keen to leave Trawler Town. Maybe it was his gentle, disarming disposition and the languorous take on the world, or maybe it was simply Marv, always listening, who can't resist chiming in: *'Tell him, be fuckin' honest, tell him the truth.'*

So I do. I tell him there's an anger in me, a general distrust of most people. Of what, or why, I'm not quite sure – it's something I don't really understand – but if I keep moving, never settling, then whatever it is, it can't hurt me. I don't say hurt – that's a step too far. But he nods as if he understands and we sit in silence before he veers off towards calmer waters with talk of family Sunday dinners. How eating food can be a healing process. I'm not sure I know what he's getting at but I suspect the big galumph understands far more than he lets on.

On a sodden evening the tournament begins. The drill hall is packed, mainly due to the weather outside I suspect and, more down to luck than skill, I win my bouts and go through to the finals to be held later in the year. As the matches are arranged in weight order, I'm able to watch Clive's bout. He loses his final fight on points, but not without proving to all that slow hands or bad feet are less important than heart and spirit. Slugger's stock has risen considerably following news of his infamous knockout and we make sure he knows it.

I am experiencing camaraderie at close quarters, whether it is the shouts of support as I absorb punches in the ring or working together to hold back water in a metal box, even the endless marching. It is the wattle and daub that builds a boy into something – but what?

At end of the boxing competition, I'm desperate to find a mirror and check my face, convinced I am bruised, disfigured, vanity driving my urgency as we're going ashore to celebrate. Clive wanders in eating a burger and offers some advice: 'Don't keep winning, mate. They'll only ask you to volunteer again.' We have, to a degree, evolved, grown. We head ashore knowing that adulthood is around the corner, and while it will be met with an air of invincibility, we are still in many ways, kids. But life has a habit of pulling you up by the roots.

As my training draws to a close the master-at-arms tells me the navy is counting on me in the forthcoming inter-service boxing finals, but HR (known as the 'Writers' Branch' in the navy) has other plans. I'm about to be drafted to my first ship, which I will join in Valletta, Malta, in a few weeks' time. So a return to the ring is avoided, which Clive considers final proof that I am something of a 'jammy bastard'.

The family don't attend my navy passing-out parades – my grandparents would have liked to but the information is never passed on. It's the same, later, when I join the police – family remain disconnected from important family matters, as ever maintaining the illusion of normality, I become a master at changing the subject when the topic of family comes up. Ma has still not forgiven me for leaving to live with Pa. Our Kid and Bruv will soon be off on their own adventures away from Trawler Town. I promise them it will be worth the wait. Neither are faring well back home. Our Kid will go to sea himself, a 'deckie' on a deep-water trawler, while Bruv will try his hand as a chef before choosing a career in the military. Neither will leave Trawler Town equipped with the emotional sturdiness to sustain them and in that respect we are no different.

There is time for one last night ashore with Clive and mates before I leave to join my ship's company on a large assault ship in the midst of a world cruise. We head for the nightspots that favour and lure young military. We are loud, daft, full of life and light on wisdom. We make plans to reunite, knowing they will likely not come to pass, but that is not the point – we have time on our side, plans are as fluid as the water beneath the ferry that carries us over to Portsmouth. One thing is certain: Clive and I will keep in touch, friends for life, forever united by the day his feet landed us in a boxing ring. Except we don't. I never see him again. He is killed six months later in a traffic accident. When I get the news, I say nothing.

'Fuck off! Why? What have we fuckin' done to deserve this? You fuckin' miserable cunts! I fuckin' hate you . . . What's the fuckin' point!' Always there, the voice in my head, wails and whispers, pretending he has all the answers.

I fly to Malta with the RAF. It's my first-ever flight, my first visit to a foreign country. I land in the early evening, the warm breeze caressing my face, alien to anyone used to the regular experience of a slap from an easterly passing through Trawler Town. From the airport, a smattering of officers and ratings – junior ranks – and I are transported directly to the naval dockyard accommodation. The ship is late arriving at the island, and I have a couple of days almost to myself. The senior rating, in charge of new arrivals, suggests once my bunk space is stowed and tidy, I explore the island, warning, 'I should give the Gut a wide berth.' I nod enthusiastically having absolutely no idea what he is talking about.

A chance to go beyond the NAAFI and out into Valletta. New discoveries with every step.

The Royal Navy is still a large presence on the island, but within a few years the UK leaves for good. Tourism is still relatively low key, and the country is some distance from becoming a Mecca for international gambling and a tax haven rocked by corruption and the suggestion of infiltration by international organised crime. While government relations with the administration of Dom Mintoff are hardly cosy, I find it to be a welcoming, magical, magnificent, historic island.

On my first night in another country I change into the duds of a teenager styled by Louis International of Portsmouth and am good to go. Long before online shopping, a small collection of Portsmouth outfitters would visit surrounding naval bases enticing young sailors to buy the latest fashion on a buy-now-regret-later basis. It would have been cheaper to raise sheep and weave my own clothes rather than pay the eye-watering APR. Still, I walk out of the dockyard and into the embrace of Valletta feeling good, a million miles away from the back alleys of Trawler Town.

Heading into the heart of the breathtaking stone beauty of the island's capital, I realise just how far away from home I am. The sweet smell of *buzbiez* – fennel – hangs in the air. Sicilian snapdragons sprouting out from stone walls add flashes of colour and scent the heavy stonework. Walking all over the old capital I somehow manage to skirt the hidden dangers of the Gut, as the lengthy Strait Street in Valletta was universally known to military in its heyday. It has a singular purpose: drink and debauchery. I remain oblivious to its charms at this point. After several miles up and down narrow streets I stop to drink tea and eat a traditional savoury called a *pastizz* – it looks like a dinky Cornish pastie but is filled with mushy peas. I'm so excited I purchase postcards to inform friends and family of the discovery.

It's barely nine months since I said goodbye, but I already feel like I have travelled a considerable distance from Ma and Pa. It is only the beginning. I sleep well and in the morning HMS *Intrepid* enters the grand harbour. Stepping aboard as the most junior rating, I am excited about whatever adventures lie ahead. I will take no part in international relations, no pivotal role in gunboat diplomacy. I will fix the odd broken loudspeaker and paint compartments in the belly of the ship, but all the while a coarser, more resilient hide will cover the boy, fashioned in Trawler Town but now to be toughened by travels in warmer climes. In the months ahead I'll travel through Europe, the Caribbean, and South and North America – far from home.

Eventually, my work brings me closer home, to Belfast on board a minesweeper, disproving Pa's theory that the navy won't find themselves in Ireland. The voyage over is dog rough, but I love being on the ship's wheel, the nearest I get to seamanship duties. At the height of the Troubles, Belfast leaves a taste that is hard to shift. Tasked with coastal security we board fishing boats and search the coastline caves for arms dumps. I have no appreciation or understanding of the political issues and entrenched difficulties of the Troubles. At 18, I might legally call myself a man, but the nature of the job, lugging a fully automatic weapon around as we board fishing vessels, does little to counter thoughts that this is an illusion. Perhaps the navy is sizing me up because when the sweeper is earmarked for a minor refit I am 'volunteered' once more. This time it's for the submarine service. I thought submariners were all doughty volunteers in the truest sense given the precarious nature of the work. I raise this with a supervisor, who quickly explains the navy doesn't make mistakes therefore I must have volunteered, adding, 'for which the navy is very grateful'.

I'm grateful for the rise in pay, less so for future travels under various oceans rather than on top of them. I work guard duty at the main gate at submarine base HMS *Dolphin*, onshore in Gosport, awaiting submariner training. In my downtime I find work as labourer for a local landscaper. I'm paired up with another labourer, Tom, who is a similar age and waiting to go off to medical school. We chat about my travels so far, of Trawler Town and family. Privately educated, he has a confidence and certainty about his future that I find alien but he's good company. It is the age of the garden rockery. We lay dozens and I have never been keen on them since. Tom asks why I joined the navy, and I say I don't really know, too ashamed to tell him the truth. With all the confidence of a man whose life is already mapped out he tells me he sees me working in something more creative. When I ask why, he says that he's never met anybody so 'loquacious' on the subject of cinema and the films of Alfred Hitchcock in particular. I've watched a lot of Hitchcock, thanks to Grandma, but I have no idea what he means, though I nod as if I do. I look up the word when I get back to base.

I'm taciturn when it comes to becoming a fully fledged submariner, as I'm constantly told complaining will do me no good and truth be known I actually enjoy the training. Part of me looks forward to further travels around the world, better paid with the bonus of staying in hotels, as submariners do not live on board when alongside. Tales of fun and frolics of long-haired submariners convince me this might not be too shabby after all. All I have to do is survive the Tank.

If the damage-control exercise in basic training was challenging, the Tank is terror on a different level. Pass this and an onboard test and I will be entitled to wear the 'Kissing Kippers', the prestigious breast badge only awarded to submariners, and walk with the air of a man one instructor describes as 'having survived a skull fuck of bodacious intensity'. The Tank will be discontinued in 2009 due to risk, cost and the reality of how submarines generally operate in areas where escape is unlikely. The morning arrives when I stand in line hoping somebody in charge knows what they are doing.

The test of the Tank is simply four pressurised ascents up a cylindrical tube of water in a metal tower, but only once your lungs and ears have been checked and certified capable of withstanding the madness. I discover, after an instructor fusses and checks over a piece of kit that I have been breathing into repeatedly, I have a VO_2 max – a measure of oxygen consumption during exertion – well above average. This does nothing to increase my confidence but might explain my obsession with swimming underwater. Eased into the process by making a couple of free ascents from 30 feet, we then move on to 60. That's 60 feet, in a nose clip and pair of speedos. Finally, the sheer madness of a 120-foot ascent. Fired out of an escape compartment dressed head to toe in a full-body yellow rubber escape suit only to be grabbed by a rescue diver who, catching you by the foot, refuses to release you until he's satisfied you do not have too much air in your lungs for the ascent, achieved by repeatedly asking for your name and service number. Perhaps he is preparing me for the precarious life of an undercover detective as many important briefings will be conveyed with all the clarity of someone speaking through a compressed air valve.

I survive and am stamped fit for service. However, any hope of further foreign travel is quashed when I discover I have, not surprisingly given my record, 'volunteered' again, this time for 'bombers'. A nuclear deterrent front-line submarine will be my final home in the navy. I buy my first car – a metallic blue Ford Escort – and head north to HMS *Neptune* on the banks of Gare Loch on the Clyde. From here I will sail as one of two operational crews on the ballistic missile-armed HMS *Revenge*. Thousands of miles in travel, all underwater and for at least two months at time. While school friends who, like me, flunked their exams but opted to resit are now contemplating university with something of a plan for their futures, I have more training before joining the boat (submarines are always called boats) and still no idea of what to do with my life.

For my first onboard patrol I discover that I have no bunk as we are carrying more crew than the boat is able to accommodate.

When we pull away from the dock, my bed is a hammock slung to the bulkhead behind a bank of computers in my work station, the missile control compartment. No chance of a quick escape from this malarkey. At least I'm given a torch to read by. Marv is less impressed: *'Fuck sake. How do we get out of here in a hurry? Why doesn't one of the fuckin' guests sleep in here?'* A fair point, although I remind him we did 'volunteer' and the visiting 'scientists' clearly need their sleep.

The months at sea are spent little further than 2,500 miles from various allocated targets, which may change during a patrol, such changes sanctioned and authorised by the prime minister. In my hammock I come to better understand Marv, the inner voice I suspect many of us have.

At the end of my watch, several weeks into the patrol, I retire behind the wall of computers to my hammock, slide the computer block panel shut – not locked: that can only be done from the outside – and read until sleep comes calling. I wake a few hours later, not knowing if it's morning, noon or night, of no consequence on board a boat. The crew of a bomber exists in a twilight world within another world, a metal tube within a metal casing deep beneath the ocean. The only sounds are the outer casing and the clicks and whirrs of the matrix, while I cuddle the computer that decides who dies first. No need to count sheep to send myself off to sleep – I simply listen to the electrical contacts opening and shutting on the Armageddon maker, hoping it will never happen.

The boat is pitching and rolling. When this happens in a submarine, you know the weather must be dog rough on the roof, the surface, and that we must have come up to periscope depth.

It can't be a dummy launch, because I would have been called to action stations, so we must have ascended for one of many other possible reasons.

I can't get back to sleep as I bash about in my metal cage. So I climb out of the hammock and discover I am buried inside the matrix – somebody has locked the panel. I've been told to tap against a certain part of the frame if the panel should be inadvertently locked, which I do. I also call out, but no one hears. I am trapped. My heart rate increases slightly as I tap, tap, tap from inside my strange world. I'm trying not to panic. Why is she rolling? Tap, tap, TAP! The boat's nose begins to sink into a dive. I tap again. Nothing. Who locked me in? Why is it locked? TAP, TAP, TAP . . . Nothing. I call out, once, twice, louder, nothing. Finally, he speaks,

'They're fuckin' with you, those cunts. One of those cunts thinks this is funny.'

'Who?'

'Does it matter?'

'No but I'm stuck behind this clicking, ticking, nuclear bomb-enabling wall of death AND I CAN'T BREATHE, I just—

'Shut up! Listen to the click, click, clicking of the machine – the clicks that have sent you to sleep every day – count them as they open and shut, one high, one low as they play their war games and relax . . . Just relax . . . and breathe.'

I listen to him because no one else can hear me. I climb back into my hammock in the guts of the boat, close my eyes and count the clicks behind that wall of metal and wire. He's right. I count and my heart rate slows and the clicks continue and the pitching boat settles as she continues on her silent journey and I fall asleep again. When I awake the panel is open. *'Don't say a fuckin' word about this,'* he reminds me. Because he has my back, because he knows, I know, it will be seen as weakness, it was a test and for the first time I have an understanding of who he is and why he lives in my head. And it's all okay.

Apart from this, the first patrols pass relatively swiftly, and I quickly adapt to the routine. There is no connection to the outside world save for the occasional 40-word telegrams known as 'Family-Grams'. Grave news, anything likely to disturb or upset, is weeded out before transmission. We live cheek by jowl in an undersea world thanks to patience; like the boat you become very good at listening. The primary aim of a bomber is to remain undetected, just as the undercover officer's primary aim is to not disturb the environment and remain undetected.

On patrol I have time to think about what comes next. This was never meant to be long term. I have escaped my family, but what now? The decision is made during an off-crew period. I have a furious row with Pa and Stepmother over a girl I've fallen in love with on my travels. I am in many ways more hardy, self-reliant. I'm too young to settle down, but crave stability, a true sense of home. The spat morphs into a row about my plans for the future. I look at Pa, content in mediocrity, and decide I'll prove to him I can do better. I'll start with policing – decision made, as if things were ever that simple. The reality is I am simply trying to get closer to him.

I hand in my notice to the navy so as not to be committed in the long term and immediately make two applications to the police service – a large northern constabulary and the Metropolitan Police – before leaving for my final patrol. The two months pass slowly, and I'm unsure of the decision and the future. Perhaps the Texan Yoda dude who I met on my travels one night on a Cartagena beach was right. A man of considerable age, once married to a Native American whose death he clearly still mourned, he told me my life will be defined by 'ages of'. At the time it sounded hokey and yet to the Trawler Town boy there was something in his slow drawl that had me transfixed.

I mull over all of this as the *Revenge* glides silently home, deep beneath the surface, off the Barra Fan to the west of Scotland. I'm off-watch, lying in my bunk (hammock long forgotten) reading, or at least trying to. Contemplating the next step – another uniform, another quasi family? Another temporary home for the temporary boy. We're four hours from land. Four hours from the patrol ending and a period of leave, followed by work ashore until being demobbed and a new beginning. I'm half reading in this halfway world when the captain interrupts: 'Do you hear there? Captain speaking. Standby to test all sea valves. Boat will dive in zero five minutes.'

I get up from my bunk, bored, ready for a brew. The boat's fore planes angle and begin to take her down as I amble up from number-one deck and pass the beating heart of any boat, the galley. Two cooks are hard at work as I head on to the forward recreation mess deck and pour a mug of hot tea from a constantly steaming urn while the boat slowly falls. One hundred feet. Two crew members chat about their plans for leave while another quietly reads, barely a nod between us – we're all ready for home. I forgot my book. Should I return to my bunk or finish my tea? Hot tea from the urn, 120 men inside another urn. I sit and wait for the drill to end. Two hundred feet. It is the end of a naval adventure inside a metal tube where we make our own air, trying to escape from a place where I felt I couldn't breathe. Two hundred and fifty feet. The boat detaches herself further from the life above as I sit and mull over the future. We are immersed within an alien galaxy we can't see and that neither welcomes nor rejects us. I take a biscuit from the tin. Gingersnaps – good dunkers, reliable. Take another. Three hundred feet. The old boat groans.

With pre-patrol preparation I have spent three and a half months away from home, but where is that really? More than three months hidden from the outer world and now my temporary home is creaking like Grandpa sinking into his favourite chair. I love that chair. I love life. I don't want to drift like flotsam, but what do I want? Three hundred and fifty feet. A new uniform, a new attempt to prove an unutterable point in a pointless exercise?

Suddenly alarms. Klaxons screech and sound. The captain, a softly spoken man, is at all times reassuring, but now there's the slightest of pauses before the order: 'Captain speaking. Close all watertight doors. Close all watertight doors. This is not a drill. I repeat . . . this is not a drill.' It's more the voice of a vicar than a warrior. I leap towards the hatch door as crewmates run towards the forward escape compartment, boots beating a drum tap for the condemned. I hesitate. *'Shut the fuckin' hatch!'* I turn around. *'Shut the fuckin' hatch!'* It isn't a crew mate – it's *him*. Off-watch crew beat against the hatch demanding entry. At four hundred feet, with a blown sea valve. Not an exercise, not anything I have experienced before, simply surreal as hands beat against the hatch.

Only two things are possible now, as somewhere in the boat

seawater pours in: if it's not stopped, it will fill her belly and we will sink like a stone, or we won't. But on we drop off the Hebridean Slope. Four hundred and fifty feet. I don't want to die in a metal can off the Barra Fan, within touching distance of . . .

'You're not going to die, you cunt, shut the fuck up!' I listened to *him* before and do so again.

BOOM! PHZOOSH! In the control compartment the submarine captain with a vicar's tone issues orders, calms his flock. 'He's blown the tanks,' says the senior rating in the compartment, a killick stoker – a leading hand who works in the engine room – known as 'Pluke' because of his chronic acne. I've never spoken to him, other than a nod when passing along a gangway, but here we are, sinking together. There are four of us in an escape compartment, which is as little use as a chocolate frying pan given the depth of the Barra Fan. She shudders, exhales. 'Now,' I say silently to myself. Four hundred and seventy-five feet. 'Now,' whispers Pluke. 'Come on,' says the junior cook who has never shaved and has his mother and father's faces tattooed on separate arms. 'Now' is the hope uttered by 120 souls. I stand, feel the bow still sinking, and, weirdly, recite the Lord's Prayer in my head – is this me or is it *him*? I suppose everybody believes in God now.

The killick rises up from his seat. So too does the junior cook, dressed in angelic white. Four new friends standing together. Bolts, panels and frames protest, contort and groan. Bow planes argue with the deep, trying to buy time. And the submarine does, gaining a little purchase, grip and buoyancy. Her bow lifts slowly off the Barra Fan. Four hundred and fifty feet. Bow planes hold the water with a firm grip and hold fast. Four hundred feet. We feel her nose shift as she continues to ascend. Three hundred feet. There will be no time to check the surface – now we say another prayer for an empty ocean above. Two hundred feet. On she travels. One hundred feet. She breaches. BADUMPH! Bow crashing on to water, a breaching, breathing mechanical leviathan lands to cheers and laughter – no more beating on the hatch. As we settle, the conning-tower hatch opens and the outside world rushes in, it smells foul after months of our own stink but tastes so sweet. We breathe in the nectar. *'Told you, I fuckin' told you.'* As *he* will again, in the other moments of crisis, in another life. The one about to begin.

Switching Uniforms

Both police job applications are successful. The constabulary interview process is an affable affair, Pa later cooing that the superintendent in charge of the process, who Pa knew, had told him my overall score beat several graduates and should be seen as a sign of great things to come. A vicarious boost for Pa, who seems increasingly low, preoccupied with the grind of the job, he claims. I assume he's just jaded, but also worry something more is going on with him. Is it Stepmother, I wonder? But Pa, as always, sidesteps when I ask.

The Metropolitan Police's recruitment process is a more clinical affair. There is the sense that candidates ought to feel fortunate to have been granted an interview: fewer smiles from facilitators, with more lines and more miles on the clock. Perhaps this was an indication of what the organisation was slowly becoming, a creaking monolith. Bud is settling well into a police career in the north, and makes the point that if it is promotion or specialisation I seek, it might be better to head south to the Met, where there will likely be more opportunity. Nor do I forget the urgency to travel as far as possible from Trawler Town memories a few years earlier, so it is I head south, blissfully unaware I'm about to join a family as broken and dysfunctional as the one left behind, equally riddled with neuroses and stymied by an unwillingness to change.

The police college at Hendon will be my home for the next four and a half months. I take the Northern line with my green canvas navy-issue suitcase. The bobbing ceiling hand-grips dance together. Nobody talks and everyone gazes at nothing in particular. I walk the short distance to Hendon Police College, and a few hundred metres from the station entrance, a young black man is being searched in the street: five or six officers surround him, and he seems resigned to what is happening. Nobody is talking to him, while several conversations take place among the officers. One of the officers clocks the green case and nods as I walk past – he knows where I've come from, where I'm going. The city has a very different feel to Trawler Town.

Hendon Police College is as vast as the many military bases I have known. Three large accommodation tower blocks loom over the sprawling site – a couple of middle-class recruits joke, likening them to council tower blocks. I know it's likely just nervous conversation, but it rankles. I arrive as Margaret Thatcher is finding her stride in the reorganisation of social Britain, unaware that as a police officer I will form the spine of a Praetorian Guard used to enforce social policies. The notion that police are generally representative of a cross-section of society has always been flawed.

I collect my uniform, equipment and manuals, and am allocated a room in one of the tower blocks – a room to myself, luxury. We are yet to enter the age of Kevlar RoboCops, with paralysing weapons, utility belts and body armour. Our equipment consists of a wooden truncheon, metal handcuffs, pocket book, whistle and a chain with an unexplained Yale key attached. The key, it transpires when I ask, is for old police boxes, redundant for decades but as they have so many left, 'You get one anyway, young man.' Perhaps predictably, some male recruits find the truncheon the most exciting piece of kit, and it's the same group who relish self-defence classes, although less so the 'milling', as boxing is known here.

Some find being away from home an issue, fussing and fretting over washing and ironing kit (those who can't, taking it home to their parents). I have an advantage here and as the weeks progress, I realise much of my past, both navy and Trawler Town, gave me a degree of life experience so that, insofar as basic training is concerned, I find things relatively easy. The practical 'street exercises' – roleplay designed to replicate common situations constables will face, the emphasis on conflict in a variety of forms – prove difficult for a surprising number of recruits. Many struggling to find constructive dialogue to diffuse and calm the situation, nervously relying on stock responses to the staff instructors acting as members of the public. More reliance on 'well, it's against the law' as the situation escalates, less engagement in general conversation to assess the situation, underscored by an inability to pause and reset. Now the reality is, one might argue, that there is less of everything: time, officers and patience.

Within the intake there is also wisdom. The oldest recruit in my class was previously an officer in Canada. Ron, a Scot with a dry humour and a good heart. He has clearly seen a lot of life. When I walk back to the class, having dealt with a practical scenario, he leans in and murmurs 'Detective.' It becomes a constant light-hearted quip: 'De-tec-tive. Eh, you know it. I know it.' Whenever I suggest I've made no decision on my future, he simply replies, 'Oh, you don't get to choose.' He has the steady presence of an individual who has known the highs and lows of policing. I enjoy studying applicable statutes, powers of arrest, case law, and find the street improvs in no way challenging whatever the situation. I can't understand why so many classmates struggle with them.

One evening, prepping uniform in the laundry room and running through case law with Ron, I share my surprise that this area of training seems to fill so many with fear. Why is there a tendency to reach for the pocket book immediately, often, it seems, in order to hide behind it? As always, Ron has a take on it: 'You see, if you've travelled from a young age, you know when to listen, maybe . . .' He reads as much from silence as words, and in this he teaches me a valuable lesson. I am one of the youngest in the class but I feel I've travelled a deal further than most. Maybe this will be of some advantage when we eventually start in earnest.

That night, looking out from my room high over sleepy London suburbs, I reflect on his comment. Maybe the past will fund a better future. As the lights flicker across a vast new landscape, I am excited to discover which part of it I will be policing in a few months' time. I don't have to wait long to find out: it will be West End Central in Savile Row, call sign Charlie Delta. The very centre of London's beating heart. I'm unsure what to make of it but unsurprisingly Ron has a view: 'Detective in two years, or my name is Orinoco,' this being the name of a fictional character from *The Wombles* series of children's books, later turned into a TV series. Pointy-nosed creatures who live in burrows and collect and recycle rubbish. First, though, is the passing-out parade. Recruits with two left feet are hidden away in the middle by the drill instructors, all ex-military and equally adept at communicating by the same incoherent screams I encountered in the navy.

One recruit, hidden amidst the uncoordinated, unable to control his flailing limbs, much to the annoyance of the drill master, will rise to chief officer rank and play a pivotal part in the Metropolitan Police's propaganda operation following the death of Jean Charles de Menezes, killed when wrongly deemed to be a 7/7 terrorist, proving far more fleet of foot with PR than on the parade ground.

Pa and Stepmother are unable to attend for reasons unclear. Ma, no longer incommunicado, has forgiven me for moving in with Pa and is delighted to attend. But in the event there is an issue and I receive a message on the morning of the passing-out parade via the main gate, who take a call from 'a very angry Welsh woman – she didn't leave a name but is unable to attend the ceremony'. I won't hear from Ma again for years.

Twenty-three recruits finish the course, little diversity, middle class catching the emerging blue gravy train, working class fleeing the last recession hoping to ring fence themselves against the next. As one recruit from Yorkshire puts it: 'Sod the pit for a game of soldiers.' Who of us knew that the police would become the flunkeys ordered to do the sodding? Some marching on parade here will almost immediately wave 'Scargill's Tenners' at disenfranchised communities, unaware this is the beginning of a decoupling of police from community.

Ron's parting advice is given with his usual smile. 'Eh, remember, never completely trust anyone in Copland,' he says. I'm not sure whether to believe him but I'll miss his wry humour.

'It's a wilderness. Here's a tip for you,' he continues, serious for a moment. 'When you meet someone for the first time and you're unsure, imagine what kind of animal they'd be, and see if you're right.' I nod, not really sure what Ron means.

'So what are you, then?' I ask.

'You tell me.'

'Mountain goat?'

He laughs, thinks for a moment. 'Good over all terrain . . . Aye. Remember, dinnae let West End lights distract you from the prize . . . De-tec-tive.'

'I won't,' I say.

'Eh, and the bosses, don't worry about them, they're all butterflies.'

'Not moths?'

'What?'

'Nothing, I was just thinking out aloud.'

I look around at the happy, mainly white families sipping tea as the commandant speaks of the wonderful diversity London offers when *he*, relatively quiet in recent months, answers.

'We never win fuck-all in Trawler Town, Ron.'

Diversity will improve greatly, particular among rank and file, but leadership, that will go in an entirely different direction.

My first shift is a late turn: 2pm–10pm. I arrive early and walk around the Portland stone-fronted building. It is a warm late summer day; before I start I have lunch in a café nearby. Sitting a little self-consciously, dressed in half blues, a civvy jacket over my uniform, I watch the world pass by. London flows far quicker than anywhere I have ever known. The only thing that moves slowly is the traffic.

I'm allocated a locker in the bowels of the building and given a quick tour of the admin offices, in the process meeting a bespectacled, slightly built PC, another Ronnie. He peers over a large ledger wearing the look of a man carrying the weight of the world on his shoulders.

'Be nice to him,' says my guide. 'He's the most powerful bloke in the building, more pull than Uncle Ted.'

'Uncle Ted?'

'You'll meet him after parade at some point . . .'

'Give the bastard my regards,' says Ronnie without looking up from his ledger.

Ronnie is the 'Duties Sergeant', a role that involves managing the movement and shift patterns of all operational officers, primarily constables and sergeants. The job given to him because no one else is as good at it, or wants it. While he doesn't look much like a beat cop, nor care for shift work himself, his skill in cajoling officers to switch shifts at short notice, to work overtime (always popular), and generally be compliant in the game of moving police pawns across the divisional board, is second to none.

I continue my whirlwind tour of 'Need to know' and 'Best to avoid' before being deposited in a large and empty parade room in the basement. Here I am, day one. The game's afoot. A dozen or so officers begin to wander in, in dribs and drabs. Some nod hello, some ignore me, a few shake hands. I am told we are short on numbers; I will quickly learn that since time immemorial police, front-line officers have always been short on numbers and always will be. This is actually part of the game, I assume. 'Shit happens,' I'm told. At least that's the official line from the canteen lawyers of which there are a few, but the real reason there is never enough foot soldiers is, as we shall see, due to poor management. Of which there is plenty.

The shift sergeant arrives. He hovers in the doorway with the air of a man who has forgotten something really important. He eventually commits to the room and sits down at a solitary desk, too small for the space, shuffles his papers and waits for the shift inspector to arrive. He looks over at me, appears to be considering a question but decides against it and resumes shuffling his papers. In the 18 months or so I work on his relief – his team – this look of earnest confusion remains. Eventually he speaks to me.

'You're the new probationer.'

'Yes, Sarge.'

'You er . . .' He hesitates. 'You er . . .' It's on the tip of his tongue. 'Was a marine. Yeah?'

'No, Sarge, navy.'

'Oh . . . Don't they have marines?'

'Er, yes, Sarge, but—'

'That was me, Sarge!' All eyes shift left.

The sergeant looks more confused. 'What was?'

'Me. I'm the . . . I was in the marines, Sarge.' Another probationer, built like a brick shithouse, holds up a hand and offers a toothy grin.

'Well, why didn't you say so instead of just standing there?'

The ex-marine's grin fades. He stares at boots as vigorously buffed as their owner.

A short and overweight Welshman leans in and whispers in my ear. 'Navy, you say?'

'What? . . . Yeah, I was.'

He smiles, 'Captain.'

'What? No, no I was a—'

'Nooo, soft arse. That's your handle . . . from now on.'

He shifts his gaze to the marine, smiles, and murmurs, 'Animal.'

This is Malcolm. Settling our new nicknames. There is a whiff of the night before on him. We're suddenly brought to attention when the sergeant issues a lacklustre command of 'Parade.' While the Animal and I stand bolt upright, the rest have a last scratch and fiddle before rising. I sense this ritual harks back to a different time. It announces the arrival of the shift inspector. Let's go with Ron's wisdom from now on, I think to myself. I look the inspector up and down, wondering what animal he is. A plump stoat, I decide. He casts a keen eye over the marine as if weighing up his gladiatorial potential. I appear to be a bonus.

'Wonderful. I thought I was only getting the one,' he says, checking his papers with the sergeant, who now looks even more confused.

Malcolm offers another quiet insight. 'Word to the wise, on no account get in a vehicle with him . . . if you can help it.'

The parade sniggers as Inspector Stoat beams at his newly reinforced line.

'What's that, Malcolm?'

'Oh nothing, sir. I was just telling Captain here, the good thing about C division is you rarely get in a vehicle.'

'Indeed, Malcolm, it's not four wheels that catches criminals, it's . . . ?'

Eventually Malcolm answers. 'Two feet, sir.'

'Absolutely right!'

Someone coughs at the end of the line while the sergeant's face suggests he's remembered what it was he's forgotten: 'A skipper and a captain on the same relief!' Is he from a trawler town, I wonder? Knows the captain of a trawler is always known as skipper, as is a sergeant in the police, particularly the Met. Sadly not, but he *is* reading a book on whaling, I discover later. He smiles as if suddenly relieved of trapped gas and moves on to police bulletins and assignments. I'm allocated to a beat and an experienced constable who will be my chaperone.

The final act of the parade is an order to 'Produce appointments', which the Stoat issues with relish. Looking along the line, I see what is expected. In the right hand, the truncheon; in the left, pocket book, whistle, chain (and redundant key), all raised in salutation. The inspector's eyes seem to be focused on me. I double-check – yep, all good. A glance to the right, however, reveals that Malcolm's stick breaks the uniformity of the line, it's half the size and looks like some kind of ancient sex toy, and there's also something wrong with his whistle. His pocket chain has extended twice as far as everyone else's, but whistle and key remain concealed.

'Come on now, Malcolm, all appointments please.'

Malcolm extends the chain further, still no whistle to be seen.

'Malcolm, I haven't got all day. Appointments. Please!'

As the line looks towards the Welshman, he tugs once more on the chain, which extends a deal further until a weathered bath plug springs from his tunic pocket and swings like a pendulum beneath his hand.

'Sorry sir, I had to borrow this tunic see . . . and well . . .'

As senior constables erupt in laughter and me and the Animal contemplate the future, the Stoat invites Malcolm to see him in his office later.

My first 'shout' (a directive over the radio of an urgent nature) involves half a dozen of us being sent to the American Embassy, then located in Grosvenor Square, in response to a flash protest. Whatever it was, it has calmed down by the time we arrive.

'What do we do now?' I ask Colin, my tutor PC for the next couple of weeks.

'Oh, wait for them to invade somewhere else . . . Shouldn't be too long, I expect.' Dry humour oils the wheels of the police machine. Colin is tall, bearded, a pipe smoker, not unlike a young Sherlock Holmes. As we walk back from the American Embassy it's clear he is a philosopher of few words, with an intuitive understanding of the politics of the police, and is not a shirker. I like him a lot. While some on the relief show signs of being jaded by the job, Colin is always available for any shout. In my first week I meet our other shift inspector, whom I call the Muntjac. It's immediately apparent he is a far more capable and popular leader. He has a limp, which no one seems to know the origins of; it gives him the rolling gait of an old fisherman and perhaps contributes to his stoic outlook. Like a Trawler Town skipper, he takes a moment to weigh up an individual or situation before speaking.

*

My accommodation is a police section house in Inverness Terrace, Bayswater, managed by a martinet of a sergeant, long past retirement age, Charlie. He runs the section house like Bligh of the *Bounty*, angrily determined to find moral weakness or error in his charges. No this, no that, and most definitely no women! Which he repeats at every opportunity, pausing at the word 'women' as if to purge himself of it. I arrive with a fellow probationer from Northern Ireland who asks, 'Well then, what about the odd man at a pinch, Sarge?'

Charlie, we soon learn, prowls the corridors with religious fervour. The only bounty he is focused on is finding an unauthorised guest in your room. 'Have you a woman in there, boy? No female guests . . . This is not a hotel.' Silence is maintained regardless of guest or not, until he eventually can be heard lumbering down the corridor in search of sin. It is otherwise reasonable accommodation at a nominal price.

One evening while in my room I hear a loud groaning coming from the back of the building. I leave my room, wander down the corridor and peer out of a window. No sign of violence or upset, but a short distance away is a hotel, so close in fact that directly opposite through open window I see two feet pointing north and a rising arse between them. The floor creaks and I turn suddenly to see Charlie. As passion mounts across the way, he notices me staring at the binoculars in his hand. 'I have known burglars float across these roofs.'

When I leave my room later for a night shift the corridor is quiet and in darkness. I flick on the lights to find Charlie illuminated and on point at the window, peering through his field glasses, ever vigilant for floating burglars.

*

The dividing boundaries of my Charlie Delta beat could not be more stark: on one side Soho and bedlam, and on the other Mayfair, dull as ditch water, the preserve of the rich and the mainly untouchable. 'Don't worry, officer, we'll take it from here' is often heard, not that it's ever really taken anywhere, which I suppose is the point. One night I'm called to a criminal damage allegation: the trashing of two hotel suites at a Park Lane hotel in a drunken frenzy. I discover it is not uncommon, with the police being called primarily to ensure the guests, often foreign nationals with diplomatic immunity, agree to pay for the damage before leaving. An inspector from another division contorts himself on the phone to his boss while the grinning, drunken suspects demand coffee be served. I am ushered to the staff canteen at the back of the building as the diplomacy plays out. At least in Soho suspects are, generally, less likely to be assessed on the basis of their oil and mineral contracts.

While Mayfair is a grind, Soho is frenetic; all of London life is found here, condensed within the few square miles of its neon-skinned beating heart. I love the raw-veined thrill of it. It drips possible arrests, 'bodies for the bin', to use the vocabulary of Copland, which I learn is important if you want to fit in. Soho offers a keen cop a slice of everything: 'We have it all here, Captain!' suggests Malcolm, the bath-plug-wielding Welsh philosopher, one morning in the canteen, as he tucks into a substantial breakfast. 'Three-card tricks, bilkers, bikers, prostitution, destitution. We have jump-ups, clip joints, pavement artists, burglary and affray. We've poncing, noncing and tomming. With hoisting, kiting, buggery and battery and, don't forget, assaults of every description.' Endless churn, a time when crime investigation is yet to be ironed out, streamlined to the point where most crimes are deemed not worthy of police attention, because if you don't record it, well, it isn't a problem. Whichever landscape, the boundaries of this fertile pasture of criminality are Oxford Street, Regent Street, Shaftesbury Avenue and Tottenham Court Road. I get to know every ginnel, snicket, corner and crevice. The fire escapes, the various vantage points from which to watch and wait – and it pays dividends. All crime is a game of patience, whoever you play for.

Being posted to central London offers an opportunity to make a name for yourself, to progress. Colin is of the opinion most cops are rarely proactive; I'm inclined to believe it holds true. As is the notion that those who are deemed *too* proactive will at some point see their enthusiasm curbed by a management that frets over proactivity: busy cops can be viewed as problematic if your primary focus is planning your career. I'm issued with a 'record of work' book, which forms part of my continual assessment through my probation, recording all 'arrests' and 'process' proceedings. Arrests are what the name implies, while process at the time was primarily concerned with minor traffic offences. I find 'process' as dull as a Mayfair beat but, given I'm required to produce proof of some degree of engagement with it, I opt for policing drivers failing to accord precedence at pedestrian crossings. If I find myself posted to the Mayfair beat, I hover by zebra crossings in order to balance my books. If nothing else, it's an opportunity to develop interpersonal skills, as the driver, this being Mayfair, is invariably inclined to debate if not argue their case. On one occasion, a traffic stop offers up a car full of stolen fish hoisted from a delivery to a nearby hotel. After calling for a van for the prisoner, the radio erupts with various 'done up like a kipper' comments, which even the prisoner finds funny. As for the stolen fish, it was the only time in my police service I was able to use my Trawler Town background to detail an exhibit.

It doesn't take me long to accept Ron was right: I settle on a plan, a plain-clothes tour of duty as soon as possible with a view to applying for the selection board for detective thereafter. Sometimes as a child I'd sit hidden at the top of the stairs and watch the 'Christmas men', as me and Our Kid called them, come to visit Pa. Northern detectives and friends of Pa who often brought a deck of cards and played long into the night, we would hear the sound of laughter and on one occasion tears and wonder what they did and why they came here and brought what to me and my brothers was the smell of Christmas – in reality, whisky and tobacco smoke. A sense of danger and excitement. While I don't intend to stick around too long in 'the job', I want to progress, while I'm here I intend to prove that anything Pa can do, I can do better. The path to becoming a detective is a single route at this time: selection board success following an attachment to a divisional crime squad, supervised by a detective inspector and two or three detectives who, in time, propose those thought ready to be put forward for a central detective selection board. I must earn the right to be considered worthy.

My first year as a probationary constable flies by, filled with long shifts and steep learning curves, the steady helping hand and advice of unflappable tutor PC Colin and other experienced officers. Colin does not let the job get to him. 'Not a game to be taken too seriously. Leave that to the butterflies.'

I remember Scottish Ron using the term at Hendon. 'Who are they?'

'Those rarely spotted under Arresting Officer's name on the charge sheet.'

I smile. The rank and file in Copland are more cynical than the navy, and he is proved right, although it takes me some time to realise it.

The Stoat offers nothing in terms of development. He is a tub-thumping bible man, myopic, and, as I discover after finding myself in a vehicle with him, probably racist. The Muntjac, on the other hand, is wise, decent and sincere, and always keen to ensure I get a broad education. He notes I've yet to deal with a sudden death but promises winter will likely bring the opportunity. He takes a keen interest in my development, and even invites me to his home to have dinner with his family. As always, in such an environment I feel awkward.

I don't have to wait long to deal with the deceased, but it's not the predicted homeless vagrant. My first sudden-death call comes while working a Soho beat, chatting to a stall holder in Frith Street. I'm sent to an address nearby, leaving the market, which is alive with noise and life, not quite sure what to expect. I've yet to see a dead body. Control room believe the address belongs to 'the Chinese tailor'. As I round the corner Inspector Stoat cuts in on the radio, telling me it sounds like the premises of 'Mr Woo' before singing his praises as a tailor, telling me he'll meet me at the location. The address is a small, one-room flat on the first floor of a premises sandwiched between two red-light buildings. I make my way up the stairs and knock; the door is already ajar.

A small table houses two sewing machines, and the objects of their labour hang around all four walls waiting to be collected or worked on. An elderly man smiles, almost half bows, and beckons me in with an open hand. His spine seems bent out of shape, or is it shock? He is clearly upset. His English is limited and dominated by the word 'Sorry'. 'Sorry, please . . .' 'Sorry, here.' He points towards a half-drawn curtain that divides the room. I step cautiously beyond. Lying on top of an old metal bedstead and neatly dressed is a grey-haired lady, perhaps a little younger, his wife. Maybe she appears younger because she seems to be smiling and simply asleep. In this small room, I realise for the first time that none of the 'roleplay' scenarios I confidently breezed through actually prepared me for what to do or say in such a situation. I take off my helmet and place it next to the sewing machines. Medicine bottles sit atop a box beside the bed, along with a few personal possessions. I pause. If ever I needed Brenda the driving instructor, it's now. The tailor follows silently into the space, takes a step back, 'Sorry. Please,' and with another half bow, noticing something is amiss, leans over and picks up a green-handled hairbrush from the box and gently brushes a lock of his wife's hair away from her face, 'Sorry . . . Sorry.' The action is so gentle, the words for her, not me.

Satisfied, he disappears behind the curtain. He isn't Mr Woo – that is just the name the Stoat has chosen for him – and he isn't Chinese, but he is a tailor; he is from Vietnam. I learn later that he and his family had fled from persecution under the communist regime, finally arriving in Soho to fix the clothes of Londoners, including the police. He returns and places a blanket over his wife, tucks in the corners and then, with an open palm, ushers me towards tea he has made. We sit on two upturned wooden boxes topped with cushions. As I attempt to note details for the Coroner's Office, he turns to look at the curtain and emits an elongated sigh, as if he has been holding his breath until someone arrived. I scribble the words a constable needs; behind me I can still hear the sounds of Frith Street market.

The inspector bowls in with purpose, along with the sergeant, who senses this is not a situation requiring bluster. I walk back to the station to write it up, through the market, the shouts and calls, empty boxes strewn across the street, life carrying on regardless. I call in on the tailor a couple of times, meet his daughter busy sewing on her mother's machine. A few months later they're gone. According to a maid tending the ground-floor business, the landlord wanted an upscale in rent that 'even two machines going like the clappers' would not achieve, so the family who arrived by boat, and are now one less, are off again.

Inspector Muntjac continues to encourage and is so supportive, dependable. A second invitation to dinner to meet his family; I am no less awkward, find the streets easier to navigate. There is no bullshit with him, no corporate flannel. He is the best of the best and will never progress beyond mid-level because of it. Barely 12 months into my probation, he starts to partner me with experienced uniformed officers working street vice in Mayfair, including Colin. It's an odd set-up, wearing 'half blues' under a civilian jacket or coat and trying to blend into the night. It's not a particularly effective disguise but I'm grateful for the opportunity. On a number of occasions we end up off grid parked up at Dolphin Square, which falls under the jurisdiction of another division: 'The shit that goes on in there . . .' By the third visit I'm so well versed on the second half of the sentence I finish it myself.

'. . . but it's never dealt with?'

'True, you been here before?'

Its reputation preceded it. An enclave of position and privilege considered off limits to police.

On the whole, though, I enjoy the work, such as it is. Often, as Colin fires up his pipe, he airs his thoughts on the politics of the police, appearing to cut to the chase, though in reality revealing little: 'The real shithousery here isn't those hanging out their arse on the street.' It's a blunt truth. One vice partner I can never quite figure out is a silver-haired dude, Troyes. He is not one to break sweat, carefully seeing his time out, but is more streetwise than many. He is full of surprises and, so long as he doesn't have to do the paperwork, capable of tossing you the odd bit of work that rises above mediocrity. Dozens of tours on the vice squad have distilled his conversation, removing the need for over-elaboration.

'So, in the navy, you fuck any toms?'

'What? No, course not. Well, there was . . . It's not straightforward because I didn't . . .'

'So that's a yes, then.'

We carry on in silence until, not surprisingly, we arrive at Dolphin Square. I wait but there is no lecture, only more silence as Troyes stares over at one of the mansion blocks. He winds down the window, spits out the word 'Cunt' into the frost and with that we turn around drive back towards Mayfair. Police cultural protocols dictate I say nothing and hope the week reveals more. It does, kind of.

It's the early hours of my third night shift with him. He drives, and while it's a bonus to be sat in the comfort of a warm vehicle in winter, there is not much conversation as we slowly creep along the deathly quiet streets and mews of Mayfair looking for something or someone.

'If you're out flogging your arse now, in this weather, you're after rent or redemption.' Rent or redemption are the two driving forces of most of the sex workers I deal with in this brief sojourn into sadness. We park up off the main stamping ground for sex workers in Mayfair at the time, the Haymarket. It may be Mayfair but it is not the world of highly paid sole-trader escorts. Troyes, not surprisingly, stays at the wheel and sends me out to hide in the shadows of a building under renovation. I suggest climbing up scaffolding to get a better view of the junction he believes most likely to produce 'tom, punter or ponce'. I've no earpiece, no covert comms, just a cumbersome police radio and a mullet to keep me warm.

'You might be up there a while . . . I admire your initiative. Watch it doesn't fuck you in the arse one day'.

His wisdom appears to spring from the reality of years of policing at the coalface until stricken with a type of 'cynical silicosis' of the mind – I remember being told in the second year of my probation that it sets in around the five-year mark, convinced it will be different for me. I scuttle up the scaffolding. It does offer a much better view of the junction, but listening to a stream of calls to Soho, this initiative is tasting a little sour. Troyes interrupts my shivering with an observation: 'Second time round, you see that?'

I saw nothing, but a few minutes later a large saloon car crawls slowly around the junction and comes to a halt, brake lights casting a red glow on the entrance to basement steps. As the exhaust pipe wheezes, a cloaked figure emerges from the basement, glances into the vehicle before quickly getting in the passenger seat. For context, Peter Sutcliffe has not long been imprisoned, and this twilight world is still cautious, on edge. I ask if he is going to pull the vehicle.

'No. We'll sit awhile. He should be back in twenty minutes or so.'

'Yes, all received' my response over the air, primarily because Marv is shouting so loud in my head Troyes must surely hear him.

'You fuckin' lazy bastard. We're fuckin' freezing up here and you, you cunt, just don't want to do any paperwork, which, incidentally, I'll be the one fuckin' doing it as always!'

'He must be a bolter, they're back . . . Receive that, over?'

'Yes, all received, over.' Distracted by my internal bickering, I miss the car crawling back around the junction, but as if for my benefit, the rear lights highlight the cloaked passenger within a soft red glow. Without a second glance, the figure slips quickly down to the basement. As quick as a clam in ruffled water.

'Right, meet you by the steps and it's your turn to get the teas.' It's always my turn to get the teas, but given the punter has now disappeared I'm not sure what it is we will be writing up over the beverage. Troyes might be lazy, but he's not daft. First, we have to go and find the cloaked figure hidden in the belly of Mayfair. Troyes is confident it will not take long, and I have the feeling he has been here before.

I clamber back down from the scaffolding and scamper

quickly across the road and over to the basement. Troyes pulls up in the car, steps casually out and takes time to button up his overcoat before sauntering over to the railings and peering down into gloom as I shiver beside him.

'Don't make us come down, Gloria. You know I'm scared of the dark.' Silence. I'm heading towards the steps when I feel his hand on my shoulder.

'Gloria, I've seen you once already this week. Remember, second time and it's a trot down the nick, so if I have to . . .'

Gloria has worked Mayfair for several years off and on. Her faintly lined face is dominated by striking green eyes that dart at the slightest movement, but, otherwise, she is not in the slightest bit fazed at being taken in. In a long-since redundant coal store in the basement she keeps a holdall, a change of top coats and a flask. It's a place to hide if police are about and a known pick-up point for her regulars. A side hustle with the building's caretaker allows her to use it as a flop to get off the street.

An unwritten rule at this time is that a warning is given to those suspected of soliciting for the purposes of prostitution, while a second stop leads to arrest and a trip to Marlborough Street court; however, Troyes has a different plan tonight. He taps Gloria for information, intelligence, and he's not interested in other working girls. It's pimps, ponces and her tricks. This is my introduction to a wholly different game to Gloria's. The slippery art of intelligence gathering, because this is the time when everything is changing so far as 'intel' is concerned. Copland is beginning to realise the value of intelligence as a commodity, and here on a cold street corner in La-La Land I begin to understand the nature of the business. As my breath congeals in the night air,

Troyes outlines Gloria's options before walking back to the car to do a name check. There might be a warrant regarding an outstanding fine, though I wonder if it is all part of his game. I turn my radio down. Gloria, unfazed, asks him to get a move on before we all freeze.

At the station Gloria produces a deck of spent underground tickets unprompted. I can't help but feel this is a routine neither her nor Troyes are unfamiliar with. With an easy dexterity, she peels off two tickets from the deck and pushes them across the table to Troyes. On them, written in a tight weave, are scribbled vehicle registration numbers, names and the date of when the ticket was bought. Two clients that she hopes never to see again, she says, as she shuffles her pack with a tired smile that indicates a non-negotiable disclaimer: what Troyes and the Metropolitan Police do with the information is a matter for them – Gloria will not be a participating informant. 'This is not my problem. I have no idea what you're talking about,' she says. Troyes nods. He's been here before. I try to work out exactly what is going on. Is she under arrest? Unlikely. Is there a warrant outstanding? Vague. Or, is the officer never knowingly overbusy stepping up to the plate and developing a work ethic?

We sit in a corner of the faded grey custody room a few years away from being rebranded as a suite. Troyes palms the tickets as Gloria shuffles her pack. I ask her if I can take a look. Her fist tightens in a protective grip, and she darts a look at Troyes, who shakes his head. What rides on the tube stays on the tube, obviously. As he reaches the door, she adds, 'Only one of those is a goer, but you know that already. Don't be long now.'

She fixes her eyes on me and says, 'I think I know you.'

Though not true, I feel myself reddening, and Troyes can't

resist: 'Really, was it when he was in Colombia?' And with that he's gone.

She thinks on for a moment: 'I love the flowers from there – bargain if you wait until late. I'm not a morning person. You?' I have no idea she is referring to the Columbia Road flower market. I can't think beyond my burning cheeks.

She doesn't wait for a reply, and I busy myself with paperwork. She sits quietly, somewhere else it seems, but noticing every movement, missing nothing, tuned in to the slightest change in the air. Experience has marked those tube tickets.

'He won't get anywhere with October . . . You should stick to August'.

The dates, combined with the names, all coded I assume, are a form of index system. I realise Gloria is a very smart lady. Trust in her world has very much declined and she's right to be careful. 'August' is a pimp and robber of working girls who frequently uses violence; 'October' moves in very different circles and feels his money entitles him to use violence. Eventually August gets a knock at his door while October is given words of advice. No doubt this happens under a cloud of cigar smoke in a private members' club while Troyes drives another probationer to a high-end neighbourhood and releases a breathy 'Cunt!' into the night air before turning the wheel.

As I near the end of my probation I'm committed to making detective. I have the highest number of arrests on my relief by some distance, but this matters not to Muntjac. In the canteen one morning he takes me aside and makes a suggestion. The chat is in part prompted by an incident with a newly promoted superintendent. A spiteful individual known as Jogger, he is the spit of Detterick in the film *The Green Mile* and as brimful with malice. On taking office he orders an officer to be stationed at a desk just inside the entrance to greet visitors, even though there is already adequate provision at the front counter to triage them, and all attempts to persuade him this is a waste of an officer fall on deaf ears. The real reason, it is suggested by some older officers, is that he craves acknowledgement of his status – the officer has to stand up and salute him – whenever he enters the building, presumably to indicate to the members of the public sat in the foyer that the diminutive, angry-looking man is someone of importance. He has been known to hover outside, hoping to catch out the officer unawares. It's a ridiculous waste of resources.

Proactive on the relief, I manage to avoid the post in the main; however, one morning I'm not so lucky. While taking an urgent message from the magistrates' court he arrives in full sail. Midsentence, phone in hand, I shout 'Morning, sir,' but this is not acceptable to him, as I did not stand up. He waits for me to finish the call before setting about a public humiliation, but he's halted halfway through by a gentleman waiting to produce his driving documents, who quietly introduces himself as a retired brigadier. With exquisite precision, he suggests that if this is a demonstration of police leadership, he fears for our future. I watch the bizarre reversal of fortune unfold as he deflates Jogger, who can't wait for the sanctuary of the lift.

The brigadier returns to his seat, sits down in smart fashion and, with a twinkle, mutters, 'In the war, we wondered how many of your chaps would be willing to collaborate and round up their neighbours if the Germans did invade.'

It seemed an odd thing to say, but it stayed with me, leading to the invention of a game to alleviate operational boredom years later when on surveillance. If ever this country was invaded and occupied, who of our colleagues past and present would collaborate and round up those deemed undesirable? There were a few names that came to mind. There's something about policing – like politics, it often attracts those entirely unsuited for authority.

Of course, Jogger has the last laugh, kind of, posting me to the front desk for the rest of the week, despite protestations from my boss. On the last day, I'm called to see the commander of the division, the infamous 'Uncle Ted'.

I'm so revved up, I'm prepared to deliver a 'Fuck this, I'm going to do something else with my life' speech before handing him a letter of resignation. Marv has raged all week while I fumed in silence, twiddling my thumbs sat at the vanity desk, but as I enter the commander's office he greets me with a wide smile.

'Young man, are your balls golden?' he asks, before asking why a retired soldier has sent him a donation for the benevolent fund, as well as a bottle of malt and praise for the calm and polite manner in which a young constable reacted to an unwarranted verbal attack from 'a very short' senior officer, and expressing concern at the calibre of policing leadership in the UK. The commander correctly assumes I will not be accepting the whisky, which he proposes sharing with the head of the divisional crime squad who, he goes on, will be receiving an application from me to join them at the first available opportunity.

'Uncle Ted' asks to see my record-of-work book, and enquires about the background on some of the arrests, in particular the

'Fighting Finnegan', a middleweight champion boxer I'd arrested for drunkenness. He listens intently, asks a few questions, lights up a smoke and calls the superintendent to say he's found a young constable with an outstanding record of work 'scratching his arse on the other front desk'. Within the month I am selected for the divisional crime squad.

It was Muntjac who'd told me to take my record-of-work book to the meeting, but not before also suggesting I should wait, spend more time in uniform, perhaps sit the sergeant's exam and then at some later point think about becoming a detective.

The wheels roll for or against you – it all depends on where you are in the bigger picture. I thought I'd made the right decision at the time – looking back, I should have listened to him. And just to highlight how uncertain the future can be in Metland, I have another near miss with the wee man.

As I'm leaving the station in full uniform, including coal-scuttle hat – and yes, you do get asked if your head goes all the way to the top – I stumble upon him again exercising his innate leadership style, bullying another probationer. He's cornered his victim, bawling him out, and I can't get around him, but he's in no mind to interrupt his display and let me pass. I stand for what seems like an age when, without warning, I hear Marv. His voice, his anger, background, his accent. Trawler Town.

'*Cunt.*'

Jogger stops, stunned. As is the other probationer, who while relieved at the intervention knows that this will not improve things.

'What was that?' Jogger's eyes raging.

I'm in shock, I know this is *him*, but before I process and reply in my own voice, Marv, as if to confirm, is on him again:

'*Cunt!*' Bolder now.

Time stands still. Jogger turns, lining up the crosshairs of his tongue on a new target. I'm supposed to start on the crime squad in a week. Kiss goodbye to that, laddie. As I hide under my helmet, from nowhere a sergeant (the Llama) who had witnessed the entire event steps forward.

'Tourette's, sir.'

'Tour what?' asks Jogger, straining his neck trying to appear taller as the Llama peers down at him.

'He has Tourette's syndrome, sir, though he'll be too embarrassed to tell you himself. Diagnosed in the navy, wasn't it? He was a submariner, sir.' He turns to me. 'You haven't drunk enough water today, have you?'

'Er? . . . No, sorry Sarge.'

'On you go. You don't mind, sir?'

Jogger nods reluctantly. It's clear he's never heard of Tourette's, and neither have the two silent probationers, me and my new friend, who stare blank faced at the Llama. As we head off, I hear him explain to Jogger how my condition developed in a live fire exercise at sea. He's so convincing that when I later receive a commendation for an incident in Selfridges, Jogger explains to the bemused divisional commander it is all the more remarkable as I suffer from 'Turrets' syndrome.

I had again escaped the bully and, that one incident aside, Marv rarely spoke in public again, though he was often in the room, watching, listening, never far from saying hello.

My education will soon continue. I have a date to start on

the crime squad but, first, in my final few weeks in uniform I leave my pals on relief with enough ammunition to rag me for months to come. I have a talent for spotting hooky – a curiosity for the not-quite-right that is often productive – but, sometimes, youthful exuberance leads to embarrassment. As in this incident. One morning, in for a quick change over (finish work at 10pm, return at 6am), I forget my boots and have to borrow a pair. They're too big and have steel Blakey's, metal tips on the heels, but needs must. You can hear me coming a distance away. Later that morning I see someone or something being chased across Regent Street, a fast-moving object that appears to be clothed in a bunch of colourful flags. Nothing over the radio, but I quicken up my pace. When I see another person join the chase, I too begin running, or at least trying to. The oversized boots and Blakey's mean it's hard to gain traction. I look like Wile E. Coyote as my feet struggle for purchase, and I call in that I'm chasing a suspect. When asked the reason why, I have no answer – I'm too far away to know.

A call to the control room from Liberty's department store confirms their store detectives are chasing a known drug addict who has stolen a selection of expensive silk scarves. I'm so far away from the suspect, only the flash of colour gives any clue as to his direction. I set off as Charlie Delta seeks updates on my pursuit as other units head towards the chase. I know all the cut throughs and rat runs and make up enough ground to finally see the suspect, whose narcotic-fuelled sprint shows no sign of slowing down. We criss-cross the division, a Jackson Pollock abstract of sweat and shouts. Officers run past each other hollering 'Which way?' Members of the public offer shrieks of encouragement and updates on the suspect's progress. The suspect's silk colours trail in his wake as my boots begin to sap my energy, but having called it in, pride keeps me going.

After 20 minutes of mayhem, our resident comedian Malcolm joins the fray over the radio, offering a pitch-perfect commentary in the style of the BBC horse-racing broadcasters of the day, Peter O'Sullevan and Michael O'Hehir. By lap two of the Liberty Stakes my radio has come adrift and is thrashing wildly about, I've lost my helmet and my legs are screaming in agony. Malcom gets into his stride: 'And the field is now looking increasingly strung out as they turn for home.'

I round Oxford Street for the umpteenth time and head down Bond Street. I can see him – he's done. His legs have gone, but still he won't give up – the slight incline down Bond Street seems to be carrying him over the line and away.

My radio battery is dead and my police whistle, which has worked free of my tunic, lolls from side to side. I stop to take a breath, a spent Wile E. Coyote watching the doped Road Runner disappearing. As much in defeat, as I have no other idea what to do, I blow hard on the whistle. A sound probably not heard since the 1950s, it has no effect on the suspect, of course, but a black cab stops. The driver shouts, 'Is that him?' pointing to the explosion of colours in the distance. Oxygen deprived, thinking he said get in, I place a weary arm on the door as he roars off, leaving me chugging at the roadside. He mounts the pavement, pulls across the suspect, leaps out and floors him. The thief, energised thus far by a particularly potent amphetamine, is no match for the cabbie, who it turns out is also a football referee.

I am present, later, at court as the arresting officer, while St

John Harmsworth presides. The suspect pleads to guilty and after listening to the facts of the case Mr Harmsworth, clearly having lunched well, asks if the arresting officer is present in court. I am pushed forward. Mr Harmsworth peers at me over his spectacles.

'I must say, I am often amazed at how readily citizens of London take for granted the extraordinary dedication of the much-maligned man in black . . . I am of course referring to the Football Association referee.'

I still have the whistle.

Pa Switches Uniform Too

At the end of the month I buy myself a new pair of trainers as well as my first suit, and I'm on to my new posting. On day one, on the top floor of the art deco building with the other new starters, I sit in the crime squad office and listen to what is expected of us. We are told that the pressure will not be for everyone, that not everyone is cut out for plain-clothed work. I think of Ron's words. I'm about to discover it is certainly a very different landscape, and the management know exactly what it will take to survive their process: 'Two arrests and two assists each and every week because this place survives on bodies in the bin.' A Hunger Games of sorts, for the right to wear a suit.

That is what's required to stay the course, and to get on the course that leads to becoming a detective. From there, the path to become an undercover officer: detective first, UC thereafter. A road not travelled unless invited. I will be the only one from this room who makes it; I feel my foot feather the accelerator.

Early days on the crime squad are once again similar to military basic training. I accept the mocking banter as part of the initiation from officers, some of whom are barely ahead of me in training, some full of swagger, while others give you no more than a side glance. Some of my colleagues won't make it to a selection board, periodically culled by management, the all-seeing eyes of a detective inspector assisted by two detectives. Some will ask to go back to uniform, knowing it is not for them, and some leave with a bias against CID, easier to bear a grudge than accept they were never cut out for the work. Once I asked Pa why he never thought about becoming a detective.

'I'd never have been home, son, and . . .'

'Yet when you fuckin' was . . .'

Marv filling the void – not that he ever felt the blows. But Pa never did answer the question.

My new colleagues are a mixed bunch, some flash, some comically ill-prepared and some who clearly know what they are doing, conscientious, hard-working, who think with their heads, rather than pointing a finger at the first suitable candidate for arrest within their own parameters of plausibility. For my part, I arrive with the highest arrest record of that year, a result of instinct and curiosity and hard work. Graft rather than grift. I'm proud of it.

I spend hours going through intelligence reports, wanted bulletins, outstanding warrants, speaking to detectives downstairs in the CID office, looking for an opportunity to shine. I don't know why or where the enthusiasm comes from other than a desire to make detective quickly, to prove I am a better cop than Pa, to prove I am a good son. It makes little sense – there was never a chance to prove anything to Ma, but maybe with him there might be some kind of redemption, for both of us. There is time enough to figure out what to do with the rest of my life. I'm young. Turns out I'm good at this and, I increasingly realise, it spikes the adrenalin like nothing else, it's almost an addiction. So I pledge myself to yet another family – it's easier than trying to get closer to one I won't admit I might never understand. But this one, this parent of bastards and saints, when it has you within its grip, it will not let you go, and like the one I left behind, it too will make promises it never intends to keep.

All the same, I throw myself wholeheartedly into my new role, patrolling the West End in plain clothes, targeting all the aspects of street crime the Welsh philosopher eloquently outlined: robberies, burglary, street-level drugs, vehicle crime are a daily diet. We have no personal protection beyond our wits. No stab-proof vests, telescopic batons, Kevlar, tasers or crime tsars, no incapacitant sprays. Just instinct and wherewithal. We also have metal handcuffs, often with no key. On one occasion a rather self-assured high-flyer accidently handcuffed himself to a desk as a jape, only to find he had the wrong key. Released several hours later, he went on to make the same mistake with a prisoner, which cut short his stay on the crime squad, though he also went on to rise up the ranks, thus proving within policing that common sense, or the lack of, is no bar to advancement.

But I love it, the challenge, the sheer blast, the ever-changing seasons of crime in London. I run and run through the city streets until my lungs burn, a lactic acid high, a good pain. I have no idea that one day the source of the fatigue will become corrosive. I now have police accommodation in Spencer Park, Wandsworth. A balcony at the back of my small apartment overlooks a green space, which backs on to a thicket where squirrels perform daily acrobatics. Most mornings I sup tea on the balcony before work, thinking this is as good as it gets. I would do this job for nothing – just feed me and let me enjoy doing something good for the city that has adopted me. During transport strikes I walk or run the seven miles into work – absolutely nothing will stop this Trawler Town boy making his old man proud, an almost combative edge to an inner drive, to which occasionally my inner voice whispers, '*Why?*'

Through their notebooks apprentice detectives are judged. The words they contain have been used through the ages to convict guilty and innocent in equal measure. It measures blind loyalty to the job in defence of the mythological thin blue line, calibrated under the auspices of chiefs who do nothing to stop the verbals, gob fulls, coughs and fit-ups that have occurred since policing began, happy to bask in the praise and reward that noble-cause corruption bestows, which, if discovered, is something simply out of the blue, never their responsibility.

When the Police and Criminal Evidence Act of 1984 is enacted, it does little to change the practices of old. Out with the verbals and in with the verbose. The legal requirement is now tape-recorded interviews and better management of officer notebooks. But look at every notorious miscarriage of justice, every major incident of police misfeasance or mismanagement, and you will find the same unanswered questions, the same pattern of behaviour, the same response by shoeless senior officers tiptoeing across well-carpeted offices to gently close the door on accountability.

In this environment, any young apprentice must have eyes in the back of the head to survive. Quickly you must realise who to avoid, who is most likely to make a quick arrest in search of overtime or admiration. An assistant chief constable told the filmmaker Roger Graef: 'Rank is much more important in the police than in the military.' The better quality of leadership I encountered in the military will not, however, be welcomed into the lucrative policing battalions. In policing, rank is the gift that keeps on giving. While some in senior positions are undoubtedly well-intentioned and dedicated officers, the harsh reality is that they oscillate in isolation and make little difference to rank-and-file officers, who are all too often blamed for the incompetence of senior management. I wear my Reeboks to the bare soles, chasing suspects across the division, and in 18 months not once do I look up to find myself running alongside an inspector, chief inspector, superintendent, chief superintendent, commander, deputy assistant commissioner, assistant commissioner, deputy commissioner or indeed the commissioner.

Crime is a perennial problem – you just have to be patient, observant, in the right place at the right time, and you will find it. There is some science to policing crime, but it is not rocket science. Do not believe the words of police chiefs justifying inflated salaries by repeating old mantras about the complex nature of crime in the modern age, a lack of police powers and resources – it's all an illusion, rehearsed political pat to mask poor performance that has been trotted out for years. Same message, different acronyms.

But for a brief summer, unaware of the war being planned in Thatcher's Whitehall, a young, aspiring detective is determined to get in, do good and get out. It is bloody brilliant! And that's despite the odd bloody nose, or nights spent on Mayfair rooftops, or high up on construction crane jibs undertaken with no risk assessment beyond 'Don't fall off.' We wait like longline salmon fishermen for burglars to swim into our net, or trawl a packed West End for three-card tricksters who con tourists out of cash with their playing cards and a side order of pickpocketry. We corner narcotics street deals, which would now be county-lined or dark-web sales. Then there are the handbag snatches, born out of the lucrative lure of chequebook and credit card fraud, and 'jump-ups' – thefts from the backs of delivery wagons as drivers leave their vans open for ease. At odds with the diverse composition of this city, I notice there is very little multiculturalism within the ranks, and there is more prejudice than I ever saw in Trawler Town, but I keep my head down and my figures up, and it works. Soon I have a date for my selection board. Pa thinks I'm too young in service to pass the selection board at the first attempt, but he's in for a surprise.

My third night sat on the top of a construction crane, looking out over Mayfair, with two more to go.

'I've put you on top of the crane, Captain, with the Dung Beetle, as you were in the navy,' explained the detective in charge of an initiative to tackle a spate of burglaries in the area.

'But I was a submariner . . .'

'Good with binoculars then, and it's all the same, up or down. That's life.'

'And he's actually with me, Sarge,' says the Goliath Beetle.

'Oh, yeah. Sorry, Captain.'

He's sorry, I think, because I'd be safer with the Dung Beetle. Instead I'm paired up with a lunatic, and in the small hours, as boredom sets in, he challenges me to see how far I'm willing to walk out along the crane's jib. My selection board is the following week; what could possibly go wrong?

I get halfway along, no safety harness, just sheer stupidity and the goading of my colleague. When the jib begins to move in the wind, I turn back confident I've won the challenge. The Goliath Beetle claps his hands, gives me his gloves and walks almost to the end of the jib. I feel nauseous just watching.

The following morning I'm at home standing on the balcony with a cup of tea reflecting on the madness of the night before when Pa calls. I pull the landline onto the balcony, enjoying the warmth of an early spring on my face.

'How's you, son?'

'Popsicle! All good. How are you?' Popsicle, my nickname for him in light-hearted moments. The line falls silent.

'Hello? Pa? Can you hear me, it's a bad line?'

'Yes, I'm still here, son . . . Just called to say . . . I'm in court this morning.' This is a surprise – he's been office bound for years.

'Oh, right, what's the job?'

A pause.

'Me, son. I'm the job . . . Your old Pa is . . .' He trails off, as always.

'Sorry, I don't understand . . . Court?'

'I've let you down, son. I . . . What's that noise? Bloody loud . . .'

The noise is another reason I'm on the balcony – it passes overhead same time every week.

'Concorde, Pa, it always flies over here . . . In court?'

I go back inside to hear better but when I put the phone back to my ear, he is already saying his goodbyes.

'Haven't got long, I should have rung you sooner . . . I have to go pack a bag.'

And in that moment I know what he means, even if he can't utter the words.

Pa is right – he should have rung me sooner, at least a year sooner. For over 12 months he has been on bail, committed to the Crown Court where today he will plead guilty to fraud charges. Over several years he has stolen Police Federation funds, an extraordinary sum, around £400,000 in today's money. How it was not uncovered sooner I do not know, and it was not funding a lavish lifestyle but a chronic gambling addiction. At two casinos in the north, Pa, once sheriff of Trawler Town, had morphed into the high roller hiding in plain sight, throwing company brass on the roulette table hypnotised by the spin of the wheel. The sum of all the numbers on a roulette wheel is 666, considered by some to be the number of the Beast. Gambling is the beast that leads Pa to this moment. Extraordinary.

It transpires he had at some point won a huge sum on the football pools, his prayers answered. Enough to cover what he'd stolen. What did he do? He paid it all back, of course – the sheriff was back, high in the saddle. Home and dry. But of course he doesn't stop. The beast has him in its grip and Pa won't back down. Pa never backs down. He spins the wheel again. And before long is back where he started. During the long period before court, having told his bosses, he told Stepmother, Stepsister, close friends and then, on the morning he too would leave Trawler Town, he told me.

'I've got to go, son.'

'Yes . . .'

'Son, don't visit. I'll be okay . . . Eh, Concorde? That must be something.'

'Yeah, Pa, it is.'

He is sentenced to two years and serves one.

That night on the jib wondering why, why me, why Pa is Pa and what I will say to my own boss about this, as the Goliath Beetle does press-ups on the platform, I walk out to the end of the jib, the very end. The long metal arm sways under my feet; you can never take for granted the ground beneath your feet. London is sleeping, and tonight Pa is sleeping in a cell some-where. I turn and walk back to the platform. The Goliath Beetle applauds.

'Knew you could do it . . . Best of three?'

The following day I find the detective chief superintendent, head of all CID on the division, in the Burlington Arms celebrating with several detectives. The DCS is a good man, perceptive, he sees my reticence to begin this sorry tale in a pub, suggests we walk back across the road to the station. I tell him everything, he listens intently and then reassures, pointing out I am not my father's keeper, that I should not worry about the selection board, confident I will fare well. Another conversation I reflect I would never be able to have with Pa. As I turn to leave, he tells me to visit Pa anyway, despite his request. I will do so, twice. It's diffi-cult. There is to be no apology or explanation from Pa, not ever, and even when he is released and I find myself making represen-tations on his behalf, I wonder why? I should focus on my career, not the ashes of his. Maybe if he helped me understand it would be easier, but he doesn't. Pa comes back to Trawler Town, takes his dogs to the beach and stares out to sea. Pa walked to the end of the jib and fell off; he didn't want anyone to catch him.

I pass the selection board. When the DCS calls me in to his office, he says, 'Make your dad proud.' If only it was that simple. Now I wait for my posting. Please, let it be busy, enough to help me forget.

The Bastard Borough

It is often said that London is no more than a collection of villages, and Stratford in east London did indeed begin life as a small village, attached to a Roman road linking London to Colchester. I arrive there on loan to a homicide inquiry investigating a gangland killing, and it has less of the village feel and more an air of a gladiatorial arena, particularly after dark. I already knew that though, living nearby.

The Pangolin, a high-flyer running the CID department at the quiet outpost I initially find myself at after passing the selection board, believes Stratford will be professionally more to my liking, so here I am – on a murder investigation. I know there will likely be an opportunity to stay on in the division if things work out. Ever since I spotted and arrested a 'kiter' (a credit-card fraudster) in a restaurant while having lunch with the Pangolin, and in doing so, uncovered a massive credit-card fraud, he has been keen to find me a posting better suited to my desire to push on.

Stratford is far from the polished multipurpose landscape that will one day host the Olympics, a desirable place to live by the River Lea with an international airport on its doorstep. It is unloved, it is the Bastard Borough, but to me it is heaven. I have already concluded my new aim is to be posted to a specialist unit within four years, and only then will I contemplate leaving the force and doing something else with my life. Maybe by then I will have proved the still unclear, undefined purpose.

In the Bastard Borough, everybody likes to talk, shout, whisper, in confidence, in the open, and I feel it is only a matter of time before they talk to me. The only way you ever get close to the truth of a crime, any crime, is to talk to people, to differentiate from the hypothetical and the hyperbolic, a skill that is withering on the vine within policing. Assigned to the homicide, I soon discover, regarding this particular killing, that if anyone talks, it is with one eye on the door. The murder that has led to an assembly of detectives is the result of a squalid turf war driven by tribal machismo and money – in this instance lucrative security contracts, and all that follows, narcotics markets primarily. It's a case where there seems to be little distance between victim and perpetrator. At least that's how it begins, but one thing is certain: homicide is a crime that cuts deep into your psyche and leaves its livid images scorched into your conscious.

I am a young detective, but I arrive in the Bastard Borough with two such images already scored into the back of my skull. A young man, stabbed in a Soho spieler, who staggered out into the night and barely made it a few blocks before collapsing, his life ending on a corner close to Oxford Street. I still cannot walk past that spot without seeing him: the sharp leather jacket – 'It's barely worn in', as was his life – his head resting on his arm, a pillow for the dying, his other arm stretched out as if waiting or inviting someone to take his hand in the last moments, but no one did. I wasn't long on the crime squad, and the victim was a similar age to me. I followed the blood, retraced his last steps to the basement railings of an unlicensed spieler and bar a few hundred metres away. His face is forever etched in my mind.

'Good lad. We got this now. Who you working for? What's your name?'

I told the detective that picked up the case, but never heard anything more – such is Copland. I wonder what might have happened if the boy had turned left instead of right. I have passed that spot a thousand times since, all seasons, all weather, with friends, with family, and he is always there, hand outstretched, sleeping. I never share what I see.

A second image is less public. I can't walk past this one, but it is equally vivid inside my mind. The victim had been tied up and killed as he sat on a kitchen chair, the remnants of the evening meal on the table and pots in the sink – a husband, father, a silhouette of sadness, the banality of evil in a suburban street. I was a new detective then, newly minted, newly posted, attached to a homicide inquiry run by an idiot. Sent over with another new detective, Jonny, we were keen, wanting to solve every case, certainly every homicide. But we wouldn't solve this one. Jonny said the way to make changes in the job was to replace the idiots and really get things done, take their jobs, take the promotion exam as soon as possible, which he did. I should have listened to him. Not that Jonny ever got to make a real difference. All I gained from that investigation was another baleful frame burned into memory. There for life.

And now it is a gangland humiliation gone wrong, the third homicide investigation I have worked. The death of Delaney – not his real name – gives me a clear insight into the Bastard Borough and how the criminal landscape is fast changing under the weight of powder and pills: cocaine, heroin, amphetamines. At the heart of the borough is a strip of clubs and pubs that also serves as a weekend marketplace for emerging UK narcos. East London loves a market, and the Bastard Borough prides itself on the diversity of its offerings, more 'Just Score' than Just Eat, a narco one-stop where all manner of drugs are readily available to enhance your visit if booze doesn't quite do it. The clubs and bars are plumbed into the market and if you control the door, you control the flow. Delaney was a low-level enforcer, a bully who ran a small firm of ad hoc door security.

I suppose Delaney's mother loved him – not that you can always be sure of that – but by the time he died on the floor of a low-rent nightclub there was no love for the man. News of his death was greeted more often than not with cheers than sorrow. His time was up. It was time to jog on, but he figured if his days of violence were over, he would now 'take a draw' from whatever scam he had going and from the doors he thought he still controlled. But there were new thugs on the block with other ideas, who did not take kindly to his posturing and fighting talk.

We later discover there were a dozen or so people scattered around the club at the heart of the strip, out for an early drink. Delaney, who had an interest in the premises, entered and sat at the bar, a pug-faced menace best left alone. The majority of those drinkers present were civilians, unaware the bar was exactly the sort of place not to be when a turf war is simmering. But one man was not a civilian – he was very much a player, out for a beer when he spotted an opportunity. He made a call to the man who was looking to take over door security in the area and all that comes with it. The gang entered in dribs and drabs, barely acknowledging the old soak on the barstool. Soon there was a disparate group ready to 'read Delaney his fortune' and a few home truths, not that he was in the mood for listening. He had been on the booze all day and wanted to play.

Delaney warmed up by 'cunting off' the assembled group in the traditional manner, and then when the new man, not known for his stature, entered, wearing his customary heavy dark overcoat, he was greeted with, 'Hello, you short-arsed cunt.' This only served to shorten the time Delaney had left on earth. Maybe he sensed what was coming next, perhaps somewhere in the recess of his alcohol-and drug-addled mind, what was left of his instinct told him to stand up and fight.

Whatever the reason, it was this decision that would kill him. 'Why don't you fucking—' He didn't have time to finish the sentence. The group were on him like a pack of screaming hyenas. First, they pepper-sprayed his eyes, then they bludgeoned him about the head, and then, finally, the howling pack used short blades to stab him repeatedly about the buttocks, a popular form of assault within the criminal milieu at the time – maximum humiliation, minimum risk of fatal injury. It is fair to say the gang probably did not intend to murder him, but they had little regard for the outcome. They returned to their seats and bought a round for the petrified clientele. After a drink or two, where no doubt succession was discussed, the hyenas decided they had better drop the man with no future off at the local A&E, confident he wouldn't talk, this being the way of things.

They checked the front of the club but found two uniformed officers leaning over the railings, observing the local nightlife, and so returned to their seats. As they sat waiting, most likely drinking to the future, their hostages trembled and the two constables, oblivious to what was playing out behind them, continued to admire the evening promenade. And in this livid tableau Delaney quietly bled out.

He was considered within his world a man no longer of consequence, a point vigorously emphasised when we came to investigate his death.

'I know why you're here, detective. Could not have happened to a cuntier man.'

'Shivved up the arse? Least he deserved, to be fair, officer.'

Delaney had by all accounts caused havoc wherever he'd gone. He'd run doors, peddled drugs, physically and sexually abused his family, and engaged, it turned out, in bestiality – it was said he would come home at the weekend after a night of excess and shag the dog. I sit slack-jawed in the incident room listening to a statement taken from a former partner who volunteers information that clinicians treating her for an STI were unable to identify the infection until it was subsequently confirmed that it was a strain of canine disease. Welcome to the Bastard Borough.

Arrests are made, charges brought, witnesses intimidated, defendants acquitted. It is like pulling teeth, and brings into sharp focus the reality of criminal investigation in a community where fear and intimidation often run cheek by jowl. And the community has delivered its own verdict on proceedings. We try hard to secure convictions, but fear and apathy combine in equal measure to ensure we can't build enough of a case to succeed.

After that, I'm asked if I would like a permanent posting to the borough, and I accept. I am reeled in, turn by turn, into this world. I'm at the coalface of policing. I feel at home here – it's busy every day, and I find the relentless grind to be a good companion.

This town is nothing like Trawler Town – there you talk to your neighbour; the famed East End spirit of the past has dissipated. It makes the job difficult, but I find my own way of dealing with things. Communication in a working-class community seems easier for me, a lad from Trawler Town, than for some colleagues. I capitalise on this – I talk to people, and they talk to me, give me information. A strange new world of the police informant opens up, and I come to understand this landscape.

Many detectives don't try, or perhaps don't want, to understand, instead preferring to get in and out as quick as possible. I understand why but I have a different perspective – curiosity. I begin to see that many crimes, including violence, when really drilled into are very often influenced by economic circumstances, which lead to bad choices. I see it daily, but our crime reports don't have a tick-box for that.

A wide and diverse variety of cases land on a detective's desk in the Bastard Borough, some truly difficult and perplexing. With little idea of how to proceed, I pick up the first case of FGM – female genital mutilation – in the division. The case has been passed around the office because no one understands or wants it, and it lands on my desk while I'm on leave. Despite legislation being passed a couple of years earlier, there's no input or training on how to deal with the matter. The social worker who called in the police has the same level of support I find in the office. Cops prefer cases of clear definition.

'I'm sure you'll make the right decision. Keep me posted,' says the Wolf, the new head of CID on the division, as he heads out the door to another meeting. Kick it into the long grass, he means. It's better than his stock phrase: 'Don't bleed on my carpet.' I notice the Wolf is choosing words more carefully since embarking on a serious push for more promotion. I have no idea who to speak to or where to begin. With no substantive female detective or indeed any specialist from whom I can seek advice, I ring the detective training school who suggest I try the local hospital or social services. I remind them it was they who raised the case; it is a classic carousel case, round and round, no help, no interest from on high. I return from a few days away to discover social services have reallocated the case to a different department. The Wolf doesn't remember the case when I mention it. The carousel has moved on.

I'm night-duty detective, on a week of night shifts. Unusually for the Bastard Borough, the division is relatively quiet, which is a good thing, as there is a dog in my car. This is my *Turner and Hooch* period. A few weeks after a visit to Trawler Town, where I saw Pa, I took myself off to Battersea Dogs & Cats Home; I don't want a dog, but I think one will be good for Pa, he's recently lost his, and seems amenable to the idea. On a second visit to the dogs home, I'm asked if I want to visit 'Death Row'.

'Sorry, Death Row?'

At this time, if a dog is not rehomed after a certain period they are put to sleep, as the home does not have the finances to keep them. *'Fuck that. Do not go in there. Do not set foot in there. You have to be joking. It's a fuckin' grizzly.'* Marv is not far wrong, or maybe he's dead set against the idea because he's worried I'll have someone else to talk to besides him.

Max is a Rottweiler, who looks like a bear and is about the size of one. I'm invited to step into his cage, and I realise later this was probably a test. Max is a big dog with a big personality, but today he sits in a corner of his small cage looking forlorn – there's a melancholy to him, a loneliness, that connects with me. 'You got a bit of doggy depression there?' I ask. Max eyes me cautiously before sauntering up, sitting down, sniffing my hand, licking it and waiting to see if this time it will be different, if this time someone will say yes, I suppose. 'How long before you . . . ?' The keeper doesn't respond – maybe she doesn't want to answer in front of Max. He is a fine dog. And so I leave Battersea dogs home with Max, complete with a new collar, lead, bowl and food.

Two weeks later Max begins his first night duty as the big dog in the Bastard Borough, unofficial of course. I don't have the heart to leave him in my flat, given what he's been through, so I opt to smuggle him to work with me. As you may be aware, a Rottweiler is not an easy dog to conceal. It's a warm night, and a late summer sirocco wind coats the borough in fine sand it has ferried from the Middle East. As the office is empty, I bring Max up. It's fair to say, in terms of slobber spittle, Max is up there with Hooch. I work the nights with an aide (a crime squad officer training to become a detective). It's not long since I was doing the same myself at West End Central. I'm paired with Dylan, who wears the permanent expression of a man expecting bad tidings, even when he is happy. He doesn't drive so I'm the designated taxi for CID and uniform management who have had a drink or two. I'm pulling out of the station yard with one of the bosses when he gazes up at the CID office window. 'I need glasses or my bed – I've just seen a bear at the CID office window!'

Max is an inquisitive dog. He enjoys his occasional tour of the Bastard Borough, but I know he'll settle in Trawler Town. I tell Pa I've a surprise for him, and he seems to perk up slightly; he's been even more reticent since his recent release from prison. Maybe Max might help him to find his voice. I tell him I'll be visiting soon.

Towards the end of the week of nights, I deal with an incident that troubles me greatly. A member of the public brings in a note he had just seen dropped at a nearby park. The witness thought it an odd thing to do in the early hours of the morning and managed to get part of the registration number of the car he'd seen driving off, a male at the wheel. The leaflet is carefully worded, inviting young boys of a specific age to meet secretly at a specific time with the author of the note in return for a sum of money. It is written by someone who would now certainly be suspected of being a predatory paedophile. The partial licence plate number of the car is circulated, and I have an idea that we still might be able to locate it tonight if we move quickly. From the witness's description, we know it is one of two possible types of vehicle, and from the information we have from searching the licensing database, we reduce it down to around 30 or so possibilities. Taking away all the vehicles outside the Greater London area reduces it to around a dozen. I ask for local units to visit the addresses without showing out and let me know if they find a vehicle with a warm engine bonnet and report back. Of the dozen visited, one house has a match parked on the drive with a warm bonnet.

By now it is almost daylight, so I make local enquiries. Nothing known, no criminality, just a married couple with children. I write it up and draw attention to the incident with a bulletin in the night-duty log for management. I walk home in the early morning light with Max and take a detour round the same park to see if I can find any more notes. A few more are handed in during the day, but I have other work to do. Later, when I check in with the office, I'm told the DI and a DS are on the way round, I assume to arrest the suspect. But when I get in for night duty later, I can't find any paperwork other than my original log and notes nor any update. Twenty-four hours later there still isn't anything. I don't understand why and still don't decades later.

When the two detectives arrived at the house, the owner of the vehicle claimed he was at home all evening, but there was a creeping tension that the DS picked up on. As they persisted, the tension grew. They went over his story, and the wife became agitated. She had been ill, but it wasn't that – it was something else. The spectre of something unsaid remained. The DS pressed on, revealing that all the evidence pointed to the car having been driven in the early hours of the morning. Silence. His wife looked across at him; she knew something was wrong. She was about to say something when the husband collapsed, weeping at his wife's feet. The DS couldn't have given a fuck – crocodile tears. The DI was more understanding. Maybe it was a ploy – good cop, actual cop, whatever. The suspect is a scoutmaster and previously unknown to police.

Four days later, when I return to work, he is still not under arrest – he has not been charged, and he won't be charged. The decision to take no further action is passed off as a Crown Prosecution Service diktat, because of insufficient evidence to charge with an offence but, really, who knows? To me, it seems like a lack of will to look deeper. The DCI says it was good work on my part, but time to move on.

'Choose your battles,' he says.

'Isn't it your fuckin' job to go into battle?' Marv, straight talking, as ever.

This is the moment the reality of policing dawns on me, not just in the Bastard Borough but everywhere. There are often unseen hands on the tiller of criminal justice. You toss the coin, take your chance. Who or what was behind the decision not to arrest or investigate further, to do nothing, was never explained.

The bitter taste lingers, and I have my first serious thoughts about leaving the job. First, though, it's time to relocate Max north to Trawler Town. But before I do, I get a call. It's Stepmother: Pa has had a heart attack, needs a triple bypass. Fuck you, Trawler Town, fuck you. Pa's bypass is a success, but while his near-death experience results in his ribcage being opened up,

I soon discover it does nothing to encourage him to open up emotionally. On that front we are no further forward. Here's the irony, though: insofar as relationships are concerned, I'm heading down a similar path, a closed book. I find Max a new home in London. Once sufficiently recovered, Pa buys a dog of his own, and meaningful conversation remains in short supply.

Flying Squad

The Flying Squad, which investigates complex robbery, was first set up as a 'mobile patrol experiment' with 12 detectives, hand-picked for 'their familiarity with the arcane ways' of organised crime in the aftermath of the First World War, when crime was on the increase thanks to rising unemployment and growing poverty. In his book *The Flying Squad*, Neil Darbyshire suggests that, at that time, the Met often struggled to deal with the issue of such crimes 'because of deficiencies in its organisational structure and territorial jealousies'. In an effort to counter this, a visionary senior police officer – observers of the current state of policing might think this a contradiction in terms, but there are some – Frederick Wensley sanctioned the development of a new unit as the country faced unprecedented turf wars between four gangs from east London, King's Cross, Leeds and Birmingham, the latter a clan recently dramatised as the 'Peaky Blinders'.

My instinct for developing intelligence in the last few years has caught the eye of the Flying Squad, now a department devoted to solving major robberies, and I find myself drawn to this elite unit. Recently, I'd sent them information that led to an arrest, and I'm advised that should I apply to join, my application will likely be successful.

It's very tempting, and though my love–hate relationship with my bastard job in the Bastard Borough continues, in the event I apply. While awaiting the outcome, a detailed five-page letter lands on my desk. An anonymous informant, keen to engage. *'You may not remember me'* – I don't – *'I remember you, yes you do know me . . . I like you, you're smart, and I hope honest enough to take this seriously . . .'* I did, but as we will discover, criminal intelligence, like any other commodity, is only considered valuable when those who control the market say it is. The author, someone I have clearly met in the past, names 24 emerging criminals on the rise, engaged in various nefarious activities in the division and beyond. A précis of their business is outlined by the writer. *'I hope it's been good reading . . . I'll be in touch.'* It certainly was, but they never reached out to me again, whoever they were. I spent years trying to discover their identity. Many of those named, over the following three decades, become leading figures within organised crime in the UK, including one individual identified in the letter as the *'brains'* of a three-man crew *'into extortion, heavy Charlie* [cocaine]*, stolen goods and protection'*. Decades later, a criminal career untouched by the criminal justice system, the multi-millionaire will be described by a High Court judge in a civil case as without doubt 'the head of an organised crime network, implicated in extreme violence'.

It shames the justice system that his stellar rise was unimpeded at any point by intervention. The letter gave early warning, identified many key figures who will go on to become crime mandarins, whose tendrils extend far beyond London. Those that survive bloody turf wars prosper as much by the collective inertia of the most senior police leadership and, no doubt, corruption in all its manifestations. Attempts to gather interest and funding to properly scope those identified falls on deaf ears, nothing more than an order to feed the information into the intelligence system, punt it towards departments with more resources, which I do. I felt at the time the letter was A1 and was proved right. I keep a copy to remind me of what I suspect will be the biggest missed opportunity I will witness in my service as an age of Home Office targets and overtly politicised policing dawns.

Around this time, still waiting on the results of my Flying Squad application, I'm approached by a surveillance officer who has another idea. He suggests I apply to SO10 to become a level one UC, or undercover officer. He is not the first to suggest it: the sergeant who intervened at West End Central, the Llama, rang the unit suggesting they take a look at me. As did a former supervisor on division. But I am motivated enough this time to visit the SO10 office to test the water. I bump into the Lion, one of my former supervisors on the West End plain-clothes unit with whom I have kept in touch. He is picking up a job, 'a bit of work', as the old hands would call it. He smiles. 'What took you so long, you little fucker? Waiting for me to hold your hand?' The Lion won't hold my hand, but he will test my mettle in the years to come. He was perhaps the only police officer I met in my career who put absolutely everything of himself into the job, and expected you to do likewise, but for now it is simply a question of putting a piece of paper into the system. I'm an outsider trying to get in, which, as things turn out, is often the nature of the beast when it comes to undercover policing. Beyond simply submitting an application, you need sponsorship, and I have the backing of several experienced detectives and, it will transpire, the very head of the organised crime directorate. If I'm staying in the police, might as well make it as challenging as possible.

I go on to pass my selection board for the Flying Squad, which consists of an interview with senior management and some appraisals. I can't wait to get stuck in, the real deal, organised crime, to wear the famous swooping-eagle tie of the elite unit. 'You're not old enough to be a detective. You in the right place, son?' asks an officer the first time I wear it.

While waiting for a vacancy there, an informant I'm running supplies information regarding the likely whereabouts of a large cache of firearms and ammunition. Still assessing the information, trying to locate the site, I'm asked by a Flying Squad senior officer not to be in a rush to pinpoint it. It is a clear signal my future employer would prefer the credit for any successful seizure go to them, rather than the division I am currently employed at. It's an indication of the territorial jealousies of policing, still in existence – perhaps now more than ever with 46 agencies vying for a share of diminishing budgets. When I mention the dilemma to my divisional detective inspector, a former squad officer himself, he reminds me where my 'bread is about to be buttered', so I do as asked.

Within a year I am posted on to the Flying Squad. Keen to capitalise on the intelligence sources I have registered and developed, I ask to be placed in the main office, rather than on the surveillance team. Visiting the branch office I will be attached to, I meet the boss, the Rhino. I have mixed feelings about the Rhino. He is fundamentally a decent individual, perhaps not blessed with a great deal of ability beyond bluff and bluster, but then, everyone seems to be increasingly winging it in Copland. The Rhino tells me I will definitely be going into the main office. When I arrive, I'm told it's the surveillance team for me. 'Well, you didn't believe him, did you?' asks the office manager. The trouble is, I did. That's the thing with Copland, you keep believing . . .

The Rhino had bowed to pressure from one of his favoured sergeants, who ran the team and thought I would make an ideal surveillance officer. A fizzing character who I name the Red Kangaroo, he is obsessed with the job, enjoys nothing more than a 'square up' to settle things. Wheels within wheels are also turning, because, as things turn out, in going on to become a level one UC, the surveillance team is probably the best place to be. My first major job is to act on the information I unearthed regarding an armourer. I had kept digging, and while it leads to the biggest weapons and ammunition seizure in London by the Flying Squad for 12 years, even I am surprised at the number of firearms a happy senior officer later tells me were recovered. When I suggest it was a bit less, the Red Kangaroo says I am a Flying Squad detective, not a mathematician. As the laughter subsides, I am given an 'elephant stopper', a large-calibre bullet, as a memento. I use it as a paperweight.

Ron's suggestion I look upon Copland's landscape as a jungle is never more prescient than during my early months on the Flying Squad. I discover you do not have to have a borderline personality disorder, suffer from obsessive compulsive disorder, or be either delusional or demented – but it might help. This dysfunctional environment – which appears to me to be common among all four of the squad offices – also contains some of the most dedicated and bravest officers I would meet.

There follows a series of training courses: firearms, surveillance and advanced driving, all necessary and welcome. Much of what I learn I know will be of use should I ever be deployed as a UC. Surveillance, counter-surveillance, handling a variety of firearms, better understanding the experience. On the range, you soon notice the 'Tackleberrys', so named after the character in the *Police Academy* movies popular at the time. They're the ones to watch, possessing fingers most likely to pull at the trigger. All cops, uniform or detective, taser or Glock, quickly identify the Tackleberrys within their midst.

Of all the armed operations I took part in during my time on the Flying Squad, two in particular perhaps captured the thrills and dichotomy at the heart of this elite squad. The first occurred when I was deployed not as a surveillance officer but as part of an arrest team.

A plain, autumnal day in north London in a quiet neighbourhood, mixed-use property, the poorer side of the tracks, where police activity is not uncommon. The constant hum of London life has buzzed across the day. I'm sitting inside a 'gunship', the nickname for high-performance vehicles used by the Flying Squad on such operations. Unlike other police vehicles, when their use is at an end, they will not be sold off at public auction but recycled at the driving school.

I run my finger down the window following a drop of rain and wonder if this will be another no-show. The way of things: 50 per cent no-show, 40 per cent total shitshow and 10 per cent adrenalin blast. We have been in situ, waiting at the location, for hours. Been here before – we have all been here before. Bored detectives, playing a waiting game. Today we wait to see if four suspected armed robbers, Jamaican Yardies, will confirm the information the squad has received. While the term Yardie is perhaps now better understood, at this time it was defined by suspicion within a policing orthodoxy that believed the term referred only to the Jamaican crime diaspora, rather than the broader sense of someone simply originating from a poorer community in low-quality, state-provided housing. We are briefed that the suspects intend to commit an armed robbery on the day. The target is unknown, but the threat level is such that we cannot let them move away from the plot, the location where they will all come together. So here we are, waiting, and watching a raindrop run its course.

'Yeah, Alpha Mike, standby all units, we have movement, over.'

The driver of a squad gunship is exactly that: a driver. But not any driver – they are the best of the best. In a world where the best armed robbers are often referred to as 'pavement artists', the driver of a gunship is an artist in their own right. They will get you into the mix or out of a fix.

'Yeah, all units, subjects are approaching the vehicle, over.' The head of the operation acknowledges, gunships copy and engines are started in the quiet London suburb. I check the catch on my pancake holster, so-called for its shape designed specifically for a sidearm to be concealed comfortably, for the umpteenth time, because now the subjects are approaching their vehicle.

Rain falls harder against the window.

'All units, all units, Alpha Mike, subjects are in the vehicle, subjects are in the vehicle, over.'

'Do you have eye on the vehicle? Over.'

'Yes, yes, over.'

'Thank you, standby, all units running to you, over.' I check the holster again, shifting in my seat. By now, Kevlar upper-body armour has been adopted for armed ops – it is cumbersome. I push the heavy vest away and breathe. Our driver didn't wait for the order to commence our run. He has been here many times. The moment the surveillance eye announced the suspects were approaching, he checked his mirrors and we slowly crept forward. He adjusts his rear-view mirror. I've noticed he always does this – it's a tic, a routine. We all have them. I check my holster again. On we roll slowly forward. I take a police baseball cap from inside the armour and place it ready to hand as the driver tightens his hands on the wheel, his knuckles whitening. The engine grumbles and my heart beats a little faster. London is unaware, as are the bandits, as four hidden gunships nudge towards a meeting, emerging from different points on the board, easing slowly forward towards the opposition.

'Units standby, subjects are on the move, they're on the move, over.'

The subjects, we are told, are unpredictable, violent, armed. By this point, the Flying Squad is increasingly deploying heavily armed tactical firearms units, but not today, because of a combination of office politics, availability and the desire not to have the operation compromised by the rigid protocols of a more strident approach to such potentially fluid situations. In short, those running the operation are keen for all suspects to be detained and firearms recovered rather than a shots-fired situation. It is never an easy decision. It is often a case of balancing reality against possibility.

We move out and join the traffic. We cannot let them off the tight confines of the estate. It must not develop into a chase through London. Four minutes away from contact, the subjects stop for a smoke – not tobacco or aromatic herb, but crack cocaine.

'Three minutes, over.'

Gunships ever closer, tightening the knot. The 'eye' updates, a little tension in the voice.

'All units, they are all in the vehicle, all in the vehicle, engine now running, over.'

'Roger that, thank you, two minutes, over, two minutes, over.'

Our driver jinks in behind a surveillance vehicle, who he knows will block traffic at an upcoming junction if need be.

I notice an elderly couple – they must be well into their eighties – cross the road, holding hands. A touchingly real moment in an inorganic scene. You remember these moments afterward as much as the tension. When they were full of youth, the Flying Squad were sat in Ford V8s.

'All units, two minutes. Oscar Papa, you still have eyes on the vehicle, over?'

'Yes, yes, over.'

A surveillance officer cuts in, 'All units, subject vehicle is on the move, on the move, over.'

The operational head's steady voice now has a little urgency: 'Yes, yes, I have eyes on the vehicle. One minute, over.'

I see the estate come into view. I see the subject vehicle in the distance. I take the safety catch off the holster as the other gun-ships slowly fall into position. By now armed robberies are on the wane. Will they soon be a thing of the past? Will this be one last cavalry charge across a changing landscape? I put on my police baseball cap, one hand on my firearm. The driver taps the wheel with his forefinger, hooves tapping on the ground waiting for the bugler to sound the charge as a light rain falls. These moments are, in a way, what I love. When I was boxing, it was the moment just before the bell rang, that brief moment in time when everything inside was calm, different, peaceful, at odds with all beyond.

The driver doesn't wait for the order, instinctively he knows it's coming. He floors the accelerator as the first syllable of the order 'Attack, attack, attack' is uttered. They see us bearing down at the last moment, slam their vehicle into reverse; it careers backwards at speed and smashes into a wall and crumples. We are out and on them. BOOM! Their windscreen is shattered by a hardwood stave. This, I suppose, hasn't changed since the days of Ford V8 Pilots, nor the shouting, the noise, engines scream-ing, officers screaming. The detective with the stave steps back and we step forward; guns bear down, we bear down, fingers on triggers. The next few seconds will determine the future for all of us. The driver's door bursts open, then another. My finger tightens on the trigger, *our* fingers tighten, as dazed and high their arms flail. Our arms are steady, ready to spit fire, spill blood. Shouting from all sides, the engine still screaming, this sudden urban vignette flooded with sound and lit with blue light that serves only to draw attention to the cacophony. What happens in this next fragment of time will be critical to the outcome.

In all the chaos one voice lifts with supreme clarity above all others – the voice of the wee Numbat. I, like many, have never taken to the Numbat – not an easy animal to like – but he steps forward, and what he does saves the lives of everyone in the vehicle. In this chaos of screeching imminent death, the Numbat raises a paw and allows his voice to rise above everyone else's – calming, focused, almost slowing time, certainly stopping fire and death and chaos.

Another voice interrupts: the Wild Boar. Often aggressive when threatened, he stands to my left. He can see a gun under the seat, maybe more. It transpires that there are many. This is no time for mistakes but that's okay, the Numbat doesn't intend to make one now. He is not in charge of the operation, but it is his voice that takes charge, reaching into the vehicle: 'Listen to me, listen only to me, look only at me!' And somehow, through all the chaos, they do – they somehow keep their flailing arms and hands away from the weapons within the car and his words calmly bring them out, one by one. Still the rain falls, but no tears, not today. Because of one man, in my opinion.

In a later debrief I ask a tactical firearms officer directly: would his team have opened fire given the situation? I was not surprised at the immediate reply: yes, he would have, given the circumstances. But for the Numbat, the debrief that day would have taken place in very different circumstances. As I say, I never really much cared for the Numbat based on what I had seen, but this time, he was without doubt a hero.

Perhaps it's true that for every hero there is a villain, which reminds me of an armed operation that had a different outcome.

Remember, information or intelligence are by now increasingly viewed as a commodity, often shaped by the desire to achieve maximum personal gain from any intelligence received. This can often entail such ambitious assessment of it as to effectively remove its original, and often obvious, meaning, rendering it something else altogether – which, may or may not be the purpose of such analysis by those with a vested interest in outcome. Funny, but I don't think I was ever involved in a major seizure of any kind that did not increase substantially in some shape or form by the time the public read about it in the press. Cops learn to read between the lines. Jean Charles de Menezes never did 'vault over' the Underground ticket barrier, but that wasn't the point.

It's a hot summer day, and we are again waiting on a team, plotted up to intercept an armed robbery. The teams are steadily declining in confidence, means and ability, moving like migrating buffalo to the greener (and safer pastures) of narcotics and fraud. We are behind – following – a low-grade robbery crew, certainly not Premiership, pitched at a briefing as Championship, and as things turn out, probably non-league in reality. I'm part of the surveillance team and away from the plot when the attack is called. 'Shots fired' rings out over the comms. When I arrive at the scene a detective lies wounded on the floor, ambulance called and already en route. I'm told he has been shot in the stomach by one of the gang – it's actually his hand but then, as I'm about to learn, nothing is quite what it seems.

Another detective and I are dispatched with the alleged shooter to a holding station. A senior detective suggests to me he will probably have confessed by the time we arrive – there it is again: God's work, corruption lite, the acceptable form. *'Then why don't you get in the fuckin' van with him and write it up exactly how you fuckin' want it!'* Because rank has privilege, Marv. He isn't the shooter, I'm certain. How do I *know* this, when I don't? It is that gut instinct, which has to a large extent been ironed out of policing, in the mistaken belief it is simply a legacy of the bad old days of fit-ups and close-ups – as in ranks. That's not always the case.

The 'shooter' looks as deep in shock as the prostrate detective as the reality sinks in for both. A detective has been shot, and he is in the frame. On the way to the holding station, clearly petrified at the thought of his new reality, the suspect states repeatedly the gun is an imitation and could not possibly fire. I have by now dealt with hundreds of prisoners arrested for all manner of offences, and sitting opposite him, I think he's telling the truth. Based on nothing more than what I see, hear and feel. I could be wrong, of course, swift forensic analysis of the gun will settle it, but I certainly won't be fitting him up in the back of the van on the way to the station. I make it clear when we arrive that this doesn't 'feel' right – and it is clear I'm not the only one who feels all is not what it seems. And so it proves.

As the dust settles on the shooting and I decline to contrive a false confession, we soon discover it wasn't a villain who shot the detective but a colleague, a case of blue on blue. It was the Slow Loris Monkey, and, oddly, no one seems surprised. As the wounded detective lay on the ground bleeding, contemplating his future, who knew what the Slow Loris was contemplating? It was an accident: he apparently did not know he had shot his colleague. Only when he later returned to the armoury with the rest of the unit and checked in his firearm, did he come to realise he was in fact a bullet short of a full gun. Had he been a better shot, Copland might have been planning a force funeral rather than fruit and flowers. The slow loris monkey is often said to be quite adorable, but its bite incorporates a flesh-eating venom, which it uses on other primates. I suppose a 9mm bullet was quicker.

The detective eventually made a full recovery, and the incident was downplayed and recalibrated to avoid embarrassment for the top brass. The wounded colleague was persuaded he was partly at fault, a rush of blood to the head making him run, unarmed, towards the suspects (presumably saving one of the suspects in the process). Whether it was the heat of the day or panic in the moment, the full circumstances are also bleached. The incident quietly tidied away. A financial settlement for spilt blood. The Slow Loris disappears into the undergrowth, to resurface several years later.

Three Numbers on the Index

Undercover detectives are given a three-digit number, which becomes your ID reference on the index of level one UCs. All the officers on this index are authorised to work within the UK and overseas. I've had word I will soon hear about my application, which was submitted some two years earlier, and by now I can't help think that those three numbers will signal an improved quality in the proactive policing I am desperate to engage in. Anything has to be better than the dross we often find ourselves occupied with now.

Today, for instance, our surveillance comms are fizzing with references to the 'Marrow Man', so called because our subject primarily arms himself with a variety of weighty fruit and veg carried inside a carrier bag and passed off as a concealed gun in the betting shops and off-licences he targets to feed his drug habit. 'I could see it was a banana, officer, but you can't take the risk these days, can you?' Which is true enough, and now the banana is personal, and the Flying Squad wait near the home of the man who has become a personal bête noire of the Rhino.

Rhinos are famed for their poor vision, and also for their

communicating through honks, sneezes and, oddly, their own poo. Rhinos can use the scent of it to discern a lot about other rhinos in the area. A bit like a Masonic handshake, I suppose, alerting others to nearby presence through endangered faeces. At times our Rhino's communication seems comparable, for all the clarity of purpose it provides. He is obsessed with low-hanging fruit, rather than more complex investigations. It is all about the numbers, at the end of the day – that's the message passed on from above and supported, it seems, by the Cabbage White commissioner. In any case, the glory days of working high-profile armed robbery cases may be over, the 'pavement artists', as they were once known, migrating towards the more lucrative drugs trade. What is required is a fundamental change at the very top, who seem tone deaf when it comes to constructive reform.

So we quietly complain and wait for our subject, the vegetable man, said to be a prolific robber of low-value targets, to appear. At this particular point in time, the Marrow Man has become the number-one target for the office, and so the entire surveillance and several other teams of detectives are plotted around his home waiting for the show to begin.

Eventually he emerges, dressed in a loud tracksuit top and a raggedy pair of chinos, all together more Central Casting than criminal mastermind. He limbers up with a quick touch of his toes and runs off, at a pace, backwards. Like a demented idiot. This is what it has come to for the Flying Squad – following a man who feeds his drug habit by robbing betting shops armed with fruit and veg, taking out covert surveillance teams as a matter of sport. We don't catch the suspect on this occasion, but then have you ever tried to follow a backwards-sprinting Marrow Man? Makes you dizzy. His quads must have been on fire. I get back to the office, book in my firearm, thinking this is not turning out as I hoped. We gather in the main briefing room with the rest of the office and await the brass, which includes an old face from the past, now rapidly on the rise, the Wolf. They are, after all, the largest member of the dog family.

He sits unsmiling as we file in. The briefing is to explain the use of an ingenious piece of new kit to be issued to the Flying Squad. A thick sleeve is henceforth to be placed underneath our log sheets, the purpose of which is, in essence, to alleviate the risk of further scandal after a series of allegations of police changing log entries, overwriting them in order to change or alter evidence after the event. The sleeve will prevent this and, more importantly, prevent an imprint of any such changes on the sheets beneath the offending page. This is the solution preferred, rather than addressing the cultural issue of cover-ups and cock-ups. The answer from on high, it seems, is not to change malevolent practice but to simply facilitate it, as people will surely find other ways to tamper with the record. One might argue that management presence confers tacit support of the tweaked status quo. From behind a desk – 'twas ever thus. Keep calm and cover up.

'When does it get to the fuckin' point of no return?' Marv wonders as I contemplate the brass neck of the brass. I'm not too young in service to be stymied by my own mental fatigue. Pa, a man forged on the anvil of policing in the 1960s, reflects on this with me one day as we sit staring out to sea, no closer to understanding our past, thinking about 'the job'. I turn to him and ask, 'Was the term "God's work" around in your day?'

He smiles, throws the ball again for the dog. 'Think it's been around since before my day, son.'

'But what did it mean . . . to you?'

He stood up, looked over the dunes and whistled the dogs. 'Oh you know, son . . .' and off he walks, without another word. No one *ever* wants to fucking talk about it. Altered notes, altered facts, altered reality. Hillsborough to the Daniel Morgan murder, before and beyond, on it goes . . .

Years after Pa's incarceration, Stepmother told me in his liberal stewardship of Police Federation funds, he would also fund officers' mortgage deposits, to be paid back at a later date. Several officers, some now of senior rank, near fainted at news of his arrest. It was another beach-front question: did God's work intervene? But that day, there was no response, just a sigh, that half-smile, and the ball launched high into the air for the dogs.

I understand why many are thinking of packing the job in; Metland is in a state of torpor under the Cabbage White. It is in this slightly morose state that I open a note on my desk that tells me I am to report for psychometric evaluation and interviews regarding my application to become a level one undercover officer. It's been so long that I'd almost forgotten about it. I didn't realise I needed to undertake psychometric evaluation. All I have to do is keep a lid on Marv and I think I've got this. He was none too quiet during the briefing – for him, the silicosis has begun.

How to dress for a covert intelligence source interview? Suit, shabby or somewhere in between? I assume that the decision as to whether I'm in or not, as with most in-house police promotions or appointments, is virtually a done deal prior to the day, subject to not coming across as 'batshit mental' in the tests or a 'total cunt' in the interview, according to one UC I speak to. Yet somehow I also have a sense that, unlike most forms of progression in the police, this actually might prove more egalitarian than any other posting.

I wear a suit, a smart one – not an 'I'm-giving-evidence-at-the-central-criminal-court suit', favoured by central squad detectives, too formal, nor an 'I'm-having-lunch-with-the-company-I-want-to-employ-me-when-I-leave-the-job' suit favoured by brass, too obvious. A suit that pitches you commensurate with the roles you hope to play as a level one UC, because they are sizing you up the moment you walk through the door. Choose wisely. Who are you? Who could you be? What commodity could you buy? A look that confidently says I want what you have and I am willing to pay for it, you can make a deal with me. Once you're in the door, it is a job for life, which at some point you will absolutely regret, as it will very probably be detrimental to your wellbeing.

This will be explained to you, but you will not listen, because you want to prove something. To yourself, to management, or maybe even simply to your father. So you wear a smart, relaxed tailored suit that stands out just a fraction but is neither flash nor stiff and you say little.

'*What the fuck is he wearing that for?*' Marv, on the other hand, immediately questioning one choice sitting opposite me.

The candidate, a pony-tailed dude looking for all the world like El Chapo's little brother in a loud suit, brushes at an imaginary bit of fluff on his jacket. He has nicked himself shaving that morning and has a piece of toilet paper stuck to his chin. I stare at the bloodstained loo roll. Do I tell him? If it starts bleeding, he may—

'It won't stop bleeding,' he says, noticing me noticing his paper scab. I nod in sympathy. Looks can clearly be deceiving, but it's not a good start. Or maybe *I* should have been bolder in my choice of suit. I've been told you only get one shot at this.

'If you would like to follow me, please.' We troop behind an administration officer and into a nondescript room where two observers watch us as we enter, inviting us to sit down and begin the test.

'*I wonder if El Chapo is part of the test?*' Who knows, Marv?

My pencil is blunt, so I take one off an adjacent empty table, immediately wondering if this is part of the test. Ultimately this – thinking too much – will be my downfall. It can be a problem in Copland.

Psychometric testing was adopted by the Met and adapted for UCs in the eighties, SO10 having looked at the working practices of various agencies in the United States. The test is a collection of seemingly random questions ranging from asking how you might react to outwardly innocuous situations to more potentially confrontational scenarios. As I progress through the paper I think I detect recurring themes. Or do I?

Marv and I can't wait to see who goes forward to the next stage. We cover the whys and the what-ifs, the stark realities of being an imposter in an often impossible world. At least the process is far more honest and grounded in reality than a recent assessment day I'd attended for promotion to sergeant, where I thought Marv was very likely to cause some kind of seizure midway through the utter nonsense of it all, comprising as it did of a variety of abstract exercises involving pieces of wood and lengths of rope. The lack of utter quackery attached to this process is no doubt due to the man who heads up the undercover unit, a former UC himself, who occasionally still undertakes the odd assignment. This DCI, whom I will call the Gazelle, has an easy manner that masks a diligent, sharp mind, but the real power behind the throne is one of the several detective sergeants who run the unit, the Bear. There are eight species of bear. They are uniform in their awkward gait and excellent sense of smell, but all are very different, and I believe their authority depends on who shares the landscape. This Bear is king of all he sees. A UC for years in the Met, the Bear is hard to read, and I doubt he would like anyone to know what's in his head, but one thing is for sure: if anybody is likely to have their own Marv, it will be this fella. Not that this bear would ever share. He is one of five sergeants who run the office.

I feel the interview went well. I know the recommendations, scouting reports and observation have gone on for a number of years, ever since I submitted my formal interest and was told this is how it would be – be patient and it will happen. And it does. I find out I've passed with a nod from the Gazelle in the corridor – official notification follows. When news of my course date arrives, I share it with the Lion: 'About time, you little fucker!' From him, high praise indeed. I wonder if we will ever work together.

I arrive for the start of my course at Hendon Police College knowing it will be intense, and I want it to be; I know it will likely be challenging, and I hope it is. I want it to pump thousands of tons of ice-cold water into this tank, this moribund, creaking organisation, I want to prove you can stop a ship sinking.

I am not alone in being sick of the bullshit that seems only to grease the promotion pole for management. I want to test myself and convince me and *him* this organisation is worth sticking with. '*To prove something to Pa rather than to yourself?*' murmurs Marv. Whatever, the only people I intend listening to over the next two weeks – just two weeks, is that possible? – are the big beasts who run the course, sniffing out weakness, snapping at the heels of imposters. Now the waiting is over. I am still young in service but have travelled a fair distance. I know I can do this.

I take the clothing I might need: a suit, casuals – a quiet wardrobe. We have welcome drinks in the college bar, and I meet two officers from the Royal Ulster Constabulary; beasting it from the off, they are doing the course as observers. They may be observers but they sleep with a sidearm under their beds. When the door to the bar opens, they clock the swing. We have it easy. I know because I see the difference writ large on their faces.

I mingle, a little conversation, more listening than talking as the Bear walks into the room. He looks around, big paws reaching out. I watch to see who he speaks to first, notice which horses in the paddock are his. What I don't know is that as for me, one reference from a senior officer in support vexes him; am I already a spy on behalf of management? The Bear likes to micromanage – everything, everyone. He looks after the firm and the firm very much looks after him, but I came up quickly on the outside of a pack chasing a place so, as an outsider, he will make sure I am put through the wringer – he wants to see how I shape up.

Day one is straightforward: introductions, why we are here, why we have been selected for the course, the promise that it will be intense, uncompromising. Forget any of the rumours we have heard, because they will be wrong. The days will be exceptionally long and at the end of each we will write up our reports and be ready to start again early the next – no break, no let up. In addition to guest speakers, other level one undercover officers will join us and give talks about how it should work, how it might not work and, if you are unlucky, what can happen when it really does panhandle into a crock of shit – who will be blamed and who, in reality, will be at fault. No bullshit, no bravado, no bang-on-trend corporate double-speak from a career projectile transitioning to the boardroom.

It is a breath of fresh air. It is as if each morning an army of cleaners roll into Hendon Police College and purge the place of all the half-baked dipshittery readily and steadily rolled out from the ivory towers with all the passion a career built on failing upwards musters. It is the most honest, no-holds-barred appraisal of how the *judicious* use of this particular form of policing can and will be effective against serious and organised crime. The words are ambrosia for the soul. For the first time since the early days after Charlie Delta, I feel like a true detective, that this really is a job worth doing. I fail to realise they are, of course, only words.

Training is practical, informal and detailed. The bible of covert policing at that time is handed out: the 'NUTAC Reference Manual', to be secreted at home and never shared or left unattended on police premises, nor the information revealed or shared with lower level operatives, test purchasers or trained decoys. It is handed out it with all the deference of a High Church ceremony, but in reality it is little more than a bunch of stated cases and schematic operational outlines rooted in common sense. As one supervisor reminds us, it is to be used as a reference when seeking to walk back often inexperienced leadership from absurd operational suggestions or ideas devoid of common sense when it comes to basic rules of evidence or safe deployment of 'covert human intelligence sources', in this context referred to as the UC and never CHIS. The manual includes the usual written reminders that we are volunteers, and a sprinkling of health and safety, and woolly mental health advice that I suspect are meaningless and will certainly prove to be the case insofar as my own career is concerned. But when you want to play for the first team, your drive is focused on getting on the pitch.

Level one UCs already on the index put us through roleplay scenarios. There's a rumour that the instructors will create a scenario whereby a UC will be kidnapped, but as the course rolls on, intense, relentless, we begin to think perhaps this is all an urban myth; we are swivel-eyed and alert to the possibility but nothing happens. We are into the last 48 hours and the final module, the major concluding exercise of the course. This is where the Bear shows why he is renowned for past exploits and his understanding of the game.

As we prepare for this exercise, which he has designed and no doubt will certainly not feel like an exercise, I learn first hand how quickly things can go south, despite the best preparation. The 'commodity', as it is referred to, is a stolen Old Master painting, missing for several years and now offered for sale through a criminal intermediary. The negotiations take place over two days, a chain of UC candidates playing the role of intermediaries, interested parties, each introduction edging closer to the prize, until the last meeting is set up, to take place at a café in London. At any point in the chase the line could break; the instructors are puppeteers and we dancing marionettes. The stooge playing the criminal middling (brokering) the deal tries to have me bring the money to the meeting, but this can't happen – this can never happen. I need to see the artwork first. He suggests a photo instead. Not good enough – I need to have eyes on the prize. More negotiation, more delay. Tick tock. Eventually he makes a call. It's not far from the café, he says. Let's go. Another person on the course is playing my minder. He's not a detective – I've gathered that much, not much more. I ask him to stay close to me as we leave the café and head to where the car containing the prize is waiting, out into the street. It's not there. He got the street wrong, he says.

'No, no, it's here somewhere,' he says as he makes another call. 'Yeah, just a street away. Once you see it, call in the money.' On we walk, just a bit further.

'Fuck this! This doesn't feel right.' But I ignore Marv and beckon my minder to keep close; he's lagging behind, nervous, thinking of himself or the same as me. But if we stay together, we can deal with the criminal, I suggest to Marv, adding for my benefit, when I get to the next junction, if I don't see the van, it's off. But what's wrong with my minder? He's fifteen yards behind me.

'Fuck this! No further.' And I realise immediately: Marv's right.

'Sorry mate, you're wasting my time, I'm—'

I don't finish the sentence. In my peripheral vision, I see the grey van pull in at speed, the side door already opening. I see the legs emerging first and immediately start to run, but whoever emerged from the van has grabbed just enough of my coat to slow me down a fraction, and in that split second the driver is out and on me. All over me, but I'm in good shape; whoever they are, they're not huge bulks. I give the first man a dig. I know it's an exercise, but by now it doesn't feel like it; it's no more than a reflex action, and it is a mistake because the driver has me by the collar while his partner gives me a dig that puts mine to shame. As I double up, they use my own momentum to push me into the van, and the lights go out, a bag over my head as I fight to get out. Pointless. They have me tied like a Christmas turkey, legs and arms snagged tight behind me. I'm gagged and the van drives away from the suburban London street in broad daylight.

One member of the public calls the police to say they think they might have seen something suspicious – that's it, just the one. It took little more than a minute to have me trussed and away. My kidnappers are members of the Special Boat Service, not that I know it then. I simply think, jeez, if these two are detectives I need to be on whatever course they've just done. While I contemplate what to do next, the vehicle speeds through London. 'Yeah, we got him, all good.' All is not good. Not for me. Someone begins to search me and doesn't ask permission and certainly doesn't want any lip from me, that's made abundantly clear.

The sodden, terrifying experience in the ship's compartment as a teenager in basic navy training proved that, even though your brain knows it is an exercise, they are not going to kill you, you will still be forced to contend with fear, your private fear and, in doing so, as you cooperate with your captors, desperate to not let this end badly, it feels real enough. As we drive through London, I am struggling to breathe through the tape, Marv berates me: *'Fuckin' idiot, I fuckin' knew it, dopey cunt, you fucked up.'*

One hand firmly pressing my head to the van floor, my skull absorbing every imperfection in the road, Marv recounting every missed opportunity to read the situation, there begins an interrogation, 'Who are you? What's your fucking game trying to mug us off, you cunt!' I could tell him, but I won't. I know who I am. Kidnapper One goes through my pockets. I have nothing to fear – nothing will be found to identify me.

'What's this, a packet of mints? So you're a cunt with bad breath. Cash . . . Not enough to stop what's gonna happen next if you don't tell me who you really are.' On he goes, pressing head to metal, all the while I rehearse my answers, getting ready for when the tape comes off. I tell him I was just trying to buy a painting. I thought I was doing someone a favour. I go through the story that got me here, discussed over and over but never intended to be examined while trussed up like a Norfolk Bronze butterball turkey.

He's thorough – shoes off, inside my lapels – and he's not finished by a long shot. We have been driving for a while when I hear the driver, Kidnapper Two, call out, 'Ten minutes, you ready?' The van comes to a halt, and One gets out and leaves me on the floor, arms and legs tethered behind my back. Surely they're not going to leave me here, I think, muscles already beginning to ache from the unnatural position.

'All you had to fuckin' do was leg it!' Marv never misses an opportunity to break balls.

I'm bundled out of the van. One of them snips my bindings

so I can walk and I am led into a building – it's cold, concrete floors. I'm stripped naked, which comes as a shock, as it does for the several observers who are watching the course which, it transpires, is run in tandem with a hostage negotiators' training course. Whether I 'survive' the exercise will depend on how I react to questioning and the skill of the hostage negotiators. One and Two go through my clothes again, searching for anything missed, anything that might contradict the legend I'm using. They bark, threaten. Kidnapper One is the aggressive one. Two is far calmer, more reasonable, but both are relentless in their attention.

'We know who you are. You're a cop!'

'Don't be ridiculous. I'm just trying to buy a fucking painting. Why are you doing this?'

'You're here until you tell us who you are, who you really are!'

On it goes. One of them produces a semi-automatic pistol, presses the barrel against my head. 'Feel that? Do not take me for a cunt!' I'm later told that one observer asked if it was really necessary to parade me naked and subject me to such abuse for the sake of realism, but this was a different time. As it turns out, the end of times, because this will be the last UC training programme in which such a realistic combined UC kidnap exercise is sanctioned. That decision was a mistake, I believe. Its realism stokes the embers of the past. The incident on the nuclear sub, locked behind the bank of computers, flares as I stay in role, protesting that this is all going too far, that I'm simply there to buy a painting, not to be kidnapped off the street. They slam shut the door on some kind of metal box, my metal coffin, as I continue jabbering, repeating they've got it wrong. If they let me go, we can still have a deal. Money might yet be my liberty. 'Greed, will always bring them to the table,' an experienced UC claimed in a lecture. I shout again and again. Silence. They don't seem interested in what I have to say. I wonder if they have left. I barely have room to move. My hands and feet are still tied. I feel my heart rate increase.

'*Don't!*'

Don't what? I can't fucking breathe in here. I twist my head, trying to get the hood off, finding myself headbutting the lid of whatever it is I'm trapped in. Because that's what it feels like. I'm trapped in here.

'*Don't!*'

'Fuck off! You're not locked in a metal box.'

'*Course I fuckin' am!*'

We bicker, clashes of the mind, inside my head, inside a metal box, inside the web of deceit. I stop whacking my head, not because it's ineffective, because it hurts.

Just when I think things can't get any worse, I hear footsteps approaching the box. Before I can utter a word it suddenly opens and they haul me half out,

I start pleading, 'Look, please, why are doing this to me? I—' I don't have time to finish before cans are tied over my ears so I can't shake them off.

'Hope you like this,' One says, before pushing me back in and slamming the lid shut, the relentless anger of heavy metal pounds away through the headset. How the fuck did they know I can't stand this shit? My heart rate competes with the angry beat levels, I scream abuse at my captors, and try not to think of my first submarine patrol. THUMP THUMP THUMP THUMP ...

Panic begins to engulf, fuelled by the disorienting rage pouring out the cans, ear-bleeding noise, a repetitive beat. Marv, never shy of telling me when I have fucked up, for once is silent – unable to raise his voice over the deafening din I suppose. And then, as will often be the case in this world, at the precise moment that doubt threatens, a solution appears. Marv. Silent because he has already proven how I deal with this. The repeating mantra of the tortured beat, just as the teenage boy on the verge of freaking out, locked in a metal box beneath the ocean, found a way to survive the moment by counting the clicking contacts of a bank of computers. I focus on the timing of the bass drum beat as if it is the rapid ticking of a clock. Tick tock tick tock tick tock.

So the day passes, in and out of the box, shouting, threats, back in the box, which they beat with poles, then more deafening music, tick tock tick tock. After several interrogations I'm pulled from the box, told this is it, they've had enough, either I tell them who I am right now or they will pull the trigger. The cold metal presses against my head and I decide that if I confirm I am a police officer, they will undoubtedly pull the trigger, so I stick to the cover story – the mild-mannered, dodgy art dealer in the wrong place at the wrong time trying to make a quick buck. I'm manhandled, moving swiftly along a cold concrete floor. Is this how it would be, could be, in real life? Right now, this seems like real life – a couple of hours ago I was having a coffee privately thinking, 'Well, this is going well!'

Hardwood doors are flung open with the force of my body, and I stumble and fall to the floor, into the light. It wasn't a few hours, it was 14 hours, most of it spent in a metal tomb. As hands unfree my own and take off the hood, I squint into the arc lights set up while the hostage negotiators set to work in parallel. I definitely would not want to meet those two soldiers in a dark alley, but it is over.

As a debrief begins, I am led out by the Walrus, another leading supervisor on SO10.

'Quality work, well done. They'd never have got me in that bloody coffin.'

'I don't eat as well as you,' I say.

He roars with laughter and puts an arm around me. He's one of the good guys, a 'funny money man', an expert in counterfeit currency. He once tagged a printing press overseas to enable an air strike, placing a bug on the equipment, well, that was the rumour. A quiet man, not one to disturb the water. Given I got caught, I'm not sure I did that well, but he tells me that was always the plan, and that it took longer than usual to lure me in. He smiles as we walk out of what I think is an old industrial building but is actually a near derelict part of the police college real estate. All an illusion, brilliantly conceived, and an extreme example of what could happen if the illusion you create as a UC does not go according to plan, as it very often doesn't.

Once I am thawed out and fully debriefed, I meet the two SBS marines, not at all obvious heavies but whose skillset proved way beyond mine in matters of extreme prejudice. Over a few beers one of the soldiers admits that despite knowing it was an exercise, I almost convinced him I wasn't a cop, and he's not sure that would have stopped him pulling the trigger in a different landscape.

We share a few laughs about the navy and submarines; had I not been posted to nuclear bombers our paths may well have crossed at some point as they clambered into the torpedo tube. To each his own. The Bear wanders in.

'Done well there, boy! No right or wrong way to play that. Good shift,' he says, and on he saunters. He won't ever consider me one of his own, I soon learn, believing I've been plumbed in by his boss. For all his genius, the Bear is a man riddled with insecurity. At the end of the road, when I leave, it will be with little respect for him.

But the course has lived up to expectations: the most intense two weeks of my life, 18-hour days, relentless hard yards, roleplays, court cross-examinations, case law, suggestions on appearance commensurate with deployment. We discuss legend building, a term borrowed from the clandestine world of the spy, meaning to construct a multidimensional fake identity capable of withstanding close scrutiny. There is insight into how to construct one, when to best use it, and the avoidable pitfalls. How to read a room, where to sit, where definitely not to sit, commodities in all forms: we learn it all. The best signals when calling in a strike, the ones to avoid, the art of dealing with management and their desires and weakness that will invariably put them first and you last.

'Just sit there, Liam, on the sofa. React how you see fit. Remember, you're buying weight, not corner shite.'

I wait for the exercise to begin.

'Hello. You still here?' She walks in behind me, unannounced. Natural blonde hair tied back, tall, athletic, casually taking out the bobble as she moves, letting her hair fall as she slips the bobble over her wrist. Wow! There is something prepossessing about her, beyond looks, a supreme confidence, like she owns the space.

'You shy all of a sudden.'

'Fuck me, she is awesome!'

'What's that?' I reply.

'Can I ask you something?

'Sure'

'Are you gay?'

'I . . . no, why?'

'You sure?' She sits next to me, shuffles up. The class, barely six feet away, shift in their seats.

'I think so, last time I checked.' She smiles at this.

'Would you fuck me?'

'Jesus, in a heartbeat.'

Fuck off, Marv, not now.

'Would you?'

I manage a half-laugh. 'What the fuck is this . . .' and move to stand.

Another voice chirps in behind me. 'No you just sit there, pal. We're all friends here, yeah?'

'Fuck me, anyone else!'

'Yeah, we are.'

'Then you would?' she says.

'What?'

'Fuck me'

'I'm just waiting to see if *we* can have a deal.'

'Is he waking up?'

'What?'

'*Too fuckin' right I am.*'

'You getting a lobby on?'

I try another smile. Sunlight flares dust particles hanging in the air. I bet she owns those too.

'Show me.'

'What's that?'

'Show me.'

'Show you what?'

'*The fuck . . .*'

'Unzip and show me. I don't believe you.'

'*Do not get your fuckin' knob out.*'

'I don't think so.' I'm not smiling now.

'*She knows you're old bill.*'

'Why not?' She leans in, her voice almost a whisper. 'You hiding something?'

'No . . . I mean you're making me nervous . . .'

'Then show me.' She puts her hand on my knee. It tenses.

'*She felt that, you cunt.*'

'Tell you what, I'll count to five . . . One . . .'

'Are you listening?' asks the mystery man.

'*Do not get your fuckin' junk out!*'

'Two.'

Fuck this. I move awkwardly on the sofa. It's suddenly boiling in here.

'Three.'

'*Don't be a cunt.*'

'Four.'

'*You'll fuck this up . . .*'

No, it's whether I'm carrying a wire.

'Fuck it, sure, why not' . . . as I stand and reach for my belt buckle.

'And we'll leave it there, thank you.'

End of exercise.

Twelve started out, a dozen, a mixed bag, the dirty dozen. Some don't make it, some I will see again in work, some I won't. Some will have their true colours revealed in time. But I've passed, another service number to add to the collection. I'm now a licensed level one UC. There are, at this time, around 110 level ones on the index, although less than half of them are active. This does not include officers participating in the shadow shitshow charged with an altogether different and dubious task, that of spying on legitimate protest, of which there is no mention nor suggestion.

To get on to the course in the first place, beyond passing the interview and psychometric testing, you also have to sell yourself, explaining your USP, what area of expertise you can bring to things. Mine, I realised, was gifted to me by Pa. After all this time, I still cannot reconcile the scale of his addiction or the complexity of it, especially since he seems not to have learned from his mistakes. After leaving prison, he becomes a penny gambler, making small, multiple bets on the horses that keep him going, topped up with twice-weekly village whist drives. A form of gambler-lite methadone, it keeps him bothered, engaged, alive. I'm frustrated but also fascinated, and in him I see an opportunity to develop a legend that might allow me to understand him, and to create an identity that will secure my place as an undercover officer with a unique USP. The horses.

I had taken up horse riding while working at the Bastard Borough, initially introduced to it by a former girlfriend. I find it's the best way to relax and, if I'm honest, I prefer the company of horses to most people I meet, in and out of the job. Authorised to carry a firearm, I often use a shooting range that SO19 Firearms operates in Lippitts Hill on the edge of Epping Forest. In time they will relocate to a vast site outside London, but for now we shoot here, at this former agricultural nursery requisitioned by the War Office in the Second World War. It became an anti-aircraft gun battery, before being later used as a prisoner-of-war camp for captured Germans. I visit a stable a stone's throw from the camp and start regularly riding out from there. I soon become so proficient that they allow me to go out alone, hacking through Epping Forest. I once took a dozen detectives, most of whom had never sat on a horse, out on a dawn hack.

'How the fuck did you persuade me to do this?'

'You're all right. Brush yourself off and get back on . . .'

It's an hour or two of peace, away from Copland.

On a rest day, waiting for my course date to be set, I go for a hack in Epping so I can be alone with my thoughts.

'What the fuck are you gonna do? Ride up to a meet and say "Howdy, I'm here to buy a lorry load of whizz"?'

I tack up my favourite horse, Ida, a Hanoverian mare. I have been bitten and thrown by the horse but don't want any other. She is as tough as old boots and quick. I decide that by the time I ride back into the stables in two hours' time, I will have the framework of a successful legend, and it will involve horses in some way, shape or form. Raindrops fall gently on the dense foliage of Epping Forest, London's lungs; perfect weather, it's quiet along the bridle path and trails, the weather may be keeping people indoors, which suits me. I've never minded wet weather, at sea or on land.

So, where would this legend place me? If necessary, I could spend time with the mounted branch, I suppose. Horse transport is also a possibility. Obtain an HGV licence through SO10 who would fund training.

We trek through the forest, me, my friend the Hanoverian mare and Marv. *'Soppy cunt, talking to a horse.'* The rain picks up, laying a wet sheen across the forest. I have barely seen a soul as I break out into a large plain that's good for a canter. Ida begins to dance, trying to get her head. Not yet, I say, and not of a mind to be thrown again. She, straining against the bit, prancing, is on edge; I stroke her neck. 'It's okay, easy now, easy.' As I whisper, I suddenly hear a loud shout.

A popular, if somewhat debatable fad at the time around parts of London was the ownership of American pit bull terriers or an equivalent ferocious-toothed canine.

Predominantly, it seemed to me, they were owned by young men either struggling with issues of low self-esteem or networked low-level narcos, keen to strut the message. Shouting at the top of his voice was a bull-necked, shaven-headed Neanderthal, his dog missile hurtling at speed towards us. Clearly no time to ask early man to get his dog under control, I rise out of the saddle to a tuck and kick on, not that Ida needs it – she too has seen what's coming, all she wants is to bolt.

I move from canter to gallop in a couple of strides, looking over my shoulder to see a frothing beast intent on locking on to flanks, and gaining ground.

'Fuck this, get a fuckin' move on,' mutters Marv. I slip the reins and lean in, clicking my tongue in her ear, asking for more: 'Come on, come on, girl, come on!' She takes hold of the bit, flying

hooves flicking churned mud in the face of the pit bull as we gradually begin to pull away. We come to a halt by a thicket at the top of the hill and look back. We've lost it. As I gather my breath and Ida snorts, shaking her head in triumph, it comes to me. What the missing component of my legend will be. Thorough-bred horse racing.

I speak to Pa to put some meat on the bones. We talk about the attraction of horse racing. For him it is obvious, and he proves extremely knowledgeable. We discuss flat and National Hunt racing, the trainers, established owners and prominent jockeys, different courses around the country, the Jockey Club. We are some way into a long chat, sat under the cover of the small Decimus Burton lighthouse that I first saw as a kid – it feels like a different time. As we stare out to the sea, he pauses and asks why the sudden interest, and I want to tell him what this moment is all about, not just becoming a UC. What I actually say is that it is connected to a case I'm working, still unsure of when my SO10 training will begin and not wanting to have *that* conversation with him, not just yet. Satisfied that I am not trying to, God forbid, understand how gambling took over his life, or discuss the impact, he settles into the task.

A few of the remaining inshore fishing vessels sail past as I get a tiny bit closer to my old man without really getting nearer to the truth. I leave after a few days, a notebook laden with information and ideas on what to do next. One of which is to attend a meeting of the Met's own horse-racing club, run by a couple of uniformed old sweats. They arrange trips to racing meets and club nights with guest speakers, and have plans to arrange shared ownership of a horse one day to run in their own colours. I begin to attend the meetings when I can, and on one occasion meet an extraordinary individual, a man with equine DNA, who once rode the winner of the Grand National and is now a National Hunt trainer, and who strikes me as being as mad as a mongoose and extraordinarily good company.

Graham is a man constantly at a gallop. He breezes into one such meeting of the club as if riding out a winner at Newton Abbot, and I immediately know that this immensely likeable man is someone who can help me. I introduce myself and a friendship begins. In time, I start to visit Graham at his training yard, and our friendship develops. I help out around the yard, mucking out, cleaning the tack. Just being around the horses is a way of relaxing away from the politics of the police, which I'm finding increasingly disorganised and unfocused. Scotland Yard is showing its age, and it seems to me that both domestic and international organised crime are accelerating away from the justice system, waving as they go. Who knows, maybe a change of government will shake things up. Things can only get better, right?

In less than six months, with Graham's help and further assistance from former jockey and racing commentator Richard Pitman, I put together a solid legend in racing, confident it will stand scrutiny. Graham and Richard have no real idea of why exactly I am developing this detailed 'back story', beyond the fact it is work related, but they appreciate the thanks from my head of unit for their kind assistance. Any covert legend is reliant on the assistance of good people.

I continue to absorb myself in this strange new world without any danger of falling into the abyss that Pa found himself in – betting's a mug's game, I suspect. I overtake the racing club by putting together a syndicate with other officers for a share in a racehorse, which sadly doesn't live up to expectations but nevertheless adds to my growing knowledge. I research different makes of horse transporters, and draw up a shortlist of the makes and models that would lend themselves to nefarious activity that I can pitch to criminals when the time comes. The smell of horse shit and piss has the potential to mask a thousand commodities. I put thousands of hours, unpaid, into developing a legend fit for purpose because I love what I'm doing. Because this, this form of policing, is pure and unsullied and I believe I have found a way to make an effective difference.

SO10 have no budget for legend development beyond the basic skillset scenarios, though I can't help but agree with one supervisor, an SO10 office philosopher, the Marsh Duck, who observes wryly that we remain able to maintain an excellent fleet of vehicles with chauffeurs for senior management. In time, this will lead to one commissioner, the Lackey, being heavily criticised for spending an extraordinarily large percentage of the Met's vehicle budget on a fleet of luxury cars for chief officers. But I believe that investment of my time and effort will bring its rewards in ensuring, as much as is ever possible, I will never be burned – exposed – on a covert operation.

Having passed the course, I chase work, finding reasons to drop into the SO10 office on the fifth floor at the Yard, ever keen to push on and get assigned. As an undercover detective, you often continue with your detective duties even as you undertake deployment; the extra yards are not the problem, or at least so you convince yourself, because you want to work. In reality, it is a ridiculous state of affairs. The Bear remains cautious, convinced I'm some kind of mole, but I learn the identity of who has been advocating for me, my former boss, the Pangolin, now head of the directorate and tipped for the very top. He had simply said to the Bear, 'give him a fair hearing in the selection process, I think he has real potential', but bears are used to building their own dens, and he interpreted this as something else – that I was his spy. Funny how a profession that loves to know the guts of everything hates the thought of it applying to them. And though I am not the Pangolin's spy, truth is often redundant in the jungle that is Copland. Soon the Pangolin will move into the private sector, never occupying the top desk. Too independent of thought, perhaps. I believe this can be a problem on the upper floors.

My first UC job eventually arrives, and it comes from the Flying Squad. There is an informant claiming access to a criminal armourer, with whom I may be able to negotiate a 'parcel' of firearms. It's a quick scope, in and out, to establish if there are firearms that need to be taken off the streets. It's a short chain, which, as it turns out, the informant is obviously pulling.

'What do you think?' the young armourer asks when I eventually meet him, as he shows me a 'taste' in the form of a decrepit firearm.

'Is this it? Where's the rest?'

'Easy, good things come to those who wait,' he suggests.

'Good things? It's a fuckin' musket!'

He is a low-level dabbler trying to middle his way up the pecking order of criminality, this being the time for dabblers and paddlers of their own canoes, while the large-scale vessels of criminality sail on, including many named in the letter sent to me in the Bastard Borough. It is not unusual at this time for operational heads to begin a briefing outlining what time the operation will finish in order to keep costs down, or stipulate time off in lieu in order to balance the budget. This was often the reality of the UC; it has led, for example, to a High Court case regarding covert officers not being paid for the hours they actually worked, the ramifications of which are already being felt. In short, it was a symptom of nothing less than a failure by leadership, a failure in truly understanding the requirements and complexity of proactive policing beyond the obvious. As for my low-level dabbler, he was eventually arrested, his musket having led to other offences.

Operation Dahlia

On another early case, I find myself in west London trying to recover a valuable painting stolen from a museum. I perhaps should have known it might not work out, given the similarity to the exercise on my training course, and on top of that the briefing team don't inspire me with confidence, save for one detective who continually rolls his eyes when his boss goes to great lengths to repeat how productive and consistently grade A1 his intelligence has been thus far. The DS quietly tells me on the side not to hold my breath, and I tell him I'm very good at that, which lightens the mood in what proves to be a very long evening. Hope springs eternal and I hope the skipper is merely jaded. There is no plan or real belief that the painting will be produced at this particular meet – the aim is simply to assess credibility and establish if it looks like a 'goer', agree to a price and tee up a second meeting on the basis of our discussions.

The operational head wants a full transcript and expects me to wear a wire, though mobile technology will eventually largely replace the cumbersome Nagra recording device that we now use. The DS is unhappy with this, realising the job is not as well prepped as it might be – such as knowing who exactly will turn up to the meet – and he is at pains to point it out that ultimately it will be my decision as to whether I wear one or not. It's clearly a concept the ops head is not familiar with – the fact that an officer of junior rank is able to counter command a senior rank. Diplomacy is key in such situations, which is why I answer and not Marv.

'He's as daft as he looks, this cunt.'

'It's like a magician working a trick on stage, guv,' I say, the detective sergeant all ears as I use the only magician I could think of at the time. 'Like, er, Paul Daniels! And his assistant . . . working the guillotine trick'. His eyes light up.

'Debbie McGee?'

'Yeah, I think so.'

'How does that relate to this?'

I suggest that while Paul Daniels is in charge of the act and the trick, it is Debbie McGee who has to agree that she is *willing* to be guillotined and only when satisfied with all the safety protocols.

'If she is not happy, there is no trick. Paul Daniels is still in charge but . . .'

'Yes, no, I totally understand, Debbie McGee, there's something about her . . . good-looking woman . . .'

The DS, a moon-faced old sweat, is too long in service to let that slide: 'So you, guv, are . . . Paul Daniels, and the UC here, well he is your Debbie McGee.'

As one of the surveillance team siting across the room closes his eyes, Marv reminds me, *'You fuckin' volunteered for this.'*

The DS is right. It is not worth the risk, wearing a

cumbersome tape at such an early meeting when it's clearly not known if the job is likely to progress. My gut feeling is it is a crock of shit and it should never have been presented as suitable to plumb in a level one UC, particularly as I'd had it drilled into me how improper use of UC deployment by lazy management wanting quick wins was undermining the whole programme. I am not inclined to criticise at this point in my career, keen as I am to work in at least one area of effective, proactive policing.

While I wait to meet the informant, the DS explains the trial and tribulations of working with the DI who runs him. It is the DI's first post as a detective and his team are counting down the days before he moves on to his next. The DS does not bother with such negativity, preferring a glass-half-full outlook. With less than three years to serve, he's counting down his own days. His positivity clearly works – he wears a smile throughout, whereas mine fades when he tells me if the job goes on beyond a certain time he will be booking off due to overtime restrictions. My gut feeling, which has no place in the new dawn, is that he is the only officer with any idea what is or might be required, even if the meeting does turn out to be 'pretty much a doddle', as the DI confidently predicts.

It takes place in a pub on the edge of parkland in the middle of nowhere. The team have provided a phone from which I will update them, particularly in the unlikely event the suspects turn up carrying a painting, which of course they don't. In fact, only one suspect turns up. As I was pitched to the informant as extremely strong on British horse racing but extremely limited on British artists, I hover like a second-rate salesman with a pair of pints and try to ascertain from the suspect if this is ever likely to develop into a recovery. After a few hours I'm doubtful and after a couple more I just want to get home, knowing I have an early start the next day on the Flying Squad. As I've said, at this time, all UC work is in addition to the officer's day job, unless it is an especially long-term deployment, and so it only adds to the pressure. When the meeting comes to an end, I find I can't contact the team, as the phone they supplied has died. I hope they'll pick up the suspect as he leaves the pub.

Except they don't. In the absence of the DS, long since gone to his bed, they look to the DI for advice. Because I had indicated in my first update that the commodity was not in the hands of the suspect, and because they can't get in touch with me, he thinks I have must have stood down, so he tells the team to do the same. As the hapless suspect wanders away free of any surveillance, I myself wander back to try and find the hapless DI. He doesn't answer my calls – he too has gone home, presumably to salivate over Debbie McGee.

It's a beautiful, clear, crisp night, and I decide to walk. I skirt through parkland, hoping that this is not the shape of things to come. The DS calls me the next day rather apoplectic with rage towards his common-senseless DI, full of apologies for the cretinous end to a dismal deployment. When I suggest that the informant might be playing the DI, he shares the news that moves are underway to bring forward the well-connected DI's move to pastures new. He continued to graze well, though, last seen in a senior position in a regional constabulary – on a still night you can hear his officers scream. SO10 run their own comb through my diplomatic update on the case. I know the DS has contacted them to apologise, and they too conclude that, all things considered, despite our best efforts, this is a case for the division to continue without further input from us.

As new policing priorities take root, outlandish and ill-thought-out requests by mission-statement junkies to use what should be 'last resort' methods will become more and more commonplace. I am booked to participate in a UC chain, featuring several detectives, engaged in trying to buy a large weight of cocaine, when an operational head leaves the top-secret case file in a briefcase on public transport. It is not a promising start, nor am I left feeling particularly confident when, deciding that my covert name might clash with a suspect's, a supervisor instructs the informant to give me a name of his choosing without consulting me or SO10. He does this, disregarding the fact that my pseudonym, legend, paperwork, credit cards, passport, everything, are all in another name – hardly robust. The supervisor blames the informant, who threatens to walk away, so riled at the verbal he receives. Luckily, I've been working on another legend under a different pseudonym – one shelved until needed – so I cobble together a framework under that name, carry a weight of cash rather than credit cards and hope for the best. It does the job. The operational chain extends, gathering more evidence and eventually leading to arrests, but there is little appetite to understand how potentially dangerous this could have been. If you take an interest in current affairs, you might have surmised that the Met are not the best of organisations when it comes to learning from past mistakes.

'A proper goer.' Words used by one experienced UC in relation to the tensile strength of any 'legend' being paramount. The past once again reverberates as I set about the task. '*Nil sine labore!*'

shouted a particularly vicious teacher as he launched a black-board duster at me, mistakenly believing I had disrupted class. A great shot, it drew blood, a bag of parched peas from the boy who was actually guilty. *Nil sine labore*, nothing without effort. The only thing from schooldays that stood the test of time, an echo I acknowledge as I set about piecing together my own proper goer. A legend gives back as much as you put into it. Don't pigeonhole yourself – you need to be adept, confident, metaphorically able to wear suits of a different cut with equal comfort. Use your forename in your pseudonym – when you hear it, you need to turn. Date of birth? Add years, don't take them off – it will play in your favour. Don't shave your head – let your hair be if you have it. Never turn up for a meeting channeling a screen version of real life. Ink is tricky if you think about it – so are vivid scars. Hammering yourself in the gym to become a muscle bosun (a navy term) is all well and good but will only be effective in one or two scenarios, if you are lucky. The more robust the legend, the less likely it will trip you up when deployed. It is organic and must be treated as such. Nourish it but also understand that any patina it has comes only with age.

Hardly surprising, coming from Trawler Town, that I also begin to look into creating a cover story around commercial fishing, because one legend alone isn't enough – you need a diversity of options, simmering on the back burner for long-term sustainability. I share this with Bud and we agree that the best man to speak to would be 'Steve', Trawler Town's own Captain Ahab with a heart. I've known him since my early teens when I regarded him as being a bit terrifying – he has that thing all skippers have of giving you the eye as they look and assess you.

Steve knows I'm a detective and greets my tentative enquiries with 'I don't want to know why' (good people that help never do). He suggests the nuts and bolts required to build a framework and, like most trawler skippers, is absolutely on point. Steve knows better than most that his world is living on borrowed time, and, in a way, so am I.

I decide to test this alter ego, this man of the sea, bring him out into the light, well, a café near St James's Park in London. Play a game with one of the veterans, the Sea Eagle. They love fish. There's a possibility we're going to be working together. It's an opportunity to test this new identity before putting him away – a skirmish with someone who would easily nail a flimsy legend. The prize is nothing more than coffees all round. We talk boats, fishing grounds, fish migration. Of course, he knows next to fuck-all about the industry but that's not the point – it's how convincing I am. And in that respect, I'm on it. And while no doubt UCs past and present have embarked on a similar project, good, bad and indifferent, I'm confident not one produced a good-sized fresh cod and filleted it before a wide-eyed barista and a bemused UC. He accepted my gift of fresh fillets with a smile and delivered his endorsement in his languid Michael Caine-esque lilt (think *Alfie*): 'Yeah . . . I'll give you that, son, that's a proper go'er.' The barista, however, asked me, despite being a good customer, never to do it again. Fair point.

In another area of London, still something of an urban prairie, yet to be reconfigured by the needs of profit rather than people, I am sitting in the chair of my *other* barbershop. The real deal, a genuine slow-twirling pole, a purveyor of fine cuts, this is the one I visit when maintaining a particular 'covert' legend. In essence, it would be Liam Curran getting his haircut, not Liam Thomas; it is Curran who chews the cud with the barber, not me: his thoughts on the day, the world, the ordinary and the mundane, the nuts and bolts of nothing in particular.

Today I am at that *other* barbershop waiting for the *other* phone to ring. For several weeks I have been trying to buy a parcel of firearms, semi-automatic pistols suspected of entering the UK from overseas. This is the intelligence supplied, but working out whether it is solid or not, aside from any 'technical' assistance from hardwired bugs or intercepts, will often be an additional task required of you, as it is here. Not all that glitters is gold – sometimes it is better to walk away rather than risk exposure for a crock of shit, as I did with the painting in the park.

At this point in time, weapons are increasingly finding their way into the UK, a steady flow that will continue to rise. A few years earlier, a police officer had been brutally gunned down in south London while answering a routine call. A good man slain, a consequence of this rising flood. Many of these weapons arrived as trophies, contraband from the First Gulf War, only to be later sold, and this illegal armoury is further augmented by subsequent conflicts in the Balkans and Middle East. And we all become more weaponised in response: more gangsters with guns and more cops in Kevlar, hurtling at speed from A to B and back.

Outside the barbershop laden with faded frames of haircuts that one day might come back into fashion, overcast skies are stained with black. This is Copland weather at its best – mist and drizzle are always preferable to blue skies. It is ideal weather to move unobserved through the city, hood up and head down. But occasionally I miss the sunlight, and not just for the warmth. Once I took a week's holiday to a quiet Greek Island – I can still see that solitary man singing on the beach. I went because I missed the simple feeling of the sun on my face. Looking back, it is a painful memory.

The barber lifts his hands away from my neck as I take the call. The barbers in such neighbourhoods as UCs will often find themselves are like priests, offering a confessional box if needed – all hearing, to the artifice, silent in reply. It's the primary subject calling me, asking if we are still on for a meet. He tells me he hopes to soon have a nice 'instrument' I might want to take a look at as a sample, me being, on this occasion, a buyer of fine 'instruments'. We agree to meet. The priest lowers his hands back to the task and continues in silence. I watch his face in the mirror as he moves around me – he really could be a man of the cloth. We make small talk as if he was a player in some massive conspiracy and not simply my *other* barber.

Often, to gain the trust of a subject, it is simply a case of making the subject like you, and being sensitive and attuned to every beat. Ensuring you are aware of anything that indicates progression or otherwise. Phrases picked up on a line – a phone intercept or probe – will occasionally offer a glimpse into operations that you hope you will eventually have chapter and verse on. But never, ever, repeat what you hear.

'What do you think about him, the quiet fella . . . you like him?' A question asked about me and picked up on an intercept in a corruption case I worked. They did. Sometimes it is about tickling a subject's greed: 'Oh, he's definitely good for the money.'

Or sometimes it was simply the promise of new opportunities: 'Yeah, I think we can deal with him, what do you think?'

If you push regardless, and often there is no other option, you can find yourself in a pickle. And in Operation Dahlia, I really did find myself in a pickle. There is not an officer deployed as a UC, past or present, I suspect, who has not been faced with such a situation.

'Sink or swim, that's all you can do,' the Bear once said to me. 'Which stroke you use, boy, that's down to you.' I have time to reflect on this when such a quandary presents itself during Dahlia. This time I decide to swim, because under the table is a 9mm semi-automatic pistol, a sample of what is on offer. It shouldn't be on offer right now and nor should it have been brought to the meet in a pub by the bull-necked, sports-apparel-wearing, gum-chewing individual sitting opposite me, alongside the primary subject I am here to meet. And while I am sure I have never met Bull Neck before, he utters a line no UC ever wants to hear: 'I know you.'

It's a strange thing, but what you most fear in such awkward moments is very often the last thing you might expect. I'm bookended, sat between a rock and a hard man, the potential for sudden violence increasing while my options decrease. I'm racking my brain for details of a long-forgotten professional situation. But more than anything, I am worried what the Bear will think of me if this goes wrong, the desperate need for validation from family. The job is seemingly heading south, a fact made more real when the primary subject reaches over, picks up my phone and begins to examine it.

'Oh, right . . . Where was that, fella?'

Negotiations now clearly on hold, the question is delivered softly as he studies my phone. I'm not worried about the phone – it's just a phone. It will pass scrutiny, which is more than can be said for me or indeed any other UC who finds him or herself in a similar situation, because in reality, despite what I said about legends, we are all made of straw – we burn easily if exposed to the wrong climate. Time now to use whatever stroke necessary. I stare at my bull-necked accuser, who looks quite capable of smashing the living daylights out of me and, more worryingly, seems keen to do so. I rattle through chance meetings, including the two occasions I visited Pa in prison, but there is no way, surely – too long ago and Pa never would have disclosed what I did for a living – that can't be it. I do have a secret: I once stood in for a victim who was too upset to go on camera for a re-enactment while working in the Bastard Borough – utter stupidity. *'You fuckin' cunt. I told you that!'* Not now, Marv, temperature rising. I thought it would never see the light of day, but what if it did . . . Why the fuck did I do that? *'Because you're a stupid cunt!'* On and on my mind races until I find not so much the swimming stroke as the mechanism, the thing I have done since childhood. I close my eyes and sink beneath the surface of reality and hope to find a solution outside it.

In the moment, I offer a small piece of me, the real me, my past. 'Yesss . . . I recognise you, Tonka's mate, in the mob, yeah?' Bull Neck snorts and strains the muscles bolting his neck to his shoulders. His partner, the primary target, looks pained at my response, but at the same time, intrigued, he calmly places my phone back down on the table.

'Mob? New York's a bit far off the manor to be fair, and I've known him a long while,' he suggests, nodding towards Bull Neck. I am not sure whether to laugh or buy more time.

The primary has a receding hairline which lifts even higher along his forehead when he talks, giving him a quizzical look. It goes into overdrive as someone from his own past walks into the pub and hollers a welcome. The distraction surprises him, and in this brief interlude I find a breath and my stride, quickly defining the idea. The Lion often takes a deep drag on his roll-up when in a similar situation – I've seen him do it. He suggested me for this job. I feel the weight. I nod at Bull Neck and smile.

'Yeah, I do fucking know you. Tonka's mate! Yes! Malta?'

It silences everyone apart from Bull Neck, who looks incredulous.

'Malta? What you fucking talking about? I've never been there in my life.'

I carry on, as fast as my thoughts will allow.

'Tonka's mate. You collected the bets in the bog. Down the Gut?'

Bull Neck, understandably, has absolutely no idea what I am talking about – a large vein on the side of his neck throbs displeasure.

'Collecting money in a bog? What the fuck are you saying?'

'Was this when you were in Spain?' asks Hairline, now all ears.

'What? No, I've not fucking been to Malta.' His pal spits in reply.

I have no choice but to plough on. I don't recognise him, which is not to say that he's wrong, but I do know one thing: he bears an uncanny resemblance to one of the prime participants in an incident that took place in Malta back when I was in the navy. I was there and now so was he. In any case, telling the story might take his mind off any suspicions.

Tonka was a stoker in the Royal Navy, the son of a senior military officer, and though he had the benefit of an excellent private education, he was entirely happy below decks. I cannot say if it was there or public school that he discovered his incendiary skill, one that I stumbled upon with riotous consequence, but I am about to pin my colours to the mast and hope that what I reveal to the table at a covert meet will persuade them I'm a bona fide armourer with legitimate military experience. Wherever the Bull Neck believes our paths crossed, he is like a dog with a bone, leaving me nowhere to go but forward.

As mentioned, the Gut was a notorious, heaving, pulsing, narrow street that seemed to stretch the length of Valletta. A livid wound of Bacchanalian butchery and brouhaha, it offered a warm welcome to every single aspect of the social and sexual spectrum. A potpourri of class, nationality and vastly different appetites, it was the most terrifying place for a 17-year-old Trawler Town boy still mainly a virgin.

Flogger was the senior rating on my mess deck and a veteran of the Gut. Once ashore, he led from the front. It soon had the makings of a suicide mission, given the ferocity with which we hit the first bar. Within minutes, a gender-fluid dwarf dressed in killer leather boots, a corset and a US Navy dixie-cup hat aggressively asked me if I'd ever had an enemy. The music was so loud, his accent so heavy, I struggled to comprehend what he meant, so I smiled as he repeated, 'Ave you enameeee?' I couldn't understand why, having told him 'probably', he seemed so angry with my non-committal answer. Flogger let me suffer until we left the bar – turned out he was asking if I'd ever had an enema. It was an early warning that nothing was off limits in the Gut, pardon the pun. At this rate I was unlikely to last, as Flogger was only just warming up.

We rendezvoused with Tonka at another bar. Flogger and he were old shipmates, and a night in Tonka's company had legendary status. By the time we arrived, I was struggling, but Flogger was not a man to be disappointed. The bar could best be described as being like the cantina in *Star Wars* but where everyone was dressed in crushed velvet. I gulped in a breath of air, warm and sticky from its passage across deserts. Focus was difficult. I was trying to tell Flogger I might take the next liberty boat (a water taxi provided by the ship's crew) back to the ship when he raised his bony arms aloft and hollered like a man demented. 'TONKA! TONKA!'

Standing at the bar with several other sailors, marines and assorted stragglers was Tonka. I don't why but I smiled as if it all now made perfect sense, but it didn't, and it was about to get a shitload worse. Tonka raised a full beer and downed it in one. I felt nauseous. Flogger charged towards his mate as I snuck away. I sat outside for a while. The fresh air seemed to revive me, and then I heard it, rising up from the basement bar I'd just left. 'TONKA! TONKA! TONKA! TONKA!'

I should have headed for the harbour, but I didn't – I followed the hypnotic beat. A ruck of bodies was trying to squeeze through a small door at the back of the bar. I followed suit, pushing and pulling my way through the heaving mass, potholing through sweat-caked flesh. The thing was, I'd heard what Tonka's infamy was based upon – I just didn't believe it. On I went, fighting through to emerge in a fetid karzy. There, in the gloom, sat Tonka. And I realised that everything I'd heard was true and I paid homage in the only way fitting. 'TONKA! TONKA! TONKA! TONKA!'

When an undercover officer participates in a buy, there is always the chance, no matter how precise and careful the preparation has been or how secure the chain, that if just one link breaks, or even trembles, it can break the entire interlocked sequence and take you with it. The tensile strength of an undercover operation can be as thin as gossamer, but it can also move mountains. But if it needs to flex, you must be prepared to think on your feet to avoid catastrophe. Often the only viable solution is to draw upon your own life experience. What I saw one night in Malta was now to be dropped into a conversation with two gun runners to keep a covert line intact. It was unconventional. It was pure Tonka. I check to see if they are still with me.

'That's where we met, yeah?' I suggest to Bull Neck as I take a sip of beer and glance across. 'You were the Bootneck collecting wagers with his mate, Flogger – 42 . . . 45 Commando, yeah?'

'What? Marine? No, no mate.'

'He's fuckin' happy having that,' whispers Marv as Bull Neck shakes his head, comfortable with the suggestion of him being a former marine. He also called me mate, so all is not lost. On I charge on back through time, chapter and verse, the tale of the Tonka, as it happened, and Hairline and Bull Neck are coming with me.

Tonka, I tell them, was sitting like Buddha, trousers round ankles, head nodding with confident certainty as he manoeuvred another 50 pence carefully into place. Inside his foreskin. He'd clearly done this before. Cheers rang out. Surely I couldn't be the only one thinking, why? And how exactly do you arrive at a point in your life where you decide the burning question that must be answered is how many of the biggest coins in the realm can you fit inside your foreskin? Tonka's looked like it was on fire as Flogger cajoled and whipped all assembled into a frenzy, a league of nations united in salutation. 'TONKA! TONKA! TONKA!' As if acknowledging his subjects, Tonka raised one arm, the other taking the weight, and roared, 'SEVEN . . . POUNDS!' The swirling, sweating crowd erupted. His adjutant, the marine, acting like a boxer's second, demanded we give his man room in the ring. Not that the navy's alternative diplomat was fazed by the pressure, unlike the end of his cock, which increasingly looked like a bag of spanners wrapped in an intestine. He took a slug of beer and demanded another coin. The atmosphere was thick with anticipation. There was a problem – only Maltese lira were now available, but Tonka, a stickler for protocol, argued it had to be a 50-pence piece. We all frantically checked our pockets without success, but with brilliant ingenuity someone stepped forward with an agreeable solution to the drunken audience.

And at this moment in the story, to keep Bull Neck on the back foot and me on the front, I step forward, placing myself front and centre in the story, rather than as it actually unfolded – a marine offered Tonka a 9mm bullet from a Makarov semi-automatic pistol, suggesting it would make a fitting alternative. A golden bullet, the final piece in Tonka's technical test. In Valletta the crowd roared approval; in a backwater London pub, the audience is silent.

'See, I had this nine-mil round from a Makarov.'

'A what?'

'Makarov. A Soviet nine-millimetre pistol, great bit of kit, reliable, been around years,' I explain to Hairline as Bull Neck, still clearly happy to be judged Royal Marine material, nods in agreement. On we go, back to Valletta, demonstrating that my interest in firearms started early. It was me who fished the bullet out of a pocket and offered up the totemic Soviet-era ordinance to the Buddha of Balls. Tonka's mashed-potato smile returned, and he raised the bullet in the air as once again his name rang out: 'TONKA! TONKA! TONKA!' And as the boy from Trawler Town thought on the night, and the UC winging it thinks right now, could this get any weirder?

Tonka placed the bullet with surgical skill, a crowning glory upon his crown, if you can picture the scene, which I realise is not easy.

Tonka rose to his feet, as Flogger led the cheering and the adjutant took the money, and Tonka paraded his genital Jenga for all to see as his name echoed across the Gut – it was as if we had just won the World Cup. And then, in the drunken mayhem, I saw the dwarf heading towards me as the piercing sound of several whistles interrupted the night. An irate owner of an adjacent bar, objecting to Tonka's show stealing his trade, had called in the 'Regs', the naval police, claiming his country's currency was being disrespected. (Two nights later, Tonka went for a world record in the informant's bar.) In the time-honoured police tradition of trying to squeeze a quart into a pint pot, dozens of Regulators attempted to bowl into the small yard and pandemonium broke out. As I struggled to unsee Tonka's bulging abstract and avoid the dwarf, Flogger grabbed me by the collar, dragged me towards a near wall and pushed me over. I remember thinking that he'd been here before.

'Whoah! Wait, wait, you put a cap in his fucking foreskin?' Hairline breaks the moment, he needs details.

'Dwarf?' asks Bull Neck, clearly paying attention.

'Yeah . . . No, I mean Tonka did, obviously. Besides, it wasn't so much inside as sort of . . . wedged. On top. Kind of . . .'

Bull Neck looks towards Hairline, but he's gone – he is still standing in a pissed-soaked yard back in Valletta as my shipmates and I bomb burst across the Gut and, in true naval tradition, carry on regardless. No one was left behind.

'And, no one asked for their money back . . .' I wait to see how we are – is it still on?

Hairline slowly nods, ruminating before addressing Bull Neck, 'That's why we are world leaders, makes you proud to be British.'

Laughter bounces off the walls that no longer seem so oppressive, and that's it. We are on.

'Seven-pounds-fifty worth of fifty-pence coins inside his fucking foreskin!' Hairline clearly did not expect this shift. 'Seven pounds fucking fifty!' He is clearly computing a different kind of tensile strength to that of a covert line.

'Yeah, I mean you had to be there, which you was, yes?' I point at Bull Neck, also conducting the same calculation, though more slowly I suspect.

I exposed a little of my own skin. I did of course serve with the navy, and had they dug further into that, asked difficult questions, but Bull Neck had to be disavowed of the idea that our paths had crossed. You have seconds to take or lose control. However outrageous the line, if you commit and they like you, chances are they will also trade. Bull Neck was wrong – our paths had surely not crossed – but in the doubt and uncertainty, I chose to refashion my legend in the moment.

Hairline rises all smiles and we move outside. Now, as we walk across the car park, there is humour, not fear. I belt up in the back of Hairline's car as we set off along the line, on the next leg of the journey. Hairline looks over at Bull Neck behind the wheel, and asks for the 9mm pistol, then slowly turns to face me. The knot in my stomach returns. I feel Marv's hand on my shoulder, as my hand lifts casually towards the door.

'*Shussh,*' whispers Marv. '*We're on, we're fuckin' on.*' But still the knot twists.

Hairline's turn to whisper. 'My mate, in Catford, bit of a player.'

'Oh, yeah.'

'Yeah. Everyone knows him. He gets about, east London mainly.' Has he played me? I wonder, my hand slowly rising. 'Yeah, handsome fucker. He'd be good for five maybe, six tops.'

The engine is running but where are we going? Five or six guns, that will do for starters surely?

'But . . . seven fuckin pounds fucking fifty! . . .'

Chasing the commodity, whatever it might be, occasionally creates an unseen dilemma: how much are you willing or able to reveal of yourself? It's a question you might only have seconds to answer, and the grind takes its toll, it's an addictive grind. All UCs are to some degree masochists, and selfish too. We befriend and we betray, and we often hurt those close to us. For many, if not all, the price I suspect is often not worth the sacrifice, but you never fully understand the price until it's over and the ashes run through your fingers, your ambition distilled to dust. It is why many UCs burn out before they are ever burned by their targets.

Operation Tulip

I have been engaged on an armed surveillance operation for two weeks, waiting for a high-street bank robbery. It's high summer in London, and the city sweats as it sleeps, praying for a storm to lift heavy skies and let the boroughs breathe, as my pancake holster bleeds into my back. The Walrus over at SO10 calls: 'Got a bit of work for you – tricky. Can you come in?' There is always uncertainty, so all jobs are potentially tricky, but if you are told it is, it's because it *is* tricky. I'll be there first thing tomorrow, I say, anything to break the monotony of the day job.

In each job, you evaluate, get a steer on the look and background required. Operation Tulip is most definitely not a suit job – it's a jeans and T-shirt job, a simple drop and go. Ensure the subject is happy with the kit you deliver, in this instance his repaired computer. The one he uses to watch and share child pornography, because he is a paedophile. This is in the years before sophisticated remote surveillance. The suspect believes you are of a like mind, though he will not discuss this with you because he does not know you well enough. He is cautious. He will, however, ask whether you have repaired the kit, discreetly.

You explain that it's all good, then make your excuses and leave. This is also a time when the full scale and enormity of this crime are yet to be grasped or understood. Without doubt, high-profile offenders have exerted influence in order to escape detection or prosecution, but even that narrative is yet to unfold. The muggy summer is still relentless as I walk to the front door of a neat home in a leafy suburb of south London, carrying my work.

Tap, tap. Come out, come out, wherever you are. Through the window I see a shadow move across the room; shadow world. He's in the hallway, looking for his keys maybe. The shadow comes to the door and I get ready to smile. The door opens to reveal a man in late middle age, out of shape, corpulent.

'How long has this cunt been getting away with it?' Shut up, Marv, shut up!

The man looks me up and down, smiles. 'God, it's hot, isn't it?' he says as he invites me in and ushers me into a comfortable lounge. 'Too hot to work. Tea? The best way to cool down, a quick cuppa.'

'Coffee?' I suggest.

I start to tell him the kit is all good, but he cuts me short.

'Kettle on first. Please have a seat.' He strides off towards the kitchen as I sit down. I am cast back to the Bastard Borough, an unrelated child abuse case, a shocking photo of a child being abused. For years I had sought to ascertain the identity of the perpetrator; I'd given up on him ever being caught. But that face, his round face, the spectacles, the . . .

'It's not him.' I know it's not fucking him, Marv. I'm not blind.

'Same shaped head though,' he persists.

I look around, take in the room, trying to shut Marv up, but he keeps up his commentary: *'Right age. Does he know him? Does he*

*talk to him using this keyboard? He's got away with the most fuckin'
depraved crimes for so long that we have to bring this into his house.'* Shut
up. *'Look at him sat there with his fuckin' tea and biscuits. You're gonna
drink tea with this fuckin' child-molesting cunt? He's taking the piss out of
you. He's been taking the piss for years.'* Shut up!

My narrative must register on my face, because he starts up:
'Oh, forget something, did I? Yes, the milk, my wife doesn't,
hang on . . .' He rises.

'He knows. He's fuckin' away. He's picked up his car keys. He's—'

I put my hand firm on his shoulder. He spins around, and my
hand sinks into flesh. He's heavy set but gone to seed. His face
says it all – he knows I know. I smash my fist into his face, and his
pudgy lip splits instantly as my knuckles grind against his teeth.
He tries to carry on towards the door, but I kick at his leg and it
catches his other, weight and momentum bring him down. He
tries to push himself up with his hand, but I stamp hard down on
the knuckles, hearing the bones crunch as the fingers snap,
knuckles floating loose – I stamp again and again and again and—

'Here we go, milk.'

A fantasy. Was it Marv or . . . me?

He puts a hand on my shoulder as he places the milk on the
tray, then, weirdly, decides to pour some into my coffee.

'Are you okay?'

'Yeah, yeah, I'm fine,' I tell him. 'I'm just a bit hot.'

'Stuffy in here. I've not long been in. I'll open the window'.

'Thank you,' I say. Birdsong floods the room. I don't why, why
now, but I think about the blackbird I shot as a kid in Trawler
Town, the old air rifle Pa brought home. Guilt. Perhaps this is
how I make amends.

'How's your coffee?'

'Good. Thank you.'

He puts his cup down. 'So, here it is,' he says. 'All good?'

'Yes, all good.'

I leave the house and step into the sultry London air. He is standing at the door, the same smile, and then a wave that seems like a salute. I nod, smile back, walk back to the van. Tick tock begins the clock. He will be caught, within the year. He pleads guilty and goes to prison for several years. He put too much milk in my coffee – it really bothered me at the time. I take it black now.

Operation Bluebell

In the 1990s, organised crime began to evolve and adapt far more quickly than either the Home Office or ACPO (the Association of Chief Police Officers), a limited company, later replaced, following bad press, by the National Police Chiefs Council. Latin America extended its markets, while closer to home the birth of a 24-hour-party-people culture fuelled a demand for instant gratification. As the landscape rapidly changed, the upper echelons of British policing proved themselves to be experts who knew more and more about less and less. Stewardship, increasingly, was poor, as I was about to discover on Operation Bluebell.

Things start badly. When I turn up for the first briefing, I've been assigned another random name. This means, with other cases underway, I'm now running three identities. The first meet, after phone calls, takes place in an upmarket hotel in central London. I arrive a little early, let the dog see the rabbit, because not a lot is known about the subject, 'Jack', and you never know who else might arrive. I've checked the hotel out previously, so I'm familiar with the layout. I take a couple of daily papers, open the sports pages and order a drink. My character likes a gamble, so I check the results of the previous day, picking one winner in order to claim I had been on it in good style. A roll of notes to back up the claim. This is a world where most like a flutter of some description, along with some sports talk – it's a gentle way into a meeting.

Jack arrives, and we ease into things. It goes well, and in fact I'm offered a large amount of isosafrole, a precursor used in the manufacture of ecstasy, a one-off purchase or possibly the opportunity to join a syndicate in the large-scale manufacture of the drug. I have established my credibility over drinks in comfortable surroundings. This is the courtship, the opportunity for him to make an initial assessment, which is often reported back to partners hiding in the shadows. The importance of first impressions.

I'm assured the precursor is good quality, stolen direct from the manufacturer and offered to the criminals I am now negotiating with in lieu of a debt. I'm told a sample can be produced. Within the dark web of criminality, everything is currency. The strange phenomenon of crypto will, to some extent, accelerate the hyper-greasing of palms across all criminality, but old-fashioned cash always works.

As the initial meeting has gone well, I'm certain the subject will want a second, though Marv is a dissenting voice. *'He'd never been in a hotel like that, and what about his fuckin' shoes? Scuffed to fuck.'* He's right, they were. I do mention the shoes to the squad – might mean something. Then again, one of the biggest stone-hearted killers in east London dressed like a charity-shop mannequin at the time. It might be impossible to be well-dressed in cheap shoes, but it means fuck-all in the drugs business. Or so we think.

'Maybe. I guess time will tell, brother.'

I don't know when it was exactly that Marv started calling me brother. I think it was sometime after a fist fight, in the rear of the smallest observation van owned by the Met between two of its heaviest built detective inspectors, escalated my stress levels off the scale. Since then, Marv's voice has been fraternal.

We don't have to wait too long. Jack calls, says he has spoken with his partners and suggests we meet, at the same hotel as before. On the day itself, he calls to say he's running late but is still very keen to meet. I land at the hotel a little late myself – my second favourite maxim is 'the only fuckers who turn up on time are the police and undertakers'. Jack bounds in, this time in different duds but the same shoes. After long conversations with his partners, he says, they can supply the entire batch of 'lemonade' to manufacture the ecstasy in partnership with me. He also has a Dutch recipe and can provide a choice of secure premises, some of which have been used to cook previously, and security. Maybe he catches my glance when he says 'previously', because he adds, 'But we will have it clean.' He will provide all other materials and equipment if I supply the chemist, for a four-way split, upfront expenses I incur to be reimbursed, of course. They are all good to go but require a good chemist.

And so the courtship continues. We share war stories. One is based in truth – plucked from the archives in researching a way in – and one not, his own. All, to some extent, an illusion, both sides are aligned when in reality we are both lost. The war on drugs is failing. However, it is a war without end. The information is assessed and on we go. I meet him at his 'home', which is comfortable but certainly not high-end. Jack is suggesting we could use it as accommodation for the chemist when a young woman appears. She watches in silence and takes no part as conspiracy invades her home while her child sleeps in another room. This is the reality of drug-trade grifters chancing an opportunity, fuelled by greed, waltzing with criminal justice. Jack's offer is born of a desire to keep a close eye on the chemist. *'And get a grip of him, get into his fuckin' head.'* Also true. It's not a problem for Jack – they will just move out, he explains, while the girl says nothing. Another partner appears, 'Tony', eyes on the swivel, a face that looks constantly perturbed. He brings with him a sample of the 'lemonade'. All the world loves a good chemist, and right now they are very much in demand. I stress this, how sought after they are, as the girl leans against the door frame, silent, angry shadows under her eyes. Tired, of what is the question.

Jack returns with beers, talks about this job and that job, how you have to seize the moment, 'keep it all moving'. But it turns out we have a problem.

'The chemist who's gonna blow up your plans, mate, won't be available for a few weeks,' hence the slow dance. This is true: I can't introduce the 'chemist' as he is on another job.

'Well, my guy is busy until . . .' he counters.

And on we dance and dance, circling, getting closer to the precursor until, eventually, I do pass on the chemist. It rumbles on for another six months.

The operation is a success – a drugs factory dismantled, lengthy prison sentences dispensed. I hope the girl with shadows stayed away – these tangential moments bother *him* and me alike, and others, sometimes discussed over a drink, often not.

I pulled the job up by its bootstraps, but my footprints will be nowhere to be seen. This is not unusual. If you're in at the beginning, you may well be a distant shadow at the end, but my absence from the congratulations that will ring out are for wholly different reasons.

Operation Kingcup

A couple of years later I'm wandering along the fifth floor with a docket when the Bear grabs me. 'I've just called you, got a minute?' It's another one of the many weird interactions with the SO10 office, given the call was from another supervisor. I never figure out this strange dynamic of subterfuge. There follows the usual 'bit of work' discussion, describing a long-term sting operation into a prolific crime hotspot in south London. It is meant to last a year or so, though it will double with side hustles. I'm still waiting to really utilise the horse-racing legend, which I've put so much into and have yet to use as much as I'd like – maybe this will be it, maybe not.

The Moose, a veteran with a dry wit, and the officer who actually made the call, is on good form when I arrive a little later at the office. 'A lovely bit of work, this. You'll be working for a right pair of cunts, but you're good at diplomacy, aren't you?'

'When do I start?'

'Well, you need to learn the trade a bit,' he says. 'Think *Only Fools and Horses* but good with guns.' So, no horse boxes this time. It's a shopfront sting in the middle of an area plagued by violent crime and racism. I'll be one of three UCs – safety in numbers, though that will prove to be a lie.

'Who's running it?' I ask.

'I told you, a pair of right cunts.' He'd get on well with Marv would the Moose. I detect a slight twinkle in his eye and wonder what he's not telling me. 'I put you up for it, and there was a lot of competition, so don't let me down.' This means don't forget to drop a bottle of his favourite tipple into the office at some point. As I take down contact details and likely start dates, the Bear wanders in.

'Has he told you? Nice job. I put you up for it.' See what I mean, always the wall of mirrors. So, that will be two bottles.

A meeting is arranged with the infamous double act, a DCI and a DI. The DCI looks like he's been sleeping in his clothes for a week and has terrible body odour about him. I try to focus on listening to the DI, who is doing all the talking, not helped by Marv's interjections: *'Fuck, is that his breath or his armpits?'* The DCI shuffles about, never making eye contact. Eventually he leaves, wishing me luck, and when he's out of the room, the DI begins a long eulogy to his smelly friend. 'Top man – ruthless. You heard of him?'

'I never fuckin' smelled anyone like him.'

'Er no, 'fraid not.'

The DI has a flat head and beady eyes: this is the Dassie. His mentor is the Tasmanian Devil.

'Listen, I don't stand on ceremony. No need to call me guv – first names only.' Marv sees straight through him: *'He's fuckin' desperate for rank, this man.'*

The Dassie tells me that the Bear has spoken highly of me,

and I ask who was it that recommended me. It seems it was the head of the unit, the Gazelle, so that's three bottles. When I next get back to the SO10 office after the meeting, the Moose hollers across the office, 'You met the evangelical brothers yet?'

'Only one really, the Dassie?'

'Ah, the sorcerer's apprentice. Good luck with him.'

The job will need me to operate as a modern-day grifter, an underworld chancer, surviving by making do and bending every criminal opportunity in my family's favour. In doing so, the aim is to identify and gain evidence on as many thieves and crooks as possible in an area blighted by rising crime and indifferent polit-ics. Our cover will be a shop, a kind of Fagin's emporium. I stay with the Flying Squad for a while longer, before working on a counter-terrorism inquiry on attachment and finding work in a second-hand furniture shop (chalk and cheese), where I learn the ropes of pricing second-hand furniture: what sells well, what doesn't: how to load and pack a box van; what kind of supple-ment works best – a bacon or sausage sandwich. All the patter banter and duds of a second-hand wheeler-dealer. How to see a profit in crap. How to be seen as all right and hooky (dishonest) in another bastard borough.

I meet the other UCs on the operation. The first is the Wal-laby, a uniform officer with limited experience in investigation. I wonder what he'll be like gathering evidence strong enough to put before a court, but he looks the part and is personable, which is important when you'll be working together for nigh on a year. Then there is the dapper Dormouse. He is in fact the Bear's mouse – they go way back, having worked together before S010 was formed in the early eighties, the years of trial and error, the years when they learned by mistakes and hoped they survived to go again. They are the last of the old independents still working. The Dormouse has a face and physicality that will never, *ever*, be considered police, because he looks well into his seventies, and when he's had a drink, which is often, even older. He loves a drink and a smoke. He has an asthmatic wheeze that he can ratchet to the max on command, nicotine-stained paws that look as if they have been under the grill and he peers out from behind bottle-top glasses as he lifts tab after tab to his thin purple lips. He is without doubt the best foil for anyone minded to take a second glance at three undercover detectives.

At the Dormouse's insistence, we get our heads together in a quiet corner of a pub one afternoon and discuss our collective legend. Two brothers and dear old dad, the Trotterati – Grandad, Delboy and Rodney – riding into town aiming to make money by any hooky means. The Wallaby and I will play on the fact that we look nothing at all like each other: 'Yeah, mate, brothers with different mothers.'

One evening, checking on the progress of the shop refit, we find the Dormouse, clearly the worse for wear, staggering around the shop berating one of the techies, who is diplomatically trying to explain the reason for a delay in completion, and dragging a paint tray around which has stuck to his foot. This could be an interesting year.

We pick up the used vehicles for the job – a saloon 'for the old man' and a box van for us oily rags – and pay a final visit to the shop to sign off before we open for business, ensuring we know where any camera blind spots are situated, and identifying the optimum locations for the secreted mics and cameras to pick up. I'm looking over the back of the shop when I notice what appears to be a concealed door. I ask one of the in-house fitters what's behind it.

'That's your way to the bunker.'

'Bunker?'

'Yeah, didn't the Dassie tell you? The only way they could get the risk assessment passed was to build a ballistic bunker, in case it all goes off. Nice . . . Kevlar-lined.'

'Really? What they fetching these days?

He smiles. 'He didn't mention it?'

'No.'

The Dassie is more preoccupied with the Wallaby. He's always in my ear: 'What do you think of him? Will he go the extra yard?' The old extra-yard chestnut – most cops know what that means: *God's work*. There's that term again. In this situation, it means posturing masculinity. He is establishing that in this world no one has bigger balls than him when it comes to joining up the dots to secure a conviction by whatever means necessary (whether that is true is a different matter . . .), and we are likeminded, he assumes; it rankles, because it is born out of culture and not necessity. He clearly believes that the Dormouse and I can be relied upon. But the Wallaby? He sees something soft, perhaps even untrustworthy, unpatriotic in a Copland sense, within the Wallaby. I'm the soft one, the coward, because all I do is suggest, diplomatically, that I'm sure the Wallaby will work whatever 'hours are required' and smile, pleased at my navigation. Dassies are known not to have the best eyes in the animal kingdom, and perhaps he struggles to read my smile. It won't be the last conversation on the subject. Such toxic culture persists because of such cowardice. I do tell the Wallaby he's in my ear about him. To my surprise, he is not surprised – he knows a little about the Dassie, they have history, and that too will be visited in time.

We fill the shop with a variety of second-hand goods, always careful not to mask the all-seeing eyes of the many cameras, and we meet the back-up team that will assist us when required – a good bunch, though the Dassie will ride them hard, no doubt. I wonder how they will fare, in their hidden base, miles away from the shop, where, in a respectable leafy part of London the sun always seems to shine brighter. The Dassie is a riddle who demonstrates initiative that leads me to suspect the job will nevertheless fare well. 'I am not known for failure,' he confidently announces. He calls to say he has set up a meeting with an FBI agent who previously worked a long-term infiltration in America – he thinks we will benefit from listening to the agent's experiences. When we get to the Yard, the SO10 office tells us *they* arranged it. As I say, Copland is a place where people fight for credit, regardless of merit. Whoever set the meeting up, it's very good value – the agent is Joe Pistone, whose infiltration of the New York mafia was later dramatised in the film, *Donnie Brasco*. We spend an interesting couple of hours in his company, and virtually every single concern and observation he raises about the road we are soon to embark upon will come to pass.

The Dassie is in his element, pleased to have his ego stroked by the ceremony of promise. You always start a job hoping management will prove everything you have known in the past wrong, though your hope is rarely justified. As he disappears, skipping along the fifth floor to chat with one of his syndicate, his chief factotum and driver, a detective whose face has long since taken refuge behind a wall of hair, lets out a sigh.

'I'm gonna have him in my ear twenty-four seven.' This is the Macaw.

'Why'd you volunteer?

'I didn't.'

'Shit happens.'

'Yup.'

'Yup.'

I like the Macaw, a decent man struggling to pump reason into his boss's decisions. Our other cover man, a job that requires to act as both UC's admin and welfare rep to the UC, is the Butcher Bird. He is the Dassie's unofficial fixer, we all assume.

The first morning we go live, I go for a run, drink in the morning sun as I power through the woods near my flat and get my head straight. I tell the girl I am seeing she is unlikely to see much of me. I want stability. I have never had stability, I've never known it, so I have no true idea what it is I actually want, unlike my pal the Moth. He at least is focused on a plan to find happy union, albeit secretly checking the handbags and bank accounts of love interests to ascertain the depth of his feelings, which often backfires. My childhood friend, Bud, married at a young age, and has his family to keep him grounded. The thought of Our Kid and Bruv settling down seems unlikely given our collective take and understanding of family and, to some extent, humanity. It's the cynicism that gets you in the end, right? Maybe the job doesn't help, and the sheen has definitely faded. As the sun comes up, I reflect on the fact that I haven't yet left to do something more creative with my life. A serial procrastinator, a hopeless cynic, a—

'You're about to play Delboy Trotter, front and centre . . . How much

more fuckin' creative do you want?' Marv, it may surprise you to know, can lift the spirits on occasions when giving me a talking to. We open up the shop. It's a quiet affair, a softly, softly, catch-them-all plan. We spread the word about the legitimate side of the business – all second-hand goods considered – and wait for the calls to come our way. A long haul in an old bus. In the first week, the Dormouse identifies a nearby pub which will become both his local and, we hope, a kind of conduit for all things hooky. We fall into a routine of answering messages in the morning, followed by visits around the borough buying up second-hand furniture and old tat. If nothing else, I might develop an interest in antiques and salvage (so it proves).

If Stratford was the Bastard Borough, this place is Tension Town. Violence never far away, a constant 'what the fuck do you want?' hangs in the air. It's like an angry trawler town, where all the inhabitants are suffering steroid rage. But we settle in, buying and selling, and gently hinting we buy anything if the price is right and the provenance bad.

On the first Saturday the Wallaby and I meet the Dormouse in his new boozer, described by the locals as 'lively', giving us a chance for dear old dad to introduce his lads. New bruv and I head over after locking up the shop. The pub is not far from the site of a brutal assault that in part led to the operation being commissioned. Paint peels from the outside walls – it hasn't felt the love of community for years and is now reduced to anaesthetising its punters, hoping perhaps that it will all end soon.

The Dormouse is already a few Guinnesses in. He sits in the corner with his tabloid open on the page-three girl, smoke from his tab coiling in the air, mixing with something else in the air that

I can't quite put my finger on. The Dormouse already knows the barman by his first name and orders three more of the same 'for me and me boys'. I see surrogate bruv recoil ever so slightly from the absolute shithole we find ourselves in, but the Dormouse is absolutely on the money – this is it, we have found our level. He is also pursuing a thirst; I secretly hope that his mashed-up old face and whiskers bring us luck and not bad judgement. As I lift what proves to be a decent pint to my lips, the door opens. A taxi driver is halfway through calling out the name of his fare when from the midst of a group of old men playing cards one shouts, 'Wait outside, you black cunt!' The driver quickly and quietly shuts the door, and I realise what it is that is mixing with the smoke: the stench of banal badness, an evil brew festered over years. I look over at the table of elder racists, the same age as my grandfather, as one silverback, eyes focused on his hand of cards, offers his thoughts: 'Think you'll find that should've been Paki cunt, Bill.' They chuckle in harmony. This is the end of week one. It won't get any easier.

As we push into week three, a routine is settling. The Wallaby and I do the rounds and deliveries around the area; Dormouse runs the shop and gets a bit testy if we're not back in time for him to enjoy a leisurely liquid lunch. And while it's already clear the booze might be an issue for him, I'm confident that, if we are given a sniff, one look at the ageing rodent will assuage all concerns.

We're soon sounded out about a bit of low-level grift, a good start. We bag our first stolen goods; I buy a few hoisted credit cards and things begin to pick up. I get a call from the Macaw while out on the rounds, saying the Dormouse is being plagued in the shop by kids from a Travellers' site nearby – it is another oversight by the evangelical brothers who put their risk assessment together and acquired the shop, the first being its proximity to a venue known to be a public order hotspot, all this meaning each Saturday we must close early rather than capitalise on weekend footfall. The Dormouse is worried the Travellers might become a problem. The Macaw doesn't want to mention it to the Dassie, the backroom staff having already worked out that as little contact as possible with him will allow them the best opportunity of survival. I suggest that we go to the site. The Macaw falls silent. If it goes wrong, he doesn't want to inform the Dassie that a flare up or worse on a Travellers' site has cut short his hi-tech operation. It's left for me to me to speak with the Dormouse and get back to him. The moment we get back to the shop, 'Dad' is keen to talk off camera – meaning in the pub. It's clear he is at the end of his tether, the Wallaby is none too keen, but I suggest we have no option but to visit the site.

Since an incident as a kid, when Bud and I were getting battered by a bunch of older teenagers and Travellers came to our rescue, I have never had a problem with them. Like all communities, there's good and bad. I figure, speak your mind and respect them. The Wallaby is not convinced. 'Well, what could go wrong?' I ask. 'We're both good with horses, and my pa was a police dog handler, so I was raised with mad animals.'

The dogs greet us first, alerting the site to our presence. We get chatting with some of the men as they step out to meet the two strangers, and I tell them we can't have the kids coming in the shop, we have a business to run. I notice a terrier with a litter of pups penned under one of the caravans. As we chat, I pick one up and ask if they're selling, guessing what the answer will be. Price agreed, I shake hands with one of them and put an extra 20 in his palm. We leave the camp with the Met's first UC dog, and a guarantee the kids will stay out of the shop, which they do.

The Macaw is pleased he doesn't have to make the call. 'Great work . . . Say again, you've bought a what?' We name the dog, a small Yorkshire terrier cross of dubious heritage, Hector. Some weeks later, when I'm buying a round of drinks in another grim pub with the Dormouse, the landlord asks me how Bullseye's doing.

'Bullseye?' I ask.

'Yeah, your dad rescued him from pikeys. They were gonna eat him, yeah?' The landlord beams.

'Oh, yeah, he's good, man . . . But they weren't breeding them for food.'

'Mate,' he whispers, 'look around you.' He flicks a gaze across the bar. Fair point.

So Hector, we now discover, has a pseudonym, given to him by the Dormouse, who forgot his name, had to 'think on his feet' and came up with the story that Hector, aka 'Bullseye', was in fact saved from Travellers dealing in canine burgers. Hector becomes Bullseye when on point, travelling with the two artful dodgers in the van, and Fagin in the shop. Notwithstanding the Dassie's rapacious desire for success, the Wallaby and I agree: if we can keep 'Dad' steady on his paws and the Dassie grounded in reality, we have a good chance of making the sting a success – either that or turning batshit mental by the year's end.

The first quarter goes like this: it's a slow grind. The reality is that we have dropped into a community whose criminality views all incomers through suspicious eyes, but we are starting to make inroads. The Dassie watches the recordings and continues to raise his doubts about surrogate bruv, along with the occasional cautious query about the Dormouse. He doesn't want to get on the wrong side of the Bear. All his specific concerns land in my ear. It is not conducive to cohesion, but he tempers his impatience for immediate results with us and takes out any frustration on the back-room staff instead, as if they can magic future arrests and intelligence from the comfort of their seats several miles away in another borough. We keep our heads down and make progress: stolen property, fraud, solid intelligence regarding the identity of individuals we should try to befriend.

A long-term infiltration asks a lot of questions of all involved. The fact is you befriend strangers and then betray them; it should, and will, have an effect. You know why you are there. You have seen a thousand victims, taken a thousand statements, watched a thousand tears fall, and are convinced that jobs like this will make a difference, that *you* will make a difference, that you're on the side of the angels. But you are not. In this world we inhabit, the only things that matter are numbers, volume, stats to make the bosses look good – how you feel is an irrelevance. How this community feels is not our concern, and, right now, everyone feels a little bit tired. Since the Second World War, every working person has endured a familiar cycle of boom followed by bust – it seems there's no other way. The recessions are always far longer than the short-term booms. I see this on our legitimate side of the business, as we sell from poverty to poverty, and it is eye-watering in its truth. I cling to the notion that despite being under immense pressure, I am, we are, doing a good job. In reality, we are pissing in the wind.

In the first quarter the Dassie's attempts to bend my ear about the Wallaby are continuing to be a significant pain in the arse: will he go 'the extra yard'? Perhaps it is me he is testing? Perhaps he has other plans? The Dassie is a man in a hurry, self-absorbed, he intends to make chief officer rank. He's told me so. Maybe we are just another notch on the maypole. After a meet in the pub where we gather potential intelligence, we go into the back of the shop and I give the report direct to camera, fresh from the meeting, relaying my notes verbatim. This is adopted by the back-up team as standard practice, releasing our pocket books from whatever mythical plans might have awaited them. It stops Dassie's ramblings. Meanwhile, the grind goes on: low-level drugs suppliers, proceeds of burglaries. We get to know the faces who know the faces as we spin round and round on the carousel.

Second quarter. The total number of potential arrests to be actioned at the end of the operation is creeping up – not hugely but enough to satisfy the management . . . for now. When we lock up the shop, we head off to the drop, where we hand over exhibits to the Macaw or the Butcher Bird and support team, and sign exhibit paperwork, write statements. We take different routes home, dry cleaning to ensure we are not followed from the shop. The hours are long – 16- or 17-hour days are routine – but adrenalin helps, as does the fallacious notion that all this will enhance the community, that it will make some difference eventually.

I've been out on a poverty safari, buying furniture from the surrounding estates with the Wallaby one morning. We are now in the swing of it. If nothing else, we must be near to balancing the books on the furniture we are selling, and if we have a quiet week, we rotate the stock to appear busy.

The Dormouse tells me a woman has been in looking for me, might have something for me, came with a fella who was giving off 'good player' vibes. As we make a brew, the back office calls to agree it's game on – they have strong intelligence on the man. But the couple don't show that afternoon – I remind them only undertakers and the police turn up on time.

That evening at the drop, I recognise the guy when shown a still from the shop. The next afternoon I meet Jessie and Blake. Jessie comes in first. She says she spoke to my 'old man', and she does most of the talking here too. Blake hangs back as if they are not together, feigning a sudden interest in our shabby collection of tired furniture. He's cautious, but hidden cameras pick up every note, and it's clear Jessie knows her way around a deal. A couple of credit cards and a pair of full chequebooks are put on the table, good currency in the nineties. A little haggling, a little laughter, done deal. Not much but all adding up – it's a numbers game, after all.

'I might have a few more if you're interested.'

'Sure, but best come in when the shop's quiet, when the old man's at the pub.'

The Wallaby kicks in a little humour. 'He can't read the numbers.'

'Not when he gets back, he can't,' I suggest.

More laughter, and I get the feeling we are going to see a lot more of Jessie and Blake and the proceeds of their dipping, kiting and general thievery. And so it proves. They are prolific. Credit cards and chequebooks are their main offerings, but an assortment of stolen goods also finds its way to our little shop of curiosities via Jessie and Blake. 'Bullseye' is appreciated by all and is proving adept in his covert role, while flatly refusing to answer to the name Bullseye. One night after we have slept above the shop, the Wallaby wakes to find he has chewed through his only pair of pants. 'Bullseye!' Perhaps he is smarter than he looks.

Blake and Jessie are keen to chew through as much of our cash as possible, and I get to know them well. Blake has been grifting in London for years, working the West End and major airports, a slick operator. Like Jessie, crime primarily feeds his habit. Jessie's life took a downward spiral following the death of her father. She was the daughter of a well-known organised crime figure who was shot dead in the street in an alleged revenge execution. It seems whatever chance she had of ending the family cycle of criminality ended that night.

'I wasn't always . . .'

Her voice trails off as she decides against continuing. The life that followed is etched deep, every line on her face telling a story. She looks older than her years, and it speaks to our hidden cameras with equal power. 'She's in the shop again, mate, waiting for you. Bit freaky when she stares down the barrel of camera one.' I get used to such calls from the base. She comes into the shop often, observed by the watchers in our Orwellian bubble as I make tea.

'What the flying fuck's wrong with you? She's a thief. What about the fuckin' people who've lost their cash and cards, and fuck knows what else?'

I'm not saying she's not, Marv, I'm just saying . . .

'What?' The Wallaby appears at the door. 'What's that?'

'Nothing, mate, just talking to myself.'

'Sign of madness that, bruv.'

I nod, take tea, and sit down to do a bit of business and talk over a cuppa. I told you the job runs on tea. Blake and Jessie like to chat, Jessie in particular. Even in character we find a lot to agree on – about the absurdity and iniquity of life – as the stolen goods are slid across the table.

In the third quarter of Kingcup, if Jessie was the first meeting to lead me to reflect on the more Orwellian aspects of the operation with a fresh perspective, then an incident that takes place as autumn approaches pulls up Marv the cynic in similar fashion.

I'm out with my partner, pick-ups and drop-offs, when I get a call from the shop. The Dormouse seems on edge, asking if we can come back asap as he's had a couple of visitors he didn't like the look of. When we get back, I see his concern writ large across his face. The two visitors looked 'too tasty to be interested in second-hand furniture'. Dormouse has been around too long to be off-kilter on something like this, even after a good lunch, so we stay at the shop to see if they return, but they don't. The back office agree with the Dormouse's assessment and inform the Dassie.

That night at the drop I take a look at the camera footage. Without a shadow of a doubt, they are not in the shop to nab bargain-basement furniture. We have just had a visit from exactly the sort of punters we hoped to be welcoming, the sort that suggest it might have been a good idea to build a ballistic bunker. They walk around the shop, ignoring 'Dad', and it is the manner in which they peer into the mirrors behind which are cameras, with such obvious disdain, that it is hard not to conclude that we have been royally burned. But by whom? This is a part of south London long believed to be the most corrupt section of the Metropolitan estate and the area rumoured to be most heavily invested in keeping its secrets safe. When I joined the Flying Squad, the advice was to avoid one particular south London branch office and its Dickensian working practices, which I dismissed as an old wives' tale, but, as time will tell, it's often wise to not be too sceptical regarding folklore. This is one of the most well-embedded covert operations in London right now, yet we have been burned, fucked of potential. The big hitters will stay away. I have become the de facto spokesman for the group. It's suggested I push the issue with the Dassie. The Dormouse: 'You have a word with him, son, he's frightened of your contacts.' Not true, and reference to a mistaken notion I once had a hotline to the brass. The Wallaby. 'He can't hear anything I say, the dog would have more chance.'

So I do, I call him, only to be fobbed off – there will be a debrief at the end of the operation yadda, yadda. 'With respect, it's not you fucking out there is it, day in day out, on the estates, answering calls from fuck knows who—' The line goes silent, it's a trait with the Dassie. I wait. Nothing. Later, the Dormouse suggests as he lights up again – he's chain-smoking by now – he probably thought I was taping him. So much cynicism, it makes you proud, keeps us going. The thin crew line.

We decide to stay closed all week to reassure the Dormouse, not in the best of health, and then we carry on regardless, scooping up more low-level grift as we do. The pressure is now on for maximum numbers. We are all getting tired. The Dassie has set up a side hustle in another part of London; he asks to see me, and at the meeting he tells me he might need me to go over and get involved. Like bit-part players in the movie industry, your eyes always light up at the thought of a gig – the next job could be *the one*, the big one. It's how they keep you on the hook.

The Dormouse is off sick for a few days, so it's just me and the Wallaby – probably good for all concerned. He doesn't look after himself, and the plain truth is that he is a functioning alcoholic – we just can't mention that because now, in Copland, such problems do not exist. All, to our shame, simply keep the wheel turning, the operation running, interested only in what comes next. It's enough to have you running for the sanctuary of the bunker, just to let rip you know who you really are.

It's late morning, a young woman comes into the shop with two small children who she tells to sit quietly. She'd been in the previous week and spoken to the Dormouse, but he wasn't interested in what she had to sell – a large collection of magazines. She has brought in a few samples: comics, Marvel comics, first editions, mint condition in plastic sleeves. I know this person, despite Marv suggesting she's brought the kids in to soft-soap me. I'm momentarily taken back. An incident in my childhood. I am about six or seven. Pa says, 'Come on, we've got to pay a visit.' He has picked me up from school, which is rare. Snow is falling in Trawler Town, also rare – big tea-plate flakes that stick to your nose. He takes my hand, buries it in his own and sets off at a furious pace – it's the only time I remember him holding my hand. Pa and Ma not big on that. We scurry up towards a row of terraces near school. He knocks at a door, which quickly opens – the snow is falling heavily now. Several people are gathered by the fire, men wearing white shirts and black ties.

'Are they policeman too, Pa?'

A woman walks out of the kitchen holding a child.

'Sorry, I had to nip out to . . .'

'No, you're all right love, I . . .'

I wonder why grown-ups never finish a sentence. There are snowflakes in her hair, melting on her face, but her eyes are red-rimmed, like a black eye but red – maybe it was the big tea-plate snowflakes. Pa hands the woman an envelope, tells her we can't stay. She nods and tries to smile, and then we leave.

'Can snowflakes make your eyes red, Pa?' I ask as we walk back.

'If they land funny, I suppose they could.'

A fisherman's tale – one who didn't come home. I don't know how he knew the woman. When I asked him, all he said was, 'Hard times.' I learned, years later, the envelope contained money.

This woman, in the shop, could be that trawlerman's wife, eyes reddened by those same snowflakes. Same look of despair. She holds her child, her arms wound tight as if to stop it escaping. 'They were my husband's,' she says. 'I . . . I have a couple of boxes at home.' My brain is drawn to a distant memory as she holds her youngest with a stillness born of fatigue. Her face has the lined and haunted look of Lange's Migrant Mother. I feel shabby, squalid, that the cameras should not be filming this, whatever it is. Not her, not me. A child stands on an armchair and pulls a face in the mirror. Only it is not a mirror. The mother apologises. I talk, to change the subject. But this moment is not hard criminal graft, it is hard times. The shop phone rings again. I ignore it. I know it's him, The Dassie.

'Yeah, no problem, what's your address?'

Hector, aka Bullseye, wanders over to the kids. I get the impression they haven't laughed in a while. Later we go over to a small flat on a sink estate a short distance away, where in a few years' time a young man will be clubbed to death simply for being in the wrong place at the wrong time. Menace is already heavy in the air. She opens the door – the apartment is threadbare but spotless. Adult shoes and kids in a neat row – a pair of sandy, worn work boots stand alone. Two large boxes sit on a small Formica table, along with two photos of family smiling. 'They're all there if you want to look through them. Would you like a tea or coffee?'

Before we can answer, one of the children speaks. 'We haven't got milk, Mummy.'

She smiles. 'Yes, there is.'

'No, remember, we couldn't.'

She grabs her child, tries again to smile, settles for a hug with her daughter.

'We're good,' I say. 'Okay if I take a look?' She nods. We are in the flat of a Solomon Grundy, the man who lived his entire life in a week. But this man was a labourer, a new job each week, his labour changing the face of old docklands into new homes for other people. New cranes replacing old memories. Married young, two children. He hoped one day they would move away from here. He put money on the table every Friday, just like his father did before him, before this area became a wasteland for many and an opportunity for a few. He wasn't a drinker, a thief or a man of violence. He collected comics because one day they would be valuable – this he promised. No need to turn the pages. He told the kids stories himself and, besides, reading wasn't his strength. His strength kept the pages of this family pristine on a sink estate where hope was otherwise flushed away. Home early one Friday, not feeling too good – a fever. He said he'd be fine the next day, but he wasn't. He was tired, needed to sleep – don't call the doctor. They wouldn't come here anyway. Dead by

Monday. The tale of a Solomon Grundy who died on a sink estate. Viral meningitis. I don't have faith, but standing here in this place, watching this extraordinary woman, the dignity, the despair, I feel discombobulated. The feeling lingers.

The following week, heading home to an empty flat, I stop to buy groceries to replace the groceries I need to throw out from last week, ready to be replaced again the following week. When I leave the supermarket, I find myself parked outside the sink estate, where after dark the howling and the prowling begins. It's no place for a country to raise its children. I look over at the flat, where one light illuminates a solitary window. Why am I here? What has me so strung out? It's not fatigue, not the Dassie, not the job – it's the total absence of kindness. See, right now, I could walk up those stairs and knock on the door to ask, 'That cup of tea still on offer? Because if it is, I have milk and biscuits, and if it's okay with you, we could sit by the table and chat, just for ten minutes, no ulterior motive, it's just, it's just, I am not, I am not who you think I am, I am not what I think I am . . . I—'

'*What the fuck is wrong with you, you cunt?*'

What is wrong with *us*, Marv? What is wrong with us?

And he knows, better than me, because he has seen more than me. '*Everyone knows Sugar Puffs help in a crisis,*' he continues. '*You can buy them round the corner. Get the family size.*' So I do. I buy the Sugar Puffs, a few groceries, circle the block and park up, but the light has gone out. Out of the van, walk through detritus dancing on the wind, up the stairs, stand at the door, raise my fist to knock . . . to do what? To do nothing. I hang the bag over the door handle and lower my fist. Back in the van, turn up the heater and volume, wondering where to cross the river tonight, dry cleaning, but some things won't wash away. I love London, the anonymity a city allows, but visibility or the lack of it is not something you can always avoid. I don't want to be in an empty flat for 24 hours, but then the cascade landline at home rings, a phone line that purports to originate from elsewhere, still useful despite mobile phones. It's a welcome distraction, an old job that had withered on the vine kicking back to life. I go through the motions on the call, realising the company of wild horses is the tonic required.

In the morning I head down to Graham's yard, just to breathe different air for a few hours. I'm not using the racing legend but I still need to maintain it. The Dassie had asked me to pick up a bit of horse manure for his garden, and I agreed; I've picked up shit for management many times. Graham is good for a healthy dose of reality – you cannot make your living on top of half a ton of equine muscle moving at 35 miles an hour towards a brush fence and not be in touch with it.

'I got to say, you look a bit tired. Mind, it's a funny world, all that up there, whatever it is you do – not that you've told me . . .'

I fall in step behind him, quickening up to his pace and breathe. I am a thousand light years away from the forgotten housing estates in south London.

I pack the van with several bags of horse manure for Dassie.

'Well, he must have a big garden is all I'll say. What's he growing?'

'His ego, I think.'

After a day here, not even the chlorinated stench of racehorse shit can spoil the journey home. Maybe one day the Lambourn Valley will be where old UCs are put out to grass.

Back on the job, management are keen to dismiss any notion of corruption. When I ask again, the Dassie promises once more that the issue will be reviewed at the operation's conclusion; if the shop's cover is blown, we will explore other options. It seems little more than froth to me. There is so much going on in this part of London we are not aware of – the rotten flesh in London's rump. I get the sense the Dormouse wants out at this point, while the Wallaby and I chip away at what Joe Pistone might call nickel-and-dime jobs, building up the eventual arrest numbers to satisfy management. Jessie and Blake continue to boost our figures, as they 'boost' anything not nailed down. My energy and focus are bolstered by the potential of the hinted side hustle management are keen to develop. But Joe Pistone was right: there comes a time when you wonder if everybody is on the same prayer sheet, or even on your side.

We head over to the Dassie's house to drop off a large piece of furniture, bought in from a legit punter and which he has coveted for a while. His wife opens the door and greets us with a livid black eye. My curiosity as to how she came by her injury is piqued by the Wallaby's whispers. The anger barometer has been rising for a while, it is fair to say we are all a little strung out. When we come to the end of a stressful week and the Dassie pushes the time and meeting place back for the umpteenth time – although we all know he will be late in any event – I find myself getting even tenser. The Macaw looks shattered, as we all do, as we wait and wait in the pub the Dassie favours. When he arrives, he orders his 'knife and fork' and sets about his pint as his driver wonders how much longer before he can get home.

There is no apology for being late yet again, not even any real discussion about the operation, and I feel we are simply here to pick up the tab. Before we arrived, the Dormouse and the Wallaby suggested again that, as he occasionally listens to me – I'm too tired to argue otherwise – I should broach the issue of our 'knife-and-fork meetings', and the lack of purpose. I'm so wired I'm not sure who will speak first, me or Marv. *'Look at him, pawing the menu. Plenty of fuckin' interest in cheeseburgers, but two fuckin' "faces" wander into the shop to mirror-gaze for ten minutes and he's out the back washing dishes.'* The music is so loud I can't hear myself think over Marv's relentless monologue. When the Dassie's food arrives, he asks us whether we're having anything. No, we ate earlier, I say. As the Dormouse sups his Guinness, he kicks me under the table, and while I try to think of what to say next, Marv comes on strong.

'Why are you always late?' The Dassie looks up surprised – clearly he doesn't recognise Marv. I try to stop him, but it's too late – he's well and truly joined the table.

'Why treat us like cunts? Do you know how fuckin' tiring and unnecessary this is?' I can't stop him now. 'I don't think you do. See, we had a chat earlier. How about we just give you the money, from our expenses? You can go out for meal anytime, you and the wife? All the hours you're doing . . .'

He rises to his feet so quickly that I think he might be choking as he turns puce. He explodes: 'I'll fucking take all of you on. You fucking dare challenge me!'

On he goes, the torrent of invective almost drowned out by the music. While the Wallaby and the Dormouse enjoy the show, the Macaw contemplates which side to back before deciding to abstain, the Dassie's young driver looking like he knows that somehow this will end up being his fault either way.

The storm passes as a few drinkers stare over at the strange angry man who now stops and looks slightly puzzled. It's as if he's unsure why he is the only one standing, so he sits and takes another large bite of his burger. We don't mention the string of cheese hanging from his chin. We have just met the future of the Metropolitan Police. The incident is never mentioned again, though the Macaw rings to apologise and check we are not going to resign.

One year in, the Wallaby and I embark on a joint operation, Petunia, a cross-border venture with Kent Police, specifically targeting firearms and narcotics. They provide funding and a cover, but from the outset I have a feeling we are being gamed, either by an informant overreaching or management allowing ambition to override common sense. The intelligence leads prove worthless, but we are asked to press on, which we do, picking up a few low-grade deals, adding to the numbers, but nothing of note. Certainly not enough to erase a sense the operation is using covert deployment as a tool to facilitate ambition rather than arrests. The cover man supplied by Kent has a lugubrious weariness suggesting he shares the same opinion. We're plumbed into specific targets – gymnasiums, a few bars and a nightclub – but every tack produces little more than a feeling that, whatever is at play, it is not productive or conducive to our safety. Increasingly, I have the feeling it is not simply overreach but that we are on board a leaky ship. That there is a real possibility the operation has been compromised by corruption, and we're being outed as UCs working the area.

We find ourselves pulled into a meeting at a bar in south London where we believe we may be able to hook into a drugs line, but from the moment we enter, it's clear that we are the subjects. It is a well-known venue, regarded as a hotbed of criminality, and we are not welcome. I see the tautness in the Wallaby's face – it's understandable, but he needs to lose it. He suggests we leave immediately. I know that would be a bad idea. *'Fuckin' turn tail now and next stop A&E,'* murmurs Marv. It's not that the Wallaby is simply scared – I certainly am, but I'm more experienced as a detective, certainly more life experience, and I suspect I have had more bones broken.

'We can't leave. We have to front this out, mate.' I tell him a story: 'Did I ever tell you about Tonka and a moneybag made of foreskin?'

'A what?'

Words are the only way to avert danger when you are outnumbered and running is not an option. Tonka and his remarkable exploits are my best shot in the circumstances, so we ignore the hard stares, hoping to project a sense of *you got the wrong guys, mate.* I tell the story, switch locations, change the names and trot it out like a stand-up routine. The barman can't help but be drawn in.

'But how did he . . . ?'

'Yeah I know, mate. I was shocked too.'

'Fuck me, how many times is another man's cock going to dig you out of a hole?' If Marv can josh, it means we're okay.

We build a fragile coalition of credulity and confusion, strong enough to plant a seed of doubt that the two expected undercover officers are not us. We stay long enough to leave safely, certain in the knowledge the whole operation has been compromised. We are very lucky to walk out of the bar intact. Our Kent cover man is not surprised at the incident, which is itself disconcerting, but at least he is honest enough to admit we have a problem, even if he's reticent to go into greater detail, either because he doesn't know or he has been told not to. We have a heated meeting at a safe house where he goes as far as to suggest the problem is a well-connected officer in south London. The Wallaby and I are fast losing faith as duplicity and a lack of transparency seem to be enveloping our shadow world.

When we raise concerns, we are continually fobbed off, stroked to ensure we stay on the treadmill. Initial suggestions that we are maybe reading too much into a situation give way to yet more vague promises from the Dassie that he will get to the bottom of it, though a look from the Macaw suggests that's unlikely. Gaslighting, you'd call it now. Over a year in now, without a break, constant pressure to keep up arrest numbers in anticipation of the eventual round-up. The fatigue is far more acute than if the operation was a slow-burn infiltration. It is not so much the long hours as the mask – it might seem exciting living behind one, having a false identity, but it's not. You convince yourself it is somebody else's skin, except it isn't. It's yours. Your other self, gagged – hoping any muffled protests will not lead to you making a mistake that threatens your safety.

The Dassie needs an urgent meeting – he asks me to come into the Yard. I suggest somewhere off-grid, given the risk of being seen and after recent events, but the Macaw calls to say it has to be the Yard, the Dassie is too busy to meet elsewhere, it's a power thing. When I arrive, any discussion as to being potentially compromised is again avoided; ever the master manipulator, he dangles another carrot. Knowing his mule will bite. He is nothing if not energetic, he wants to talk about the other side hustle he has going, bizarrely operating out of a squat near a large sports stadium. And, because I am a delusional detective – most are, a belief the next job will be different, better, improved by your involvement – I ask what I have to do.

At the time, commercial premises in London are being hammered nightly by corporate burglaries, the thieves looking for one simple commodity: computer chips. Before the advent of the cloud, these memory chips were vital to computer networks and extremely valuable – with a massive and rapid expansion of information technology underway, they are more expensive than bullion. The Dassie has a techie working out of the squat, whom I'm told is contracted to work for the police as a civilian. The Dassie initially got the Wallaby to oversee it, another test, but he is struggling with the aggressive attitude of the thieves, who increasingly demand a higher price for the chips. The Dassie wants me to lower the pressure in the room, which is making the techie a nervous wreck, while also, as always, upping the arrest numbers. He asks me to put the issues of our cover being compromised to one side, promising it will be addressed at a later stage. I suggest it might not be a good idea for me to get involved before we know the extent of the leak in south London, but he's having none of it. I see from the paperwork on his desk he is prepping for a promotion board – more pressing matters.

I leave the meeting via a side entrance, deep in thought. I'm barely 200 metres away from the Yard when I hear my name called.

'What you doing up here, man?'

It's Blake. He runs across the road with a man I've never met before. I don't assume he saw from where I emerged because I was exceptionally careful, but . . . I do know I now have to spend a couple of hours in his company to be sure. His companion doesn't say much. I hope it's Blake who heads up the pairing. I keep walking, don't answer the question, telling him I have a thirst. I need to get as far away from the Yard as possible. Luckily every street in central London is as good as a mile, and off-duty cops generally stick to the same watering holes. We dive into a scratty pub, and Blake is the first to speak.

'You look fucked.'

'Want to know why?' asks Marv as I take a deep draw on a pint and nod. I wait for Blake's mate to take a leak before asking who he is, saying I'm not comfortable talking in his presence. I declined the Dassie's offer to walk out of the Yard with an ops docket, but I did take a sample of memory chips to play with and learn how to hold them correctly, so as not to put sweat into the contacts. Blake's eyes up light up when I show him the small but extremely valuable prize. He has no idea about the commodity but immediately grasps how criminal markets change. When his mate returns, I pocket the sample and say no more.

Operation Rose

On the Monday I meet the techie. He's as wired as the compo-
nents he breaks down to extract memory-chip gold. It becomes
clear he is a participating informant working on the promise of
payment and a reduction in sentence for some kind of computer-
related scam that brought him to the attention of the Dassie and
'that other evil bastard'. It's unclear whether my primary role is to
act as a minder to a lunatic, coerced into working for the police
with vague promises, or deal with the snipers – thieves – rolling
up regularly to offload bags of memory chips. I soon realise why
I was kept in the dark as to his status: he is a ticking time bomb,
quite possibly mad. He clearly hates the Dassie and the other 'evil
bastard', convinced he is a spook when he is patently a police
officer. I assume he means either the Tasmanian Devil or the
Butcher Bird.

The role is, however, a welcome break from the grind of running the shop and all its politics, notwithstanding the new set of
politics. I've barely set up in the squat when I take a call from the
back office monitoring the product. A message from management: the techie needs to rein in his invective against the Dassie.

I welcome the clarity in simply dealing with aggressive thieves as they try every trick in the book to leverage control of the flop, the squat we run the operation from, and pressure us for a higher price, inevitably laying down more information in front of the hidden cameras as to where they boosted the memory chips from, all within the confines of another rundown building earmarked for repurposing in the next cyclical reboot of the economy. Despite all that, I am finally in the bear pit I'd hoped the shop would prove to be.

Through this utter shithole we buy most of the stolen memory chips on offer in London at the time and pursue other criminality – drugs are ever present, as is the dipshittery of our understanding of the issue. Narcotics are a problem the UK has consistently failed to address properly, but narcos are not the only cartels making millions out of a trade that blights the lives of countless people around the world. Agencies spending hundreds of millions have not made the slightest difference to the proliferation of the trade or corruption it engenders. Not one dealer I hoovered up or dealt with in my entire police service made the slightest difference in the grand scheme of things, nor, I would suggest, did any major seizure of the last 40 years. Until individuals within the upper tiers of policing and government agencies are capable of sustained cathedral thinking, we will get nowhere. So I wouldn't hold your breath.

Meanwhile, Operation Rose fluctuates between its highs and lows. I'm heading in early one morning to the squat when the Macaw calls to tell me to divert immediately to a safe location, well off the plot, as it looks like we have been blown. He says the Dassie is spinning, and that he'll find out more and report back.

'Fuck him! He fuckin' should have listened when we suspected we'd been compromised,' rages Marv as I acknowledge and spin the vehicle away from the plot.

I ask the Macaw what he knows so far – all he's been told is that somebody scrawled 'Under Police Surveillance' on a wall with an arrow pointing at our door. He promises to get back to me. I drive over to the South Bank, park up, buy a coffee and watch craftsmen building Shakespeare's Globe theatre. Two hours later, still no news, so I ring for an update. They're running through tapes to see if they can identify who was responsible.

'Where are you?' asks the Macaw, breathless.

'Watching a new theatre go up on the South Bank.'

'High fucking drama here. The Dassie has taken a look and is preparing to throw everyone under a bus.'

'Did they use paint?' I ask, referring to the arrow.

'No, a piece of paper taped to the main door.'

'Surprised they could spell surveillance,' I say.

'Ha ha. No, it just said UPS, with a big arrow.' I feel myself began to bristle.

'Right, so we're certain it's not U-P-S, as in the delivery service?'

He pauses. 'Good point . . . Can you repeat that, mate?'

An hour or so later, the United Parcel Service makes a scheduled delivery next door.

We don't have long to dwell on the comedy moment, as the opportunity to get into a possible illegal armourer comes our way through the squat. Buying firearms of any description is an altogether far more satisfying proposal – whether it's just one or

a parcel, you feel an immediate sense of satisfaction that somewhere, someone has been spared pain and despair, vicariously or
otherwise. In Operation Rose, I chase the offer of firearms
around London with varying degrees of success. Unlike the narcotics that flow into the UK as often as the tide, firearms control
in the UK has been, to a degree, a success. But the break-up of
the Yugoslav federation and collapse of communism across Europe, along with the Second Iraq War, has seen a proliferation of
weapons coming into the UK, and while I'm dealing with a target on Operation Rose regarding a large amount of cocaine, I'm
asked if I am interested in buying a parcel of handguns. The offer
of business comes from an interesting source – a public sector
worker, urbane loquaciousness masking a dangerous menace. He
always carries a bag with him – I'm curious as to what it contains.
He runs with a pair of friends-cum-minders and plays a very
tight game. There is caution at every step from both sides as we
skirt around business, slowly getting to know each other, but he
represents a welcome challenge after months of bullshit and bravado from the memory-chip snipers.

There's a pub near the flop; and there, over countless games
of pool, we get to know each other. The pool-table area is a clearing house for much criminality operating within the still largely
working-class community here. It might be argued that while the
Square Mile, a short hop away in the City of London, plots a different kind of thievery over fine dining, grassroot graft is often
discussed over a pint and pool. The subject clearly has access and
contacts, and this is proven beyond doubt when he brings a semi-
automatic pistol to the pub as proof of potential. This could be
problematic for all concerned, because you don't want to let the

gun run, but, equally, it's not the prize, and we need time to exert more control before we can make a deal safely. I have a plan, but unbeknownst to me he has his own ideas about minimising risk and satisfying himself I am bona fide. He poisons me.

Gut feeling, instinct and intuition are now largely discouraged if not outlawed by Home Office mandarins and police chiefs as they navigate through, it must be said, constantly changing political landscapes, but the reality is that a little intuition goes a long way. It's nightfall outside the flop when I take a call from the 'Bagman', who wants to meet in the pub nearby. The Wallaby is with me; regardless of moving the job along, a pint appeals to both of us after a long day in the company of the 'techie hostage', whose behaviour is becoming increasingly erratic as he protests at his treatment by the Dassie. It's become routine for the team monitoring the cameras to call and ask if I can keep him in check, as they fear judicious editing will be required to spare the Dassie's blushes when evidential disclosure takes place at any future trials arising from the operation. Once the informant is shepherded away, the Wallaby and I head over to meet the Bagman, who is already into a game on the pool table. He wastes no time in hinting he is happy to trade without going into detail. After a few games and a couple of drinks, he's suddenly keen to retrace past steps – how do I know the Wallaby, where do I live? When this happens it obviously flags caution. These are the sort of details you know can ignite your straw house. But I feel it's all okay, just a few more checks to reassure himself, no threat. It's late, and we don't need to force things – that never works. Next time – there's always a next time. I answer his questions, confident we are moving closer to the prize.

I take a leak, and as I come out of the toilet I catch just the briefest of glances from the Bagman to his friend – the kind that, when you look back, was far more important than first thought. I finish my drink and we agree to speak over the phone in the next couple of days, but the Bagman wants me to stay; if my bruv needs to leave, he says, fine, but why don't I stick around, have another drink. He suggests a new bar that's recently opened not that far away – we should pay it a visit. He knows I need to leave, but he's persistent. I have thousands of pounds of memory chips to book in as evidence at the off-site drop. As I suggest another time, I suddenly feel very clammy. A pressing need to get out of the pub, also propelled by the fact that I urgently need to take a shit. Why does my mouth suddenly feel so dry, and why have the colours in this dated old pub suddenly taken on a vivid aspect? I leave the pub with a quick wave, followed by my partner.

'You okay? You seem a bit wired.'

'Yeah fine, feel a bit clammy all of a sudden, did you notice . . .'

'You're gonna shit yourself.'

'Did I notice what?'

'Right now! Gonna fuckin' shit yourself!'

'Fuck off, Marv,' I say, the room spinning.

'Marv, who's Marv?'

'What?'

'You called me Marv . . . you okay?'

I'm now speed-walking towards the flop, clenching my arse like there's no tomorrow and wondering why the sky seems strangely iridescent. I barely make it to the toilet in the squat – it's a grim affair, just about serviceable as a place to take a piss but best avoided if possible. It has no chance of coping with what I am about to do to it. It's so bad I think I've quite possibly shat out Marv. As I stare at peeling paint on the walls, the flakes seem to flutter like early summer butterflies while my arse explodes. The Wallaby knocks at the door.

'Are you all right, bruv?'

'Think so, just need a minute.'

'You've been in there half an hour, mate.'

I find this funny, and start laughing. 'I don't think my arsehole works, bruv.' Something has gone terribly wrong, and not just with my bowels, as I laugh uncontrollably. He taps again.

'It sounds like it's working, bruv.'

By now I'm too busy wondering if the butterflies in the toilet are from the wall or my arse. I shout out to my partner, 'I think we've a problem, bruv. Did you have eyes on my drink when I went to the bog?' as I continue to purge with abandon.

Not that it matters now – the problem is how to get me out of the place safely. When I finally emerge from the toilet, erstwhile bruv is straight to the point: 'Fuck, man, your eyes are insane!'

I try to examine my own dilated pupils – I'm sweating and filled with a desperate thirst. The Wallaby is understandably keen to get me out of the flop but at the back of my increasingly agitated mind I'm certain the Bagman is out there waiting. I need to share this with him, but before I can, I head back to the toilet for round two, and I start to hallucinate. Whatever is happening to me, it is about to get very dark.

The Wallaby and I have lived in each other's pockets for well over 18 months. I have got to know him and like him, insofar you ever get to know another cop. Cops cling together when oscillating in their own world. They rarely make lasting friends or good partners, primarily perhaps because they don't believe anyone understands their world. And in my experience, rarely evolve until breaking free of Copland's gravity and for some that proves impossible. But, that night the Wallaby takes care of his 'bruv', hugely helped by a young member of our support team from the base nearby. They get me off the plot, taking care to check the Bagman is not with us, forced to listen to my paranoiac ramblings as my heart thumps to its very own boom town rhythm. In the back-up officers' apartment, I spend the night hallucinating, tripping through the hours until just before dawn.

Whatever drops the Bagman or his mate administered, I saw the look inside the pub: we got him. I should have known. It did not produce a good trip by any stretch of the imagination; in fact, it pulled my imagination forcibly from skull and out through arse. A hallucinatory, sweaty romp through fields of dark dreams with Marv. Where it would have led to had I gone off with the Bagman and his pals or got behind the wheel is anybody's guess, and the scale of incident doesn't seem to register with the Dassie when he is told.

'He was probably pissed. It's been full on – let him let off a bit of steam. It's a one-off.'

The only steam I want to vent is at the suggestion we were simply the worse for the Guinness. I want to get a blood test, whereas the Dassie only wants me back on the horse. Only the numbers count at the end of the day – the gospel according to the Bear at the training school – and the Bear was right, not that I choose to speak to him about the incident. He's got his own problems, locked in a room at the back of SO10 because of a civilian accountant at the Yard who has planned his retirement by 'buying big chunks of Scotland' with stolen covert funds, the exposure of which is causing palpations on the fifth floor for a group of senior officers. I suspect the Bear is busy with an audit.

So on I go. The Macaw tells me that the Dassie is being an 'overbearing tube', fretting about promotion, consumed by news of a rival getting the next rank ahead of him. Such rancour is not uncommon in the police; once while on the Flying Squad, waiting to get an urgent intercept authority signed by a chief, the office secretary confided with barely concealed contempt that we would have to wait until he had gathered himself after weeping at the news a rival had made commander ahead of him. The Dassie not that long previously had told me of his plans to get a staff officer's job to better position himself; he advises me to focus on promotion, and I remind him that my hair is too long. He gets the reference, allowing himself a smile; the rank structure plays an important part in ensuring careerists feel better about themselves.

In the midst of Operation Kingcup, I had failed a promotion assessment. After a long moratorium on promotion for junior ranks and those long qualified for promotion, a selection centre had been convened. When I told the Dassie I intended to do it, he'd asked me if I was sure, given I was undertaking a long-term undercover operation – why not wait for a couple of years? I'd already done that. Unlike any other department, UCs are given no allowance for the nature and demands of deployment, for fear it might appear unfair to less operationally experienced candidates. I had a crazy head of hair at the time: it worked for the sting operation but stung those running the assessment centre. Given a half-day off to attend, this involved taking a circuitous route, to ensure I hadn't been followed, to a hotel near the location of the assessment centre, where in the toilets I'd changed into a suit more in keeping with the task at hand, then a cab from the hotel to the location.

I was confident, despite the odd circumstances in which to prepare – I was the only candidate working in such an unusual situation – I'd give a good account of myself, until a moment in the assessment made me realise it didn't matter what I did.

Much of the assessment process was set up from the perspective of a uniform sergeant dealing with issues in and around a fictional police division. It is my belief that often the most capable minds in the police are in the CID, but it is the uniform branch where power and authority lie: 'If you want the best career, wear a suit; if you want the best pension, leave your uniform on.'

We were on the last role-play scenario, with two assessors in the room. One, clearly the senior, had shuffled uncomfortably in his seat when I'd walked in. The scenario hadn't been too problematic, and I'd confidently worked through the protocols of the module. Throughout, there had been a sense that the senior assessor wasn't on my side, but maybe I'd just been overthinking the situation. As I'd come to the end, I'd stayed in character and said I was going off to familiarise myself with the division. I'd reached the door when in all seriousness the grumpy assessor had said, 'You'll find the barbers at the end of the high street.'

There it was: to him I was a detective who couldn't be arsed to get his hair cut and clearly didn't deserve a promotion. *'Cunt.'*

Not for the first time on the job I'd thought to myself, why don't you deal with this Marv? I'm tired. I'd turned around and walked back towards the assessor. Like so many of the cowards in authority I'd met in the police, he'd looked away and stared down at his extraordinarily polished black shoes. The other assessor had the look of a man who was thinking, well this should be interesting. I'd extended my arm to shake his hand – a proper Trawler Town handshake – and stepped towards Mr Grumpy. 'I'm sorry. I came straight from work,' I'd said. He had the sort of handshake that leaves you feeling a little soiled.

'Very soft hands,' I'd added. 'Watch out for splinters.' Marv is full of surprises, unlike the job.

When I'd got back to the plot, the Wallaby had asked how I thought it had gone.

'Fancy a trip to the valley this Sunday, company of horses?' I'd asked, which had answered the question.

We are in the last throes of the shopfront sting now; the original plan was a year, but that has run on another eight months. The realisation that this area will not change for the better just because we visited a while is hard to avoid. At another weekly 'knife and fork meeting', which have carried on regardless since the mini rebellion, the Dassie once again asks about manure – can we get him more? The Wallaby suggests he can have as much as he wants. That weekend we fill our large box van with tons of manure, arrive at the Dassie's house and drop it on the driveway as instructed, and much to the surprise of neighbours. Over tea, his wife asks if it is a steaming metaphor. We ask what he could possibly be doing with it all. Turns out he is selling it to allotment gardeners, £5 a bag. He's doing dime deals in horseshit – no wonder he always kept us waiting.

Early one evening, in the final month of the operation, I'm negotiating a buy, trying to recover more firearms not far from the estate where we bought the comics from the young widow. As we walk away from the pub, joshing with the subjects, laughing at some nonsense – the usual talking-bollocks dance of implied criminality, we turn the corner and I see her again, the angelic Migrant Mother, walking towards me with her children. I'm about to speak when she puts a protective arm around her youngest as someone in the group whistles. Her arm tightens around the child. We exchange the briefest of looks, and in that fleeting moment, I see what she is thinking, feel her scorn. I want to say, 'No, you're wrong. I'm not that person. I am . . .' As the garbled white noise of criminal enterprise rings in my ears, I glance back, watch her walk her family briskly away and think I will never have anything like that because I don't know who I am.

The operation concludes the following year with more than 70 arrests and in excess of £1 million of stolen property recovered. Like the end of a long-running theatre production, the players gather to make promises they will never keep and say their goodbyes. Some I will meet again, in wholly different circumstances. When Jessie finally gets a knock on the door, discovering the truth about the corner shop, she smiles, thinks a while, then as the arresting officers search her property, whispers, 'Tell him no hard feelings.' In custody she writes to me. It is a difficult read, not one acrimonious word, only regret that her life had led her to make poor decisions. She hopes prison will enable her to get clean but will miss looking out on the world from the shop and trying to understand it. The Dassie, in his warped wisdom, ever content to twist the knife, wants me to visit Jessie in prison and recruit her as my informant. I leave it to SO10 to explain the operational, legal and moral reasons why I won't. The Moose looks up from his papers, 'I told you he was a cunt.'

I have months of leave to take, and first off I visit Graham's yard, muck out and sit on the back of the tractor. I take a holiday where skies are less grey. I float in rejuvenating warm seawater and sink beneath its protective layer. I'm not sure I really like my world, or is it me, my life, nothing to come back to. Perhaps that's why I am already thinking about the next job. Following several weeks of rest and boredom, I'm sounded out about various central squad jobs, but I have no interest, not after years of observing the poor calibre of leadership. I resign myself to the fact that if I'm staying in, there's little point in sacrificing years working for nothing more than a tie and cursory thanks for enabling the careers of those behind a desk. I'm done with that. We have no assistance in finding a new job, no aftercare – you hawk yourself like a desperate swipe-righter searching for love. I opt for a central London division, simply to be close to the Yard, Marv and me parking our despair at a world where management fails upwards, determined to navigate our own path towards fulfilment. Securing promotion and more undercover assignments – surely the two are not incompatible, and it really does get into your system. All the speed of crack, and just as addictive. Addicts are the first people to say I'm in control, and the last to say, actually, I've *not* got this. Happy to be abused in return for another hit.

I move to the CID office at Belgravia. It is run by a quietly spoken, gentle Anglo-American DCI, who is also on the UC index – he'd recently recovered Edvard Munch's *The Scream*. This is the Kookaburra, who specialises in high art recovery. I'd first met him when he'd given a talk on my UC course. With a wry smile, he'd spoken about a case that had gone spectacularly wrong for him, the tale highlighting fine margins between success and failure. The Kookaburra is self-deprecating and devoid of any pomposity, and, though he doesn't disclose his source, he is aware of a truckload of horseshit delivered by two UCs to the home of a tyrant. It tickles him greatly.

'Well, I can't promise the whiff of Yard bullshit won't occasionally venture here . . . "For that sweet odour which doth in it live"' – it's fair to say the Kookaburra is very much a one-off – 'but you are most welcome here.'

Later, when police politics becomes too tiresome for him, he packs up his books and takes retirement, working with considerable success for the private sector recovering stolen art.

Despite a long period of leave, my sense of covert cold turkey is only accentuated by returning to the torpor of a seemingly rudderless Metropolitan Police, the Cabbage White commissioner contorting and prevaricating in his handling of the corrupted investigation into the murder of Stephen Lawrence. What I'm unaware of at the time is that this ineptitude has, to some degree, set about a chain of events that will nearly kill me.

For now, though, I breathe in and set about becoming a divisional detective with gusto again, waiting for the Met to open its promotion book eventually. Being new to the office, I'm quickly loaded with as many crime reports as possible, a pattern of operation unchanged since my time in the Bastard Borough. In time,

I move on to running a plain-clothes operation dealing with street crimes in the area. I feel unfulfilled professionally, and my home life is no better. An on–off relationship with a remarkable girl, Liz, is now back on, my refusal to ever commit based on a perverse belief that any investment in family or love is a poisoned exercise from which I am better excluded. I have an immovable sense that early life in Trawler Town forever damned me and my brothers in matters of family, coupled with an emotional immaturity that convinces me 'the job', for all its wretched truth, is my only true family now. In that regard, I need to constantly prove my love – it's a toxic love–hate relationship. I do what I have come to expect of myself. I chase and pester for more work from SO10, and more covert jobs come in as I develop my existing legend and begin to build the framework for two completely new identities.

The first of these I put to the test in the case of a family being blackmailed for the return of deeply sentimental personal property stolen in a violent robbery. A dangerous thug claims to be 'middling' the property, selling it on behalf of another criminal. I pretend to be a meek, rather hapless HR manager, simply negotiating on behalf of the victim – who is both a colleague and a friend – still too traumatised by the original crime, an aggravated burglary. The blackmailer mistakenly believes the crime was never reported to police and the victim has asked me to negotiate the return of stolen property. Through a series of long conversations, a catalogue of terror is captured on tape. Once the thug feels he has the measure of 'the pussy sent to deal', he embarks on an A to Z of what he will do to me if he does not get his money and, eventually, warming to his task, spouts chapter and verse on the horrific crime itself, the details of which only the perpetrator would know. Another three-way conversation, you might say: he calls me a cunt, Marv calls him a cunt and I tell everyone I'm really not used to such language. It ends successfully with a knock at his door and a prison sentence.

I rumble on, quick in-and-outs, pick-ups, drop-offs, links in the chain. With some jobs, you see the sweat, hard work and dedication, and sometimes you just smell the stink of personal ambition. The Kookaburra calls me into his office. Sat at his desk, covered in art-related magazines and reports, he looks more like a director at Christie's, something I suspect he'd be much happier doing. He tells me that SO10 has asked that I be released for a week or two to work on something in Europe with the Lion. 'Whatever the job is, it won't be boring,' he says, and so it proves.

Operation Cornflower

The Lion is a force of nature – irreverent, uncompromising and curmudgeonly but without doubt the most honourable, and pound for pound toughest, detective with whom I ever have the privilege of working. He is both a mentor and a friend, a man who can smell bullshit rising, and who walks his own path his entire career. Looking like a character from a Sergio Leone movie, he is not easily forgotten. Rarely changing his look going into a job beyond cloth or tie, his schtick is aided by speaking a passing level of criminal in several European languages.

I'm initially told I'm travelling as his cover man. We fly to Berlin, the job a two-strand operation: a high-value recovery of stolen goods and a possible shipment of firearms routing through eastern Europe. Within days working in this environment, I realise that the scale and proliferation of international organised crime is expanding at a rate way beyond public understanding, as well as beyond police capabilities, and I also morph from cover man to UC, which was perhaps the Lion's plan all along. Unlike his long-time partner the Bear, his nerve is, I think, undiminished. He's still at the top of his game, even if, due to poor management, we are often just 'pissing in the fucking wind'. But as he is apt to say, it doesn't stop you from trying.

I'm hurtling through the far outskirts of Berlin with Lion and a member of the Bundeskriminalamt, the BKA (Federal Criminal Police Office), as the Berliner Fernsehturm comes into view. Epitomising perhaps not only the unification of Germany but also, given I am on my way to attend a meeting of pan-European criminality, the television tower is a symbolic beacon signalling the merger of criminal enterprises across borders. As we park up near the Nikolai Quarter, the guy from the BKA – dressed for the cold, wearing a permanent grin and peering out from under his ushanka fur hat – looks out on the city as the Lion checks his watch.

The BKA driver taps the steering wheel and says, *'Berlin ist eine großartige Stadt.'*

He slowly turns to me in the back of the car, winds down the window and lights his umpteenth cigarette as the cold night air pours in. *'Willkommen zum ersten internationalen Gipfeltreffen, wo wir einen Ausblick in die Zukunft kriegen. Bitte passe gut auf ihn auf, mein Freund.'*

I nod, certain he was talking to me, and as I get out of the car, buttoning up against the cold, I ask the Lion, 'What did he say?'

'Told you to look after me, you little fucker.'

'He's obviously worked with you before,' I say and the Lion chuckles, at past memories, I suspect.

We walk towards the warmth of a restaurant in the heart of the Nikolai Quarter. The scene that unfolds is indeed *ein Ausblick in die Zukunft* – a glimpse into the future, as the BKA man also apparently said – a portrait of where we are heading. The setting is the back of the small restaurant, which has been booked specifically for the party. I see why it was suggested – I am wearing a good suit, but it is wall-to-wall Armani. Many of the attendees have brought along their partners, or at least their partners for tonight. The Lion is stuck with me. There is much conversation and laughter, good food and wine, agreements are reached, decisions taken, cooperation agreed. And I barely catch a word of it, because of the 15 people around the table I am the only person who speaks just one language. The future will not be bound by one language or border.

Late in the evening, an east European national, known to the operation, leans over and asks about my suit, a Pal Zileri – I must have made the right choice. He says he has enjoyed the evening; like me, his position at the table is indicative of his lower status in the hierarchy at play, but you do have to be invited, and we are. In heavily accented English, he asks me why I don't speak any other language. 'You need to change this, yes?'

'Man, sitting here, I hear you.' We clink glasses and he laughs. The Lion notices, all eyes as he chews, listens and entertains. My new friend pours me a glass of wine, and I suggest I'd rather have a beer.

'Yes, beer, me too,' and in the same breath, in perfect German, orders two cold beers. When they arrive, we clink glasses again and chat about London, and all its attractions, as he savours the German hops for a moment. Leaning into the table again, intent on underscoring all that I have seen this night and flush with bonhomie, he says quite calmly, 'You want to know why London is appealing?'

I smile. 'Sure.'

'In my country, the police, they harass criminals. Con-stant-ly. In your country, they talk about them. Con-stant-ly.' He laughs loud at his own joke.

'We will be there soon.'

'Might not go all your way, Benny,' suggests Marv as our glasses chink again. 'Benny', another term that crept into Marv's vocab as he got older. Who knows from where?

The pan-European organised crime fraternity sitting around the table will end their turf wars and expand their own vocabulary by forming cross-border international partnerships that in 20 years will flourish across the length and breadth of Europe. As I listen to several languages bounce around the table, police agencies across the UK wallow in inertia, fighting their own turf wars that rumble on for several more years, leading to the formation of SOCA (the Serious Organised Crime Agency). Two decades on, even that will barely scratch the surface of organised crime in the UK. In Berlin, I realise that this is the point at which police stand at a crossroads, the point at which action is required. It's an opportunity to seed the criminal landscape, not with the ambitions of pan-European organised crime but a long-term strategy to vaccinate against what is undoubtedly coming using both covert and proactive multi-agency resources. But we do neither – we are still too consumed and driven by personal agendas and private political ambitions. This abject failure will culminate in our withdrawal from the Schengen Agreement and the humiliating ramifications of unilateral boosterism. For all the scientific and technical advances policing makes, unless it is prepared to take risks, to mix long term in the company of devils, it is doomed to failure. Water freezes from the top down, I remind myself, as we head out into a mind-numbingly cold December night.

I journey by express train across Germany, then find myself in a vehicle travelling at over 130 miles per hour, driven by a lunatic I've met only an hour earlier shouting 'Schneller, Schneller!' at the wheel, as the Lion takes a nap in the back. The driver, one hand on the wheel, then removes a Glock 17 semi-automatic pistol from his waistband and asks if I could break it down with my eyes closed.

'Is he fuckin' mental?' Marv wonders.

The driver closes his eyes and offers to demonstrate, answering Marv's question in one terrifying moment. When we pull off the autobahn and into some woods so the Lion can take a piss, the lunatic sidles up to him and, fearing the worst, I'm about to hit him with a rock when the Lion, attempting to prove he can still piss over a five-bar gate, shouts, 'Did the fucker tell you about his mate's foreskin?' Thus proving two things: that the lunatic is our lunatic, and the tale of Tonka's wonka is now travelling across Europe.

With the Lion it's on to Warsaw, to liaise with the Policja Kryminalna, which is setting up its own undercover unit. It's now keen to distance itself from its history under the communist regime as an organisation that had little concern for issues of human rights and transparency. Concerned at signs of rising levels of national and international serious and organised crime, it is keen to implement a covert programme committed to the rule of law that is both effective and subject to new-found safeguards now that the country is free of totalitarianism. Both the senior

detectives and potential recruits are keen not to erode new free-
doms or find their country overrun by energised crime syndicates.
Kind and hospitable hosts, I'm surprised when the Second World
War is mentioned by the Poles, the stance the UK took when their
country was invaded still very much not forgotten.

I witness two striking reminders of the aftermath of this
troubled history. As we near the central police station, the senior
Polish detective, a man with the crumpled look of a senior librar-
ian, asks the driver to pull up short of the main entrance. 'Watch
how the people react when they near the gates,' he says. As
pedestrians near, they pick up pace, pull up their collars or simply
cross the road. No one looks at the building for fear of finding
themselves inside, or perhaps recalling a memory of a loved one
who did. A stark reminder of the undoubted horrors of the
past. The detective sighs. 'This is what we are trying to change.'

A couple of days later, in the middle of the morning, we are
in the chief's office when his phone rings. A short exchange in
Polish pre-empts a sudden clearing of all paperwork from his
desk, all quickly hidden away. Once again language limits my
understanding, but the chief and others present are clearly
agitated.

'Everything okay?' I ask. The Lion nods and rolls a ciggie.
The chief's jaw seems a little tighter as we hear footsteps
approaching along the corridor outside. I have been shown the
cells that morning, walls scratched with words no doubt etched
in pain. The footsteps echo louder and then the door bursts
open.

'*Dobroye utro vsem!*'

They didn't knock. I'm introduced to two Russian officers

from the embassy, visiting to offer their compliments of the season as Christmas nears, bottle of vodka in hand. Glasses are produced, and while I am not a fan of hard liquor, and certainly not at 10.30 in the morning, a quick look from the Lion suggests this is not optional. We toast, the drink is necked, and glasses are slammed down on the table and then refilled. Marv groans: *'For fuck's sake, what about breakfast?'*

Two shots deemed sufficient, the two Russians embrace the Polish detectives and leave, after which the chief utters something I doubt is complimentary and spits on the floor. Two customs, I suspect, also rooted in the past.

I enjoy the company of the Polish detectives, who enthuse on the merits of undercover policing. I feel they are genuine in believing, as I do at the time, that it is one of the few areas of policing that if used as intended, and as a last resort, will rarely be contested, as the evidence is often overwhelming and invariably has the support of all aspects of a fair judicial process.

When I eventually walk away from the duplicitous jungles of Copland to preserve my sanity, I lose touch with the Lion. Recently, I learned he died suddenly, in unusual circumstances, during lockdown. He was found dead in his garden in eastern Europe, having lain there for several days. A few weeks prior to his death, he had installed a comprehensive security camera network at his home. When the police discovered his body, the system's hard drive was missing. The Lion departed, as always, leaving you guessing.

The Gazelle invites me up to his office at SO10 around the time I fly out to Warsaw. He asks me to close the door as he tells me that whatever decision I make at the end of this conversation, the subject must remain a secret once I leave his office. He pauses, always considered, each sentence ruminated on as he peers across London through blinds. 'I have a job for you. It's likely to be . . . difficult . . . for a host of reasons, and lengthy too.'

I don't know why, but I instinctively think it's children or cops, abuse or corruption. Either way, I have a sense it will be difficult. There's a bastard for every year. As the light filters through into his office, in the silence, a flashback. The Lion sits quietly in the canteen at Vine Street police station. They knocked the place down eventually, perhaps it died of shame. The Lion is working on a complex organised paedophile ring. As he stares into the dregs of his cup he reveals the incident room was broken into, not once but twice. His thoughts private, his advice free: never work kids or cops. It will fuck you up. Marv suspects I'm about to ignore his advice. *'Don't be a cunt, it will blow up, fuck with your head.'* You already fuck with my head, Marv, remember.

I am tired, because at the same time I'm running a unit I've set up to deal with a spate of robberies in central London, part of my day job on division, in addition to the ongoing day-to-day crime investigations.

'What's the job?' I ask. 'I'd been told I might be away with the Lion again soon.'

He turns away from the window. 'No . . . I've said you're not available. I need somebody I can trust not to talk about this, at all . . . not even up here.'

'What's the job?' I ask again.

'Operation Foxglove.'

'It isn't kids, it's cops.' That's Marv's gut feeling.

'You'll be working for Merseyside. Drug-money corruption. Complicated. They want somebody able to focus on the job, not see it as . . . something *else*.'

What does that mean? He returns to the window, ruminating. The better view is on the other side of the tower. They say herds of gazelles have no leaders – perhaps it's this that gives him an easy way about him.

'You won't have an . . . agenda, being from here.'

For a moment, that acidic doubt in the gut, I have a bad feeling about this. I ask if the Bear knows about the operation, because the Bear knows everything. 'No, just me. So you speak only with me. Merseyside will provide everything, including your cover. Contact me, if need be, no one else.' That is a surprise, even in this tower of constant surprises.

An early first meeting is arranged, up there, in the wild west. The unit is set up off-grid at an old military camp – most of the inquiry team are there, though I don't know why as it's early days. I realise later it must be because they have been going at it a while. One of the team, keen to talk, suggests, 'They're really good, this mob. Need to have your wits about you. They can smell snide.' He points at my watch – it's not fake.

'Right,' I say. 'Good to know.'

I get acquainted with the three officers whom I will see a lot of when the operation goes live in a different kind of wilderness. The Meerkat, the SIO on the anti-corruption unit, the Possum, who heads up their UC unit, and a cover man, who will be mine for the duration, the Badger. All decent sorts, perhaps magnified simply because I'm back in the north, far away from the at times stifling torpidity of the Met.

The Badger drives me back to the train station and we have time to talk. I like him – he's not a UC, but it's clear he knows the drill inside out. 'Sorry about that, lad. With the watch, I could see it wasn't snide. I didn't think you needed to meet the team, but I was overruled.' It's a fair point, given the supposed secrecy.

'Shit happens, eh?'

'It does, lad.' His eyes twinkle with past experience. Sometimes you implicitly know the good sort.

From there I take the opportunity to zip across country, a brief trip to Trawler Town to visit Pa and Our Kid. Bruv is away soldiering. When Pa was released from prison, he soon settled into a routine: Stepmother out to work early in the morning leaving him to potter with his dogs. A decade on now, and still no conversations with his sons as to the how and why. His gambling addiction remains the love that dare not speak its name. I think he doesn't know how or where to begin, and sometimes I think our relationship doesn't help, or rather the scars, my scars.

'It's complicated, Pa,' I say when he asks about my job. I have spoken carefully about the nature of what I do, picked his brains when building the horse-racing legend. It is all something of a flummox to Pa.

'But they . . . they give you a false passport?'

'Yes.'

'A different name and, credit cards? Do they work?'

'Yeah, it all works, Pa.'

'I feel like an old man – can't get my head around the ways of the world. Bloody different in my day.'

'It was just fuckin' bloody, actually!'

Stop it. Give him a break.

'He fuckin' gave you some.'

Fuck you . . .

I'm not sure Pa ever could get his head around the ways of the world – perhaps he should have stayed a butcher. I think part of me wants him to see that what I do. I am doing it, in some tangled, complicated way, out of a desire to rehabilitate his reputation and our relationship.

'That's fucked up.'

I know, Marv. But it's just him . . . he's the only Pa we have.

When Grandma passes, her house stands empty for a while. Aunt Kath is long gone. The places of respite. I visit her house with Pa. He wanders round, checking windows and doors like an old village bobby, and in the empty terrace I hear the echo of distant conversations and sense the smell of after-school tea, a meal always accompanied with buttered bread and the special gravy. Post meal, Grandpa's challenge to a bout in an altogether gentler ring than I knew at home. A spit on the railwayman's hands and shouts of, 'Now, will it be the Marmalizer or the Discombobulater?' ringing out to peals of laughter. This childhood sanctuary is about to go on the market. I don't want to see it go out of the family, this last connection with something good.

Pa's inspection complete, he wanders in. 'You look deep in thought.'

'What if I buy it?' I ask.

The area has taken a turn for the worse in recent years, and he is surprised but secretly pleased when I buy it from the family. Later, I realise why: he needed the money. He'd lost a sizeable chunk of his police pension after his arrest, and he was also being pursued by casinos – the gambling Meccas that once feted one of their most valued customers are now kicking the addict hard. Not that he discusses this with me – if only.

On the train back to London, I sit alongside a young family. I watch the parents interact with their children. They laugh and tease, and love weaves around them like a protective web. I wish . . . I wish . . .

'Yeah, that would work in your world. Every cop you know with kids is a shit parent.' The old-before-his-time cynic's voice in my head.

Watching the love across the aisle, I wonder if this is what's missing from my life. But by the time the train pulls into London, Marv, the Trawler Town mauler, has given my head a wobble. The family disappear into the masses, and I walk away from all that . . . stuff.

I also buy Grandma's old house, prices being what they are, knowing I could use it to backstop a legend. I frequently allow another undercover unit to use it, the last of her Accringtons introduced to my other problem family for no other reason than to keep one foot in a happy part of the past. It would have tickled her: 'Eee, chicky. It's a rum world out there, full of dead eyes, but I do love a thriller.'

Operation Thistle

I meet a pair of dead eyes in the next deployment, while I wait to hear more about Operation Foxglove. It's a relatively easy excursion north of the border. Memorable, because I'm told if I pull it off it will go into Scottish statute as a stated law, and set a precedent for the future use of undercover officers. It involves the Scottish crime of 'reset': the possession of property dishonestly appropriated by another, knowing it to have been so obtained and intending that the owner should be deprived of it. In this instance, the 'middling' of the proceeds of an armed robbery on a factory in the Silicon Glen stealing £2.5 million worth of computer memory chips, the 'bullion boards' much in demand by criminals in search of easy cash. This particular firm saw an opportunity to hit a soft target.

I work with another UC on the index from London, the Lemur. I'm introduced to the seller through a covert source and make the call that starts the negotiations that takes place over a few days. The Lemur and I have thrashed out a cover story. A minder of sorts and a bagman for the planned scenario. He loves a coffee, so we have several, and by the time we finish we're both vibrating like a pair of plate machines. I tee up a meeting in

Glasgow while en route to Heathrow; the Lemur's deployed with me for the last leg of the buy. We stop for yet another coffee on the way and rehearse our back story. He's flustered – problems with the child minder. I've worked with him previously. The Lemur loves his wife – anybody who's ever worked with him knows this. He talks endlessly about her – maybe it's his way of dealing with nerves. For me, it's Marv – he does the trick. Marv doesn't fancy him for this job. I'm not too sure either. It's nothing to do with a physical presence – he has a hard exterior – but he has a gentle sincerity that doesn't seem right for the scenario. En route, we gossip about 'Ten', SO10. Cops love to gossip – for some of them, it's primary evidence. We chat about who's in and out of favour, who runs with who within the department.

Arriving in Glasgow we meet with Strathclyde detectives and the procurator fiscal, who states that it is his intention to use this operation to establish case law and 'allow the expansion of covert officers'. To the Lemur and my ears it sounds like 'culvert officers', which is about right in terms of the life and times of a UC. In an aside, the senior investigating officer reveals his nephew is a professional footballer playing for Manchester City. 'Two left feet and the wee shite earns more in a month than I do in a year.' The detective is a tough, no-nonsense individual, with far less a veneer of self-serving ambition than I often encounter in the Met. I immediately warm to him. 'Buy money' totalling £100,000 is produced, checked several times and locked away. 'Buy money' always sends shivers down the necks of the chief officers signing it out, which is ironic given how free and easy they often are with public funds to bury scandal or protect the brand.

The Lemur and I move to the hotel where the sting will take

place. As I prep the room, he talks more about his marriage, and I whisper that the support team in the room next door might be sound checking his marital bliss. A bang on the wall confirms they are. I wish I could relate to his happiness. I give him six months. Six months before he walks away from 'culvert work' and never looks back. In six years' time, I'll wish I'd walked with him.

We test the sound levels across the room, moving furniture to compensate for dead spots. The Lemur takes the money to a separate room before we reconvene in the hotel lobby. Now we wait; it is always a waiting game. Waiting creates boredom that whittles your mind, creating a space for Marv to play. As the Lemur orders drinks, I sit with the *Racing Post* and settle in for the beginning, hoping Marv will sleep. Repeat mantra repeat: 'You are a career criminal, you steal, you sell what you steal, this is what you do, this is who you are.' Create the appearance of success not criminality – handy, but not a rough-edged scrote. Career criminals don't like that.

The target calls to say he's running late. I don't believe him – I think he's close. I think he's watching. Marv says nothing, and the Lemur is also quiet, but I can guess what he's thinking. An hour or so later, a man I've never spoken to before bounces across the hotel lobby with a beaming smile and full-on banter. 'No on the whisky yet?' And so it begins, our courtship of illusion.

Like me, this guy is also an imposter – he is most definitely not the man I have wooed over the phone. He is a test, a fizzing bantam cock in a T-shirt cut to emphasise his build, all posture but bringing no parcel to the plot. 'If Dill wants to change our agreement, he should tell me himself.'

I tell him he's not who I've been dealing with for weeks. He's fired up, angry, threatening, before remembering where we are and offering a conciliatory smile and the suggestion we sit. I return the smile and stick to the plan: get them in the room. 'If you no longer have the parcel, fine, I'll go home.' I give him my room number and tell him I'll be there all afternoon. As I walk towards the lift, I can feel his rage. I don't know how it will all pan out. But it has begun.

We don't have long to wait to find out. A firm knock on the door. As I open it, Tam, as we shall call him, charges in, and behind him saunters the man we've been waiting for, Dill. He smiles as he passes me.

I've barely closed the door before Tam starts in on me. 'Cunt! You fucking shite. Who the fuck are you, eh?'

'*Not who you think,*' says Marv, getting in first.

Tam's on me – his rancid breath and fur-tongued spittle peppers my face. He revs himself up quickly. 'Cunt! Do not fucking play games with us, son.'

Dill moves around the room, opening the bathroom door and looking in before sitting down and waiting for his hired firework to burn out, but Tam's not finished yet. 'We've no come to play games. You better be fuckin' genuine or I'll fuckin' shoot you, you cunt.'

'*Properly fucked now. That's set bells ringing, Tam.*'

Tam has no idea that his threat has indeed just escalated events. In the adjacent room, one of the many listening detectives makes a call that will dictate the terms of how the arrest will happen – and it will happen.

Masculinity asserted, Tam sits spent on the edge of the bed. He catches his breath then, suddenly, fluffs up the cushions. *What the fuck?* wonders Marv.

Dill takes over. It was always his deal – we all know that. If there's one true villain in the room, it's not Tam with his biceps and bad breath. It's the quiet man. It's often the quiet man. We get down to business.

'Do you have the money?' Dill asks.

'Yes.'

'Here?'

'Nearby.'

'His wee fuckin' minder will have it . . . Eh, where did you get your suit?' asks Tam, refusing to be defined. The small talk continues, tension fades. I suddenly feel tired, dog tired. Tam stares blankly out of the high-floor window as somewhere way below a tactical firearms unit moves closer to the hotel. I join Tam at the window, in part to reassure myself and Marv that there aren't any marked police vehicles below. As fatigue battles with adrenalin, I look out over the skyline and wish I was somewhere else.

I call the Lemur to the room – a slight delay. Lemurs live within a female dominant society, so perhaps he's calling home. Always crack a joke to yourself if you want to appear totally relaxed. When he eventually enters, Tam and Dill's gazes fix on the briefcase. I place it on the bed and ask the Lemur for the key. Tam leans in. Dill remains seated. The Lemur can't find the key. He empties his pockets, later swearing, unconvincingly, that it was all an act. Finally finds it. Sight of the money relaxes Tam and energises Dill. We get down to business. The provenance of the memory chips, the armed robbery on the factory they were stolen from, questions disguised as joshing to try and ascertain if they were involved in the armed robbery or are simply 'middling' the parcel. The conversation a rope, released bit by bit, that ties the pair ever further to their criminality. As the light fades we agree the deal: the Lemur will take the money to a vehicle outside the hotel where the exchange will take place and we will all raise a glass thereafter. With that, they're gone. Silence. Not even Marv. Just the sounds of Glasgow at night. I sit on the bed and wait for the kettle to boil.

I wait a bit more, and a short while later, as the Lemur walks towards their vehicle, armed police emerge from the shadows. It runs as it always runs. Aggressive shouting of strict compliance orders, blue lights blending with grey Strathclyde skies. I should feel elated, yet I'm not – it's a victory but I don't feel like celebrating.

The SIO calls the room, 'Time to go, fella. Absolutely bloody spot on, that.' I'm moved across town to the Hilton, where later the ops team raise a glass – they're set for the night. Scotland's first level one undercover operation has resulted in two arrests in textbook fashion, all documented on hi-fidelity tape, photographed, cut and dried. I'm dog tired, back to London tomorrow, back to a squat in Oval, Pal Zileri suit switched for a sweatshirt and jeans, back to sweat and beans. They give me an upgraded room. I can't wait to sleep. I should be happy. I did it – my pseudonym will go into Scottish statute. I close my eyes, and as I go under, Marv taps: *'Don't be a cunt. He won't let it happen . . .'* He is right – the Bear doesn't. He'll take that prize for himself. But we've a way to travel yet before I discover why.

Operation Foxglove

I begin Operation Foxglove not long after I get back from Scotland. It will be a cold call, with no participating informant, no visible line into a tight-knit group that I'm told consists of global drug traffickers, compromised senior police officers and TV celebrities bound together in grift and graft. It sounds utterly bonkers, yet somehow is rooted in reality.

The main thrust of the inquiry is directed towards two ranking detectives, believed to be in cahoots with a high-profile drug runner, and the wider cohort, 'who pose a serious threat to the integrity and safety of individual officers', after a contract was taken out on the life of a police officer who witnessed a shooting in a city-centre venue. It is considered too much of a risk to use an informant to introduce me to the group for fear of betrayal given the stakes and money at the disposal of the drugs syndicate.

Cold infiltration is never easy. Where to begin with these two, the Caribou, the main target, and the Capuchin Monkey. I read all the available notes and reports over and over. The intelligence briefing highlights a pub used as a regular watering hole, and this, I think, might offer a chance. I ask to be partnered with another UC, a female officer who could play my partner and give us a reason we are there, the reason why I am in the area, but they don't want to use their own staff for fear of compromise. The Gazelle introduces me to the Storm Petrel, a funny, attractive, streetwise Welsh fireball of a UC with the mental toughness of a trawler-town matriarch. Perfect. A female UC will often move quicker along the line than a man. I don't understand why there are not more on the index. Well, I do: the secret patriarchy.

The Storm Petrel tells me her partner, also a police officer, is obsessively jealous, partly driven by the fact that she can't share much about her activities as a UC. When she flies back into London on one occasion, she spots him perched behind a column at the airport. 'Dippy!' she thinks as she smiles and walks on. One fact about storm petrels is that they are monogamous.

We don't have much time to get to know each other – we run backgrounds as we drive north in a Mercedes, top-to-toe dressed to impress. We are driving to the location as strangers but will have to share a bed, because you must always assume the other side is watching. You gloss over with your partners that in covert Copland such realities exist. 'We will teach you how to lie to family, partners, loved ones,' they said on the course, and they were right.

Having the Storm with me is the reason we establish a foothold quickly. A rich criminal businessman and his good-looking, funny partner. We project just the right balance of hooky and success that deflects any potential suspicion.

One evening we're having a meal in the hotel restaurant,

which we know is used by criminals of special interest to the inquiry. A surprising choice at first sight, chintzy, more Women's Institute than organised crime group. We are stunned when a group we don't recognise settle at a nearby table. They ripple the air. *They* are players, no doubt, gut feeling again. This is confirmed when we hear names of interest to the inquiry as they discuss an arrest that has caused some disruption. We pass on the intelligence we manage to grab, along with vehicle plates. The Meerkat confirms they are known and of interest to the wider operation.

We now know we are in the right circle. Nights in the bar become more expansive and expensive as our circle also expands. This is where I test my skill for holding several conversations at once, like playing several games of chess in your head. You are speaking to the person opposite you who may be of little interest to your purpose, but they are near someone who is, so you are also listening to that person – they are of course speaking to somebody else, and you pick up a little of this conversation too. While seemingly utterly focused on the person opposite, functioning like some kind of directional sonar, you filter out the white noise and register the important echoes. I'm good at this, really good. But it's a head fuck – do it for too long and it catches up with you. Words becoming barbs to unpick your mind. And though I've never really thought about it, maybe Marv has something to do with it.

One night, several months into the infiltration in the bar of plenty, our legends now so accepted we are in the midst of a lock-in, and I stand behind the bar pouring drinks for me and our new friends, shifting to the beat, the air alive with bants and bravado. In among all the white noise, I see an opportunity to establish if the scale of the threat to the officer's life is substantial. Over the room, three faces are always watching us: the Caribou, the Capuchin and, another, the Hyena – sharp teeth, I suspect, and keen to have a trade, too keen, but what is his business? Who is this other civilian with Hyena? The Storm Petrel and I dance in the circle, the Storm proving herself adept at sidestepping probing questions and hands. I'm getting on well with the Capuchin, but the Caribou is far more aloof. It's how it goes sometimes – at odds with the intelligence. I add another layer to our intrigue by suggesting I have a business issue, involving narcotics that I do not want discussed in front of the Storm.

I suggest to the SIO that a hospitality box at a northern racecourse could be wired for sound and vision, previous operations having demonstrated the feasibility and evidential value of such product, and although it's never been done before in such circumstances or this type of venue, the Possum and Meerkat agree. I book the hospitality box, arrange catering and ask the Possum to look into bringing other UCs to move through the box on the day to upscale the event, allowing others to develop legends and giving it an air of criminal legitimacy. It comes together, but the tech department aren't able to fix cameras without revealing it is a covert operation to the course authorities, so they settle for secreted microphones in a section of the box. It's good to go.

On the morning of the day itself I drive to the racecourse early to check the equipment. As I'm getting out of the car I bump into racing pundit Richard Pitman, there to commentate for the BBC. This wasn't in the plan. Richard, a huge help in helping me to develop my original legend, takes one look at my car: *'I'm thinking I shouldn't ask why you are here.'*

'Richard, if you see me again today, you never saw me before. For both our sakes.'

For a man who made a living flying by the seat of his pants towards inevitable injury, this seems too good an opportunity and he's keen to help: *'Do you want me to say hello, you know, bit of window dressing?'* Nerves of steel, this one. I politely tell him I'll have to decline the offer and ask him to simply say a prayer I make it round the course. He heads off chuckling. I take a breath and hope that's me done with surprises for the day.

My stock is high with the group. Having previously suggested racing tips that went on to win and which some of the guests backed, the box is full, rocking. But of the two subjects only the Capuchin arrives. As the operation unfolds, it transpires that the Caribou has other, more pressing problems that will lead to his early arrest, after he is caught agreeing to pass on information, for £10,000, on the shooting that led to the contract on the officer's life.

I was told the Capuchin will be difficult, highly suspicious. His wife is also a police officer, attached to Special Branch. *'They kept that quiet.'* Marv misses little, but, as things turn out, against the brief, he proves easier than expected, and a friendly relationship is quickly established.

Our guests are made up of players, civilians and the curious, all enjoying a day at the races courtesy of the police. The day begins, and as the racecourse comes alive I move through the box socialising, clearly successfully, as one guest suggests we meet when I'm next in the area to see if we can do business together on some level. We both know it's not legitimate business. The Panda, a 'businessman' who we feel acts as a conduit for criminals, asks if he could have a word with me on the balcony. He takes a full plate of food with him – he has paws like shovels. When something like this happens, here's what often runs through your mind, both minds: why does he want me away from the group, and who does he want me away from?

'On the fuckin' balcony? It's not mic'd. It's too noisy.' Marv mutters.

The Panda has taken umbrage – apparently I'm not showing him enough respect, having spoken to somebody else from the jungle ahead of him.

'Are you fucking joking or what?' he growls, plate in hand.

'What? Mate, I'm not following you here.' I certainly need diplomatic skills now.

He steps in close so his two minders, who have followed us out on to the balcony, can't overhear, and whispers, 'You, you cunt. I'll throw you over this fucking balcony right now, treat me like that again.' I look deep into expensive dental work and nod submissively.

'The race is over there on the fuckin' grass, not in here, you cunt. What's your hurry?' Marv's right – no one hurries in this situation except horses, certainly not a UC. The Panda drags his tongue across a sliver of blood-red jus, paid for by Merseyside Police and which is now staining his lips. He pauses to line up another bite: 'You seen me waiting to talk and you blanked me, talked to that other twat instead. What's he want?'

I can smell the fruit in the jus and freshness in the bread as he wipes his plate. 'Nothing, just chatting, that's all. I don't know everyone here. Anyway . . . what time has your suit got to be back at the funeral parlour?'

The Panda puts down his plate. Marv stiffens: *'I think you might be about to take a short cut to the betting ring.'*

'Cheeky fuck, you, eh?' He pauses. 'Ten o'clock tomorrow, fits like a glove. You need to get a busy on with the fella. You asked him yet?'

I've intimated to the Panda that I need access to police databases and am willing to pay. He thinks the Capuchin will be happy to help. Staggering really, and a surprise even to some on the ops team. The tape goes up on the first race as our own two-horse race begins in the police hospitality box, will it be the Capuchin? I ask the Capuchin for a quiet word, making it plain as the day that the real reason I am here is that I am acting on behalf of criminal associates. We need to discover the circumstances behind a recent large seizure of Class A drugs and related arrests, the implication being that we want to know whether an informant was involved or the drug runners are feeding their paymasters a hooky line, so to speak. If the Capuchin supplies the information, I suspect his race will be over. The seizure is a genuine case the SIO has suggested I pitch to him. The Capuchin agrees to help.

I can't believe it's taken so little effort to get here beyond creating the illusion of wealth. The job, I sense – the wider job, the effective policing of corruption in the police – is without doubt singularly doomed. Here I am, with someone prepared to willingly compromise his career and his life. A degree of rank, settled in the organisation, yet so disillusioned with it he willingly agrees to betray his office, because he no longer believes enough in what he is doing.

'Fuck you. Fuck this! Give me your fuckin' rank. I could do your job. Gizza job. Gizzus your job. I'll do it a fuckin' sight better than you,' Marv rants in my ear as we tuck in to champagne and posh sausage rolls – not very Trawler Town; not very hopeful for the future of policing.

A smile of gratitude from the Capuchin as I top up his glass and Marv catches his breath. I suddenly have a hankering to be back in Trawler Town, and a part of me doesn't want anything to do with the Capuchin, but simply to go home. The reality is that my position is also precarious now. If he makes any checks on behalf of the man he believes me to be, the question of whether he poses a threat to the safety of a police officer in relation to a major narcotics network will be answered. But in the shadow-lands, it is never an even road, and a seismic intervention in the Meerkat's operation is about to unfold that will have far-reaching implications.

I rejoin the rest of the party, full of winners and losers now. The hospitality box has done its job, and my suggestion of using it as an opportunity to layer up existing legends has been taken up by other units. I'm pleased to have helped, but I hope they have been careful not to overexpose anything that will be compromised in any subsequent disclosure. You know the pitfalls, and you remind the ops teams, but in the excitement they don't always listen.

Drink flows. I'm on the balcony with the Panda and a few others, and there he is again, Hyena and his silent friend, who likes to watch from the shadows. I think he's on – he's a player. I'd often seen him around the pub we've got the foothold in. When did he arrive? Who with? Look at all of the 64 squares:

who are the pawns and, more importantly, who are most definitely not? I raise a glass in his direction. He nods. Time to find out more.

As I go to walk over, the Panda grabs my arm. 'All good, then. He going to sort you?'

'Yeah, man, yeah . . . all good.'

'Told you.'

Panda is enjoying his afternoon, and unexpectedly, given our earlier exchange, he grabs me in a bear hug. Here we go again. And on we go, the carousel keeps turning with more banter, circling around the edge of criminality. I break away from the Panda and the Capuchin, but the Hyena and his pal, the man who likes to observe, have disappeared, off to collect their winnings, I'm told. Not that I know who will be the true winners and losers today.

The job is done for now. I stay within character, continuing to build the legend, making the man of straw stand on his own two sheafs. A lead singer from an eighties band is in the box now, and this adds a little shine. We talk movies and music. I loved their major hit – something about the lyric that fits this situation. It writhes in my head, an earworm. Watching the guests, I recognise the braggadocio, the desperate wanting to ingratiate themselves, just to feel edgy, sexy, important. But predators are waiting on both sides of the fence.

I'm invited by a few of the attendees into the city for drinks at the end of the day, always potentially a double-edged sword, you're tired, but you want to relax – you can do that if they are all civilians. And it has been suggested that the operation might extend beyond the initial remit. There could be an overlap with other areas, particularly Manchester, a city once described to me by a career criminal Londoner as the northern giant of corrupt association. It's a city the Met will soon export another senior officer to, as head of the Greater Manchester Police, and which will end in tragedy and rumour in the ever-spinning wheel of chief-officer churn.

Tonight, Liverpool is bouncing. I meander through this extraordinary city, accompanied by the singer and others from the afternoon, taking in the nightlife. We find ourselves talking politics as the evening progresses. In one bar, there is the suggestion that the politicisation of law and order accelerated under Margaret Thatcher's leadership, which is not something I expected to hear here. We all know, all of us here, that the criminal justice system will always be more geared towards focusing on the soft targets of the poor and disenfranchised while crimes of state, institutions or corporations are by definition and sometimes decree excluded to protect the mighty. It's easier that way, I suppose.

I relax into this mix of politics, football, life. I am a Trawler Town lad back in the north, disguised as a crooked London businessman who understands these grievances. Anyone who grew up in a trawler town and watched it die would understand. A UC is an outsider, one who takes something of themself into each job and hopes it reveals nothing about who they are.

By the end of the night, I'm weary, filled with an enervating heaviness. I think of the long days on the job: weeks, months, years, waiting for what? What I want is a job that proves completely worthwhile, from the root to the fruit. Part of me likes the Capuchin – he's affable, and I even recognise something of the 'job apathy' in myself – but I despise the fact he seems to have given up and is so blasé he thinks nothing of associating with those suspected of threatening a police officer's life. Part of me wants to smash him in the face. And I despise that part of me too – the thoughts and rage lurking within, a little bit of family, waiting to prove me wanting.

Perhaps it's the weariness that clouds my mind, which means I don't pick up on the change in atmosphere, signalling something isn't right. Somewhere among the meandering booze and debate, all of us playing a role to some extent, Marv tells me it is time to head back to the hotel. It has been a long day for both of us, listening intently to several conversations at once, and my brain says enough. Time to think of nothing but the peace and quiet of my room – time to sleep. I'm heading out of the neon-lit bar when I hear my name. I turn around. There he is again, the Hyena, and his shadow man.

'All right, lad, how's you?'

'Has he fuckin' been in here all night?' It doesn't matter, Marv, we're off.

'All right, mate, yeah good, you?'

'Yeah, sound mate, sound. Good day that, lad.'

'Yeah, it was, long day, man.' I tell him I'm heading off for some sleep – busy day tomorrow. But he has a plan, and it involves another drink. It's on the way back to my hotel.

'Come on . . . just a couple of bevvies, eh?' but in the manner of: we *are* having a beer.

'Sure, why not?'

'This bar, yeah, the girls, the vibe, telling you, totally boss.'

The city is far from sleepy, but as its glow mellows into one mash of colour, my eyelids become heavy, voices bleeding into a soothing hum.

Our Kid and Bruv would have loved a night out like this, in this city; in fact, I remember Our Kid making an unscheduled stop in the port for some reason aboard a trawler to fix a problem. 'It's like the north, our kid, but different.' Both of them are now away from Trawler Town's hard stare. No doubt what has a grip of this city, and many others, is illegal narcotics. In the eighties, heroin took hold of Liverpool, anaesthetising the disenfranchised when northern unemployment was of little interest to the powers that be in the south. From the brown to the E and on and on. As I meander through the city, Colombian marching powder, cocaine, is top of the drops. And the drops in this part of the world are prolific.

I'm on the verge of falling asleep under the weight of pointless thought when Marv's sharp edge pulls me back. *'Wake up, you cunt!'*

I am awake. What's wrong with you . . . ?

The car reverses off the road slowly, backing into an alleyway. The Hyena sits on my right, the artificial light of Liverpool nightlife fading the further we progress into the alleyway. I say nothing, but I am sure now that something isn't right. The Hyena's mate keeps his eye on the rear-view mirror as he reverses ever tighter to the wall. Clever – I can't get out. 'Always sit in the back of the vehicle, if you can. Gives you more options.' Who was it that said that on the course? Good advice. I should have known – I'm stuck now. You never stop learning.

'Go on then, lad, answer me, who are you?' the Hyena asks.

'Me? I'm the man who has just spent several grand on a

piss-up because ...' I don't have time to finish the sentence because with a smile and speed that suggests he's done this before, he whips out a semi-automatic pistol and shoves it hard in my face. It catches my lip – I feel it bruise.

'Seriously. See I think you're a fuckin bizzie.'

'A what?'

'A fuckin bizzie.'

'We're always busy, you cunt.' The shadow man at the wheel hasn't moved an inch.

'I'm always busy,' I say. The Hyena's eyes are dead as cold cod. He reminds me of the Bastard Borough psycho. Shadow man still hasn't moved a muscle.

'Eh, don't try and be funny lad. Are you a fuc ... kin' ... biz ... zie?' He taps out the phonetics against my teeth.

'What the fuck is that smell? Have you shat yourself?' With the barrel that close, I can smell it. *'It's been up his fuckin' arse!'* No denying it, Marv, a strong possibility, fitting the surreal absurdity of the day: a covert operation at the races, on a scale never done before, that I thought had gone very well but might now end in an alley with me and Marv wondering if a semi-automatic pistol tapping a beat against my teeth has been shoved up someone's arse. As I run through my options, I hear a dog bark in the distance. These oddities stay with you.

I believe, as much born out of personal experience than anything else, that in moments of serious threat or crisis your immediate thoughts are rarely what might be expected. Fight or flight perhaps. But often there's no time for panic or heroics – you act according to instinct in the moment. What is in you, that's what shapes your actions and thoughts and, very probably, decides the outcome. Here, now, heart racing, scared witless, yet unable to get the thought out of my head that this shooter has definitely been too near someone's arse.

'A what?'

'A bizzie – a fuckin' cop!'

And in this moment, in the seconds you must fill convincingly or face uncertainty, Marv shouts the answer: *'Say yes. Say fuckin' yes!'*

The exact opposite of what I chose to do on my training course. Wholeheartedly, with absolute conviction, I do as he says: 'Yeah . . . you're right, mate, I am. The place was full of them today . . . that's you fucked.' The city dog barks again in the distance, breaking the silence that follows.

Like my brothers, I was never fearful around Pa's police dogs, but I'm scared now. Reality elongates time. I wait for the Hyena to speak, not taking my eyes off him. Did he just glance at the driver? The mute driver, the shadow man with one hand on the wheel, so relaxed. Engine running. It's not the Hyena, I realise, it's him, the shadow man. This is his call. For the first time I notice his watch – that's not a cabbie's watch. 'They'll spot snide a mile off, lad,' said the team . . . The Hyena howls, throws the gun into his other hand.

'Fuck me. Careful, you cunt.'

'We better get a fuckin' drink in then, lad.' The Hyena roars with laughter, and I see the slightest smile from the driver as he slips the car into reverse and we glide slowly back towards the light – the smile is just enough to convince me that he should be sitting in the back.

They think it's a joke. I'm not laughing but Marv, Marv, Marv, he has saved me again.

As the journey goes on, the driver has still barely said a word, but I catch looks in the rear-view mirror and another sight of his timepiece. Nice watch for a driver, clearly more than a ferryman. This man is driving something else, but what and for who?

There are always surprises – the water can change in a minute – but right now I'm certain I'm not the only one in this car with a story to tell. I complement him on the wristwatch. He smiles, says little. In the next bar, he buys the first round of drinks, then raises a glass and catches the eye of someone whom I suspect he knew would be here. The Hyena is right – the bar is totally boss. More drinks, but not before a quick trip to the toilets, bile in the belly, heart rate still a little excited. I empty my stomach and pop a mint into my mouth, not wanting my bad breath to give off a bizzie vibe.

Who knows, in this city of surprises? The strobes mirror my fragmented thoughts. I sip at a beer and rise to the pounding beat. A mad, sweat-inducing incident to end the day that I now sweat out on the dance floor. All part and parcel of this wild west coast. The Hyena wants to carry on partying, but the quiet man, the shadow man, the so-called 'driver', is there one moment and gone the next.

I take a taxi back to my hotel, wondering if I'm being followed. It would make sense – it's what I would do. I'm a little drunk, a lot tired and hungry having left anything I'd eaten in the Hyena's bar. My eyes fight against an urge to sleep as I replay events. Best wait until the morning before speaking to the ops team about this left-field incident – not that it will make a difference. I already know what I should do. Nothing, the reason complex but sound.

'*Why are you such a cunt? It's fuckin' obvious.*'

Just tired is all.

'*Wake up!*'

Take your licks . . . Who said that? Or was it *sleep* on your licks?

'*It's on you that . . . Cunt!*'

Yup.

I wake up to a housekeeping trolley rattling past my room. Disorientated, I think it's something else, the shadow man returning, then sink back into the bed. I look out of the window across the car park. My head hurts, the inside of my lip Liverpool red. If I report the incident, they might pull the operation entirely or, although unlikely, look to put someone else in. I hear the Lion's voice ringing in my ears: 'If you tell the fuckers about every threat, every punch, they will lose their arse.' A born cynic but one of the best at this game.

'*What you gonna fuckin' do, then?*'

Not now, Marv, my head's pounding. A shower. Long before Wim Hof bellowed, I realised a cold shower does the trick and makes *him* shut the fuck up. It energises you from the off, and your first thoughts are usually the soundest. Probably because of this, I realise I'm working for good people. I don't think they would lose their arse, certainly not the Meerkat, and he is not the only one to suspect this will yield heavy players beyond corrupt police. It is just that, like them all, he keeps his cards close to his chest.

I decide not to say anything about the incident with the gun, but I do protect myself, because I've learned that nobody else will. Never forget: there is always an agenda, and you are often not on it.

Back at base, the team are pleased with how the day went. The Possum is pleased, claiming he wishes he had officers with my vision within his unit. I know he's stroking me, but he is a decent man in a landscape where it can be difficult to accept praise or know when it's sincere. Soon, I'm back in London. I'm still waiting for the long-delayed debrief on the long-term sting, but the Dassie is always too busy to discuss the issue, the corrupt corner of London no one ever wants to talk about.

Before I head back south, I pay a visit to Trawler Town. I once again sit under Decimus Burton's shelter, the architect's gift to the town, a fading legacy of the splendour that might have been. An early attempt to give Trawler Town an air of affluence, now serving as the place for two detectives to sip coffee and watch the tide shift. Without going into details of who I'm working for beyond an outside agency, I share the incident with Bud. His career is flourishing in his northern constabulary, yet he knows he will soon reach a ceiling set by others. 'You know how it is for the likes of us, fettler. Trawler Town, mate. Outsiders us.' Bud's right.

This is a special friendship. When you have been friends since short pants and comics and Vimto, there are no secrets. He agrees they might well pull the job or at least change the parameters. I don't want that, because I privately believe the driver will come again, and on that occasion he will bring his friends with him and whatever commodity it is that he peddles. Because this job will run and run, and expose the mendacious heart of the police, masquerading as protectors of the public but in reality protecting nothing but their own position. I intend to see it through to the end.

Bud met the Dassie when I did a cross-county job involving his specialist crime unit. He didn't take to him – thought him a great advert for the soap industry. 'Well, at least you're not working for that slippery fucker,' he says.

I still have my day job to attend to, and you're given no credit for any covert deployment, so it is easier to just get on with it. If you make a fuss, you're less likely to be released. Often, while you are away, extra cases find their way to your in-tray.

'Mad that, mate. They'll squeeze every drop. Best come back before they kill you.'

As our laughter settles and a low winter sun shimmers on the estuary, I spot a solitary trawler putting out to sea. Bud knows what I'm thinking: 'Not many left, mate.' We both know Trawler Town's death rattle sounded long ago and, in that, it has much in common with a police service not fit for purpose.

'Not worth dwelling on, mate. Fancy a pint?'

'Fuck aye.' One of these days, I think to myself, I really must introduce him to Marv.

'Yes, mate. One before we sail, eh?'

And on Operation Foxglove sails. I meet with the Capuchin and over a meal explain in greater detail my rising concern that the recent seizure of a large consignment of Class A narcotics of interest to criminal associates of mine was compromised by an informant, who may be one of the individuals arrested, and that I need access to police intelligence databases. I'm sure there is no way he will go through with it, compromise himself for the sake of a good meal. I'm instructed to offer £5,000 for access to the database, and part of me doesn't want to accept the idea a blunt in your face offer will turn him. The Meerkat is more confident. This is his turf. I watch the Capuchin cut his steak – very precise, a method to it. Completely at ease, he chats amiably, cutting through the succulent steak. Two men discussing business.

'No problem.'

I hesitate, maybe I misheard. He doesn't want the money. He'll leave any form of 'thanks' to me but the money is not necessary. Besides, he's enjoying my hospitality. We are getting acquainted. 'Maybe one day you'll give me a job or something,' he suggests. I nod, take a sip of wine and pause. It was that easy, I'm in. He has handed the keys to all I want for a piece of blood-red meat.

I think about the ramifications of this last supper – if the drugs operation had involved a UC, how their safety might have been so easily compromised for the sake of a good meal and a promise. It is of such little importance to the Capuchin, really?

I thank him, take another sip of my drink and watch him eat. I've known dipshittery, cowardice, corruption and God's work compromise and threaten the safety of jobs and individuals, but a steak and a bottle of good red to tee somebody up who in the worst-case scenario could be disappeared? The job still has the capacity to surprise.

The Capuchin asks me to leave it with him. At the debrief, when I express surprise at his willingness to potentially hand over information that might threaten life, my cover man sighs. 'Told you, wild west up here, lad.' Hard not to agree.

The Meerkat's operation might be sailing on, but there's nothing plain about it. The implications of this high-profile arrest are felt across the region, and everything goes dark for a while. But in time, with an itch unscratched, the Meerkat rolls his last dice as the dust settles on the Caribou's arrest. He asks me to call the Capuchin direct and repeat the request, which I do. Confident and at ease with me, he gives up the details over the phone.

There is still no news from the Dassie on either the compromise on the cross-border operation or the heavies who visited the shop. Our cover man on the Kent operation has a good idea, his boss who is 'on the square' (a freemason) suggested that we were burned by a corrupt detective sergeant or inspector based in south London.

Politics aside, I dive headlong into another promotion assessment process, line up another job, delivering money to offshore banks as part of another long-running operation.

Despite no assistance, and my coming out of a long-term deployment, I return to divisional work at Belgravia with a degree of spring in my step. Promotions are opening up, and there are far more vacancies this year, we are told. Assessment centres still govern the application process for promotions, albeit having been reformatted yet again. Now we are pre-scored going into the process. I leave nothing to chance. As the date nears I decline new UC deployments, focusing on the assessment centre process, and, ultimately, find myself put forward as the number-one candidate from the entire division. 'With that pre-score, you'll have to be catatonic to fail,' suggests the Fruit Bat, a quiet introvert who has replaced the flamboyant Kookaburra as chief of detectives on the division.

The following month, the Dassie asks for a meeting. He has an offer for me. Straight off the bat I again ask about the burns suffered in south London – about the fact that corruption almost led to the abrupt end of two operations. Asked by the Kent cover man not to mention his source's name, I do however ask the Dassie if he has heard similar rumours and remind him we were promised a full and proper debrief. He gives me the Dassie smile, the one that promises you everything but means nothing. He nods, deep in thought, and eventually reveals why he has called me in. His caravan has moved on. He has now joined the Met's internal affairs, what will become in time the Directorate of Professional Standards (DPS). According to him, it's the place to be. 'Corruption' is the next big thing. He invites me to join his team. 'Forget DS, you'll be at least a DI in no time. Big future. Might have to look at your firm. How'd you feel about that?'

'SO10?' I ask incredulously.

'What? No, no.' He almost chokes at the suggestion of looking into the undercover unit, fearing the Bear's wrath no doubt, gatekeeper of all secrets. 'The squad,' he clarifies, a term everyone in Copland know means the Flying Squad. He takes a long slug of his tea, which I'd paid for, obviously, and waits for my response. Of all Flying Squad offices, the most notorious office, often viewed with suspicion, was the one where the Dassie had himself served. Years earlier, when counselling opinion while contemplating applying for the elite unit, the Lion wryly advised that I should avoid this particular office, describing the unit 'a hard place to hang a picture straight'. The Dassie, almost salivating with enthusiasm for the future, tells me I'll be doing God's work.

'*Go on then. Fuckin' give it to him!*' Marv is wont to bristle in the Dassie's company.

He smiles, 'Ha!', and changes tack in a beat. I've pushed his buttons too hard. It's in the eyes.

'What you working on at the moment?'

He can't possibly know about the Merseyside corruption inquiry.

'Oh, a few bits and pieces,' I reply.

I've a plan once my promotion is confirmed (I'm now the acting DS on my unit), and it won't involve working for the Dassie, under the cloak of God's work or not. As his pitch of great adventures and riches for those who join him draws to a close, I have no idea that in diplomatically sidestepping his proposal, I may have shaped the future more than I realise. He names some of his new crew, including the Macaw and the Butcher Bird, new recruits to internal affairs, a department whispering in the ear of the Cabbage White, a man increasingly under siege over his leadership of the Met.

All commissioners of the Metropolitan Police eventually find themselves at some point encircled, having to face questions of competence, capability and value, which is perhaps not surprising given the expectations and rewards that the office brings. During my police service, I must confess I served under the some of the most striking examples of individuals promoted to their highest level of incompetence. Commissioners come and go, eventually winging off to the House of Lords or catching the blue gravy train. The Cabbage White is a commissioner shifting through the political gears pursued by increasing scrutiny, specifically his handling of several high-profile cases, none more so than the racist murder of Stephen Lawrence.

My personal crusade is simple: promotion. Make it better by joining the carousel. I can't see a plan beyond that. As soon as I am confirmed in the rank of DS, I will take the final promotion exam for inspector – a doddle, if past papers are anything to go by. Make detective inspector and then, only then, consider an exit plan, if that is what is right for me. On my terms, while still young enough to pursue a career path of my own choosing with a skillset that will lend itself to a variety of options.

My love of theatre and cinema continues unabated. On a trip to Liverpool, I almost fall over one of the guests from the hospitality box as I'm leaving a cinema – no escape. The film is *Secrets & Lies* – ironic. There are moments when I think I'd rather pretend to be someone else on-screen – less stressful. Maybe I should have listened and stayed on in education, maybe even stayed in Trawler Town. There's a thought.

'What's fuckin' wrong with you? Snap the fuck out of this. You're an excellent detective, one of a small group of elite UCs. Prospects, you cunt! Here's your fuckin' future!' Marv's right. What's wrong with me? See, I never talk about him or me, my future, with anyone – issues of trust and I am not a good communicator in any emotionally mature sense, compounded by a commitment phobia. 'Why settle down, son? It rarely works out.' Pa's words readily adopted.

Maybe that's why I flourished in the Bastard Borough, where everyone seemed adrift. I am not really afraid of anything other than becoming a detective stuck fast behind uncertainty, and there's no way home because I have no home as such, not even the foundations of one. In a rare moment of reflection, Our Kid once said to me, 'I don't think we are a *family*, our kid. We're like the Plughole Pirates. Sailing from one island to the next, trying to find one to call home.'

I should build my own family, my own island, another conclusion reached sitting in the flickering shadows of a cinema, escaping the solitude of my inadequacy. My on–off relationship with Liz, currently off again. A distance away from understanding love, how to recognise it, certainly how to embrace it.

One night, early in what will become year zero, I'm busy balancing all the plates being tossed at me, about to go overseas, when my heart – not the emotional one, the other one, the actual organ itself – goes into overdrive. I'm sitting watching an old movie, John Frankenheimer's *The Train*, when my heart suddenly begins to thump erratically, pumping like the protagonist Labiche's steam engine. Eventually it settles, only to return with a vengeance in the middle of the night. A full-on body sweat combined with limited understanding of biomechanics convinces me and the girl I'm with that night, that I'm having a heart attack. Like father like son. In the local A&E, a casualty doctor confirms there is nothing wrong with my heart, instead diagnosing a panic attack. I've never heard the term. Asked about my work, I say it's all good – maybe it was simply too much coffee. I keep the incident a secret from work – I do not want to stop working. A new addiction has taken hold in the family, but unexpected cold turkey awaits.

All of which is the last thing on my mind as I leave hospital and dive back into work as if there was no tomorrow. But something has changed. Running away from any form of commitment is the issue. I call Liz, and she and I get back together, and then I ask her to marry me. I rush headlong towards what I think will be the making of me, of us, with no real understanding of why other than an idea born out of a panic attack.

I ask the Moth to be best man, for two reasons. First, his former partner introduced me to Liz, and second, he's been down in the dumps over a number of things: being passed over for promotion and the fact that his girlfriend ended their relationship after she caught him prying into her private life and finances. I am no better than him in terms of successful relationships. But I feel that the very act of marriage will resolve everything, make me a better person, better at something other than merely being a cipher in Copland. And so I proceed with new confidence: haircut, new suit, no whiff of being a human covert resource, I leave the assessment centre that month knowing without fear of exaggeration that I have smashed it out of the park.

I work through the summer on division, setting up a robbery initiative and welcoming a new detective sergeant who joins the crime squad to take over from me. This is the Wombat. He enjoys a drink, the Wombat, and the drunken Wombat is a very different person to the sober Wombat. Still, the promotion results will be out soon. I'll be out of here, making my own way to far better things.

The day the results are out I'm in early, and the DCI calls me into his office. I'm ready to celebrate, but he looks as though he's in shock. I failed. 'You have to appeal,' he says. 'It can't be right.'

No, it can't be right. The news hits me square in the guts, and Marv goes into expletive overdrive as I try to focus and listen to the DCI. All the while, a grip takes hold – rejection. It won't let go – its impact will last for years. I'm due to get married in a few weeks' time. I can't think straight. Everything runs through my mind at once: am I doing the right thing? What's wrong with me? Liz deserves better than this, better than me. I'm incapable of even a nailed-on promotion in a dysfunctional organisation. I was told I would have to be catatonic to fail.

'You useless cunt!'

I muddle on, and both division and SO10 support my appeal in writing. I'm encouraged by all the support, but the melancholy lingers. Liz and I do get married, and I briefly perk up, convinced that all will be well, that happiness will begin with this moment. The Moth makes a speech at the reception. It's at times odd, at others humorous in an off-the-wall kind of way, but mainly odd. 'He has always needed someone to look after him,' he begins. Have I?

'He has an odd walk to him, your best man,' observes Pa dryly. 'No one else was available?' I laugh – we haven't done much of that lately. Although disappointed at my promotion news, he makes no comment – life was always full of surprises to Pa.

After a short honeymoon, I return to work. The Fruit Bat greets me with news that my appeal was unsuccessful. Once again, we share a similar look of disbelief. I don't and can't accept it, beginning my own enquires and discovering evidence of what looks like a cover-up or a cock-up or both. An assessor who recalled my attendance and who is brave enough to raise his head above the parapet confirms I was anything but 'catatonic' and that the assessment centre was 'on edge' over something.

I march into my bosses' office, and there's a sudden reversal: in the circumstances, management feel I should drop my appeal – there'll be another opportunity soon enough. I don't, then a few months later three former detectives from the same Flying Squad office I served in are arrested stealing 80 kilos of cannabis following a covert operation. Their arrests are directly linked to my failure on the promotion board, though it will take a few years to work this out. No officer at that particular Flying Squad office passed that year, sullied by association with what is yet to be made public, while the 'on edge' comment may have been linked to the fact that a supervisor at the centre was later arrested for selling exam papers the following year.

The drugs were planted in a sting operation by the Metropolitan Police's internal affairs department, targeting a former detective suspected of corruption, the Komodo, and involving another retired officer, the Sloth, and a serving detective, the Slow Loris Monkey. It seemed like a slick open-and-shut case, but while the police rumour mill accelerates into overdrive, I'm more consumed by despondency and anger about my own situation.

When I made detective at such a young age, it was often assumed I was a freemason, but when I was invited to join the secretive fraternity, I turned down the offer – I didn't think it was my thing, and certainly not Marv's. Maybe I should have joined, played the game. Such are the random thoughts occupying my mind as Liz sleeps and I watch a spider crawl across the ceiling above me as dawn breaks one morning. It leaves a line of silk behind it in case it falls. I know this because Our Kid told me. He likes to pepper otherwise sparse conversations with nuggets of trivia, believing his brother will use them when engaged in the work he doesn't talk about. He's right too, not that I tell him.

He's a little lost at the moment, Our Kid. He didn't come to the wedding. It might be time to visit Trawler Town again, or maybe I simply need another UC deployment to take my mind off things. The spider hesitates before continuing. He has almost completed his journey when there is a loud knock on the window, followed by an insistent buzz on the doorbell that wakes Liz. I pad half-naked to the front door of the flat, open the door and there, beyond the security gate, stand several plain-clothes police officers, most of them staring at their boots. The Macaw is up front, and the Butcher Bird hovers behind him.

'Hi mate, sorry . . . We've a warrant to search the flat.'

And that's how a new chapter begins: 'Hi mate.' The Macaw tries to make light of the situation. The Butcher Bird says nothing. No wonder he's been avoiding my calls pestering him regarding the Dassie's promised debrief on Operation Kingcup and our Kent fiasco. The inspector in charge of the search steps forward, nervous – he struggles to read prepared lines. I don't recognise him and will never see him again after today. He hands me a list of offences alleged to have been committed by officers from the Flying Squad and states I was one of them. The list is staggering: theft, robbery, dishonestly handling stolen property, conspiracy to pervert the course of justice. Given I was working at the office for less than 18 months of the period stated, I would have had no time for anything else.

I'm experienced enough to know there is more to this document than meets the eye. It appears to have been cobbled together for impact, to frighten the life out of the officer receiving it. It bears all the hallmarks of a managed production to facilitate a desired outcome or strategy. The Macaw tells me it is a result of the arrest of the former detectives but gives no details. The phone rings, and there is no attempt to stop me answering it, I note. It's a journalist friend on the line – I've known him for several years. He asks if I am one of the officers about to be suspended. 'I've heard a rumour you're on the list.' I confirm his 'source' is spot on, that the DPS (Directorate of Professional Standards) are still at the flat. He tells me to 'keep my chin up'. Odd thing to say, in the circumstances. What else did his source say, I wonder?

Our home is a small one-bedroom flat, and were it not for the seriousness of the situation, so many officers attempting not to trip over one another would be comical. There are so many that eventually some give up and leave. The Butcher Bird, Janus-faced, hovers, clearly wanting to have a word in private. I put the phone down and offer to make tea. Inside I'm boiling with rage.

Liz sits at the small table in the kitchen, stunned by events. Married a matter of months, this is not in the plan. She knows, I think, what this will do to me; I have no idea what it will eventually do to her. I force a smile, tell her I will be back at work within days, that all will be okay. She nods as a tear falls. They drink their tea, shuffle about, bag up my paperwork, a few files. I wonder if they will bag up the cascaded covert phone line fixed in the hall. 'We need to take your passport, driving licence, credit cards,' referring to my covert bag, all registered in pseudonyms. Butcher Bird explains the Bear specifically asked that they be collected and returned to him. I ask if they want my SO10 operational manual, locked and hidden in the same place.

'Oh yeah, thank you, best take that I guess,' says the Macaw.

I put a call into SO10 to advise them what is happening, and the Bear actually picks up. He claims he had no idea this was happening. I say nothing, finding this call and his deceit more painful than what is actually happening in front of me. Presumably protocols will lead to Merseyside being informed regarding Foxglove, which I assume will now come to an abrupt end.

The Butcher Bird hovers once again as I hand over my passports, credit cards and ops manual. I also give them a couple of covert notebooks. The Macaw peers round the kitchen door and hands me a large calibre bullet, found on my desk – the one given to me after the arms recovery as a memento from the successful Flying Squad operation. I wonder if this one bullet from several hundred will now be used to dispatch me as a disciplinary offence, but no: 'Best keep that safe, mate.'

'They must fuckin' know where it came from!'

'You haven't asked how I got it,' I say.

'Best not to complicate things,' replies the Butcher Bird.

'Fuckin' complicate things?'

Looking back, it was as revealing as the fact that a prominent journalist had heard I was 'on the list'. What list, and who gave it to him? It must have come from the inside.

I can't begin to compute the enormity of the deceit playing

out. The senior officer who gave me the memento will remain untroubled by his token gift. Back in the kitchen, the Butcher Bird still loiters. Given the size of the flat, he's struggling to get an opportunity to speak in private. Finally, he asks if we can talk. Here we go, God's work. The Butcher Bird and the Macaw are a double act sent by the Dassie, of that there is no doubt, but they clearly do not want to speak in front of Liz. They suggest she carries on as normal and goes off to work. Liz makes it clear that whatever is to be said, it will be said in front of her; she has no intention of leaving. This is clearly not part of the plan. He hesitates, but the search is all but over, so it's now or never. He looks like the condemned man, but surely that is meant to be me.

He stresses that he is merely the messenger, a statement which he repeats several times. The Dassie wants me to know that if I cooperate, and while there are no guarantees, if I am to receive a custodial sentence, he will personally see to it that I serve it out within the safety of solitary confinement. Another tear forms in Liz's eye. The inspector who is supposedly in charge of the search suddenly appears at the door and suggests they leave. This does little to assuage my anger, and it certainly doesn't silence Marv: *'You fuckin' agreed to this!'* His anger directed at two officers I knew so well. And cooperate, how exactly? I hold up the disciplinary notice in my hand. 'This? Really? You really believe this is me?'

For nearly two years, night and day, Macaw in particular came to know me, as I gave my all to an operation where safety was comprised, undoubtedly on occasion by corruption which their master refused to address either at the time or subsequently.

'Solitary confinement? Are you fuckin' serious?'

If I am stunned by the surrealism of the situation; the Butcher Bird is clearly disturbed too, while the Macaw now suggests he should never have been assigned to the search. I ask if it was a policy decision, by the SIO, their attendance? It was, the Macaw tells me, as is the decision to suspend me from duty, which will take place later that morning. When the officers leave, Liz points out they have forgotten to take the bag containing my under-cover papers, passport and credit cards. I walk them out to the cars. 'Oops,' says the Macaw, clearly glad to be heading back to the office. 'Hopefully you'll have them back soon.'

'When I get out of solitary fuckin' confinement?' Marv shouts after them.

I'm convinced I will soon be back at work. All I can think of now is protecting the integrity of my covert identity and case-work. I put a call in to the commander's office and speak with his staff officer, asking for the formal notice of suspension (which I'd been told would be carried out on police premises) to be done at a non-police premises. The commander who will carry out the procedure agrees to the request. Yet when I arrive at the agreed location, I am met by a Police Federation representative, who tells me the decision has been overturned by the DPS, and I now need to attend police premises to deal with the formalities of suspension.

'All bit full-on this, mate. Bit of a show, eh?' says the rep.

It is, and the show will run and run. When I finally meet the commander, he apologises and states he was overruled by the DPS. He takes my warrant card and explains a welfare officer will be in touch with me soon. Then he adds, 'I'm sure this will all be sorted out soon.'

I don't think I have ever heard a more sincere apology from a senior officer; I was left in no doubt he meant it. Maybe it is already dawning on management that this is wrong. Maybe I'll be back in a week or so. I walk out into the low winter sun. There's a nip in the air – should have brought a coat with me. I wasn't thinking straight. Still, I'll be back soon. I ring Liz and tell her that she should go to work, that all's well. This is Day One, Year One, of my new life.

One Flew Over the Cock-up Nest

As Year One unfolds, I have plenty of time to reflect and consider the issue of police internal affairs. Professional standards have a chequered history, managed – some might suggest manipulated – to a large extent by police themselves. Never initiate an internal inquiry with political or reputational consequences until you have already decided the outcome. To a degree, I get over the initial shock and mask my seething rage by doing what is asked of me, and remaining confident I will soon be reinstated. That all will soon be resolved, and I'll be left a little rankled perhaps but eventually promoted, dusted off and redeployed. So chin up, chill out, crack on.

I figure that given the tight parameters and management of the inquiry, no senior officers will be joining us, and so it proves. Within days I'm sitting in a meeting with Police Federation solicitors, along with 18 other officers who were all suspended on the same day, all having served with the Flying Squad within the period in question (many were still working there at the time of their suspensions). We're told to expect the numbers to grow by the week. According to the Cabbage White's public broadcasts, there are up to 250 corrupt police officers in London, so this can only be only the tip of the iceberg. As to the reason I'm frozen within it? I'll deal with that when the time comes, I think to myself. As for Marv, well . . .

Every other day, a senior officer gives a briefing to the press on the scale of the corruption problem and their efforts to combat it. They emerge from behind desks to discuss with the press over a good lunch the trouble they've known. The rank and file are castigated and morale plummets. There was and clearly remains corruption in the police. Even as I write this, years later, one might argue it has reached new levels, new scandals surpassing old. The claim is always that it is just a few rotten apples, always from the rank and file, but I believe this is a line used to muddy the waters in order to allow the bigger fish to swim away. My first meeting with the Federation solicitors is a sobering experience. I have to fight against the despondency it generates, as we sit in the large meeting room of a solicitors' practice in receipt of a lucrative contract from the Police Federation. I nod at the faces I know, most of them from a wilderness inhabited long ago. The majority will be battered and scarred by what follows, while a few will be proven to be rotten apples, but the orchard will prosper. It matters not for this group because now we are all damned, tainted, the entire Flying Squad past and present. The very manner of the process will make suspicious minds of everything and everyone. Day One of Year One is a small taste of what is to follow.

Adding to the absurdity, over tea and biscuits, talk of the weather and police work interrupted, we are encouraged to take notes by the Police Federation representative, who sits in on the meeting. It's clearly years since he worked at any coalface. He shovels biscuits away by the handful and offers his opinion on all matters with the gusto of a deranged Jonathan Pie – he has, after all, paid for the biscuits, or so I suspect he believes. By the end of the meeting, covered in crumbs, he will suggest we should all retire for an ale as if it's the cricket club AGM.

The meeting itself is convened and chaired by a senior solicitor from the firm. He looks youthful, only his grey hair indicating his vast experience. With the air of a school master, I think in this landscape he is the Orangutan. At times he looks as stunned as the rest of us, this disparate bunch from the Copland wilderness, drinking breakfast tea and nibbling Hobnobs – all very civilised. All very fuck you very much.

I look around the table. The Gnu, a Flying Squad detective I barely knew when I worked in the unit, looks over at me, curious. I don't fucking know why either, I feel like screaming back at him. Marv, meanwhile, does, repeatedly, into the void of my skull. There's little doubt we are the stock from which the DPS aims to produce a feast for the Cabbage White and his nymphs, because the leadership of the Met at this time is starved of what they need: positive headlines.

In the early weeks of Year One, it becomes clear that of the three arrested in the cannabis sting, two are now being treated as supergrasses, a term first used in the seventies to describe criminal informants whose information implicates a large of number of people. In this instance, it appears they are only informing against officers they served with while they were on the Flying Squad, within a specific time frame, and not against any officer of senior rank. All three, the Komodo, the Slow Loris Monkey and the Sloth, I knew professionally during my days with the unit. We are told the Komodo and Slow Loris Monkey have made allegations against up to 80 police officers, past and present, while the Sloth denies all allegations against him. Where are the rest, I wonder? The rest of the 250 corrupt officers the Cabbage White has announced to the press? Will I end up tea-and-biscuiting with whoever compromised the south London operations?

The suspension and searches are neatly choreographed and accompanied by supporting news bulletins, headlines designed, I suspect, to buy time. And the high table at Scotland Yard needs time. Some journalists, however, are thought to be too inquisitive when they begin to ask awkward questions. They are sidelined. Those in favour, meanwhile, are invited to feed direct from the hands of the senior management running things.

My friend, the journalist who called me the morning I was suspended, is a chief reporter for a large news group. He asks to meet, telling me he was contacted by another journalist, one clearly deemed on-message as he was already in possession of a list of names of officers past and present whose homes were being searched on the day it all happened. He'd casually scrolled through the list, apparently, pausing at my name and commenting 'an interesting character' and going on to disclose to my friend that I was a UC. Though I had known my friend since before my first posting as a detective – he was even a guest at my wedding – my friend did not know I was a level one trained UC because I had told no one beyond my immediate family. And yet, somehow, this other journalist knew.

It could only be that the DPS had compromised my safety, as well as every case I had worked on, without any thought to the consequences, handing over my details to a journalist who had presumably proved suitably supine. But in this moment, in spite of all of this, I cannot see beyond a desire to get back to work, so I simply note the fact and bury the reality.

Years earlier, addressing issues of noble-cause corruption, the Cabbage White had informed a Commons Select Committee on Home Affairs that the police service no longer relied upon confessions and that police officers no longer wrote notes together, to ensure their reports were independent. This came as a surprise to all officers and detectives across the Met, who were doing exactly that as a matter of policy, and under the supervision of senior management too. A few weeks later, in a BBC *Panorama* documentary, he claimed that 'quite often truth was the casualty' in the business of securing the prosecution of criminals, suggesting, perhaps a little too conveniently, that in the past 'a minority of officers were prepared to bend the rules . . . to massage the evidence'. Here again was the age-old inference of a few rotten apples in the lower orders acting rogue. Any one from a trawler town will tell you a fish rots from the head before spreading.

The form of corruption he was referring to is generally deemed an acceptable form – corruption lite, if you will. It is the very essence of God's work and acceptable because we are all in it together, the war on '. . . well, whatever war we are fighting this week. The judiciary, one can probably assume, turn, if not a blind eye, then one with something of a squint. There is a hope that foot soldiers have not overstepped the mark. Which of course they do, often, as the number of high-profile miscarriages of justice exposed over the last 50 years would suggest. Perhaps the Cabbage

White is privately contemplating the shit storm brewing over the activities of his secret unit, the SDS (Special Demonstration Squad), which infiltrates protest groups, a unit he takes a very special interest in. Visiting an SDS unit ensconced in a covert flop the year of his *Panorama* appearance, he presents them with a bottle of whisky, another old practice still practised, to thank them personally for all their efforts. Because he needs all the help he can get.

Allegations having been made against me, I have no choice but to go through this internal process to confirm my innocence – I get that – but already, this early on in the process, I don't believe there actually are *any* allegations against me beyond vague generalities which seem designed for impact. I'm certainly not given any specifics. So I remain stubbornly confident it will end soon enough, that my 'family', my police family, will see sense. It leads to gallows humour, and I suggest to the Orangutan we will need a bigger meeting room and better biscuits when all of the senior ranks join us. He points out that they, the senior ranks, are not represented by the Police Federation: 'I fear the spotlight is intended only for the servants and not the masters.'

At this meeting the Impala looks across and smiles. He always struck me as a kindly, decent man, but now, behind the smile, he looks shattered. I wonder what else he knows. Meanwhile, I contemplate my own secrets: I will not compromise the Merseyside corruption inquiry by speaking about that here. I will not allow anger to toss a match on all the cases I have running. I am strong enough to deal with this setback. I recall one officer sharing publicly his own despair at being similarly accused. He went on to make chief officer rank and, I will discover, is one of the main architects of the methodology now being exercised. I am also surprised to realise how much the job of detective means to me, more than I own up to. It is important. *Why*, the psychology, is more complex, and that too will take time to understand.

Soon, though, six months have passed, and I'm still no wiser as to what it is specifically that I am accused of. The lack of contact from colleagues in this time is expected to a degree – cops are frightened by their own shadow when it comes to matters of promotion and self-preservation – but it's disappointing nonetheless.

A former colleague will later describe suspension as being like a deadly virus that cops fear catching. The DPS through design and crude application creates a fear of association so that friendship in Copland is often without depth, based primarily on mutual dependency and little else. The unwritten rule is that if you appear to have dropped in the shit, don't expect contact from anyone with the faintest hope or desire for advancement. If you want sympathy, you'll find it in the dictionary, somewhere between shit and syphilis.

This fear of taint regardless of guilt or innocence renders cops inert.

Nevertheless, I find it difficult to stomach, particularly from the officers I've worked closely with in covert operations and, latterly, on the divisional unit in which I have invested a lot of time and effort in helping colleagues hoping to make detective to develop. Only the Lion is steadfast in his support, having called me at home the day I'm suspended. The Moth is now notable in his absence. I get it, a passed-over inspector, now carefully managing his friendships.

I occupy these long, empty days running or swimming, mile after mile, length after length, reflecting on the months prior to my suspension. I'm replaying the odd incidents and strange behaviour of others – dismissed at the time, with the benefit of hindsight, where perhaps they shouldn't have been. Maybe failing the assessment centre in such unexpected circumstances was not a clerical balls-up – perhaps I was blocked by the DPS. I'm hit by another memory: plain-clothes officers asking that I be the detective present when they executed a drugs search warrant they'd initiated, which turned out to be an empty apartment containing a large amount of cash sat on top of a TV. They asked if we should simply leave it, rather than seizing it and booking it in. Experienced officers suddenly behaving like morons; phone calls asking for intelligence without proper authority – were all of these set-ups?

Eventually I learn the supposed parameters of the investigation. A specific three-year period is under focus, limited to one precise area of London and involving no white officers above the rank of inspector. Beyond that, though, the inquiry is entirely without boundaries. As Year One continues to progress, regular group meetings with the Police Federation solicitor suggest that transparency or speed is unlikely if the operation that led to the arrest of the bent cops – on the surface a solid covert operation – is anything to go by. It proves to be riddled with incompetent management. The speed at which the Met's internal affairs department seeks to act on their 'information' is not matched by those charged with managing the sting that led to the arrest of the corrupt officer. It becomes clear that of the 80 kilos of narcotics planted by the DPS in the sting, only two-thirds have been recovered. Despite unlimited funding and resources, the man in charge chooses not to use any form of surveillance to track the movement and whereabouts of the drugs – as a result, the other third goes missing. This leaves the DPS open to all kinds of issues, allegations that might compromise an otherwise good job. The Federation solicitor suggests, probably accurately, 'They appear not to be too concerned with probity at this point.' I wonder to myself who ran the operation. When I find out it was the Dassie, it comes as no surprise that the police service has seemingly redistributed 30 kilos of narcotics back on to the streets of London.

It does little to fill me with confidence as I settle into my new routine of exercise and daytime television, gradually becoming well acquainted with Richard & Judy. I think Richard Madeley may be unwittingly contributing to my slow decline, with his cheery disposition and perma-tanned smile a constant companion as the long year unfolds. Alone in the flat I bicker with Marv as we debate for hours without resolution the reason for this bonhomie. I head up to Trawler Town for a weekend alone, to clear my head, and as I walk into Pa's house, Richard's beaming face glistens out from the TV and Stepmother suggests I sit and watch.

'Take your mind off things,' she says, looking at the screen. 'A happy chap, isn't he? If he were a cream cake, he'd eat himself.'

Pa's health has been up and down, and with nothing but time on my hands I want to see how he is doing. Maybe this unexpected extended leave is an opportunity to better understand him and our relationship. He's busy in his small greenhouse, too small for his bulk, really, but serving as a hideaway from Stepmother. He tends his tomatoes gently, pruning, fussing, chirping to himself – another discovery.

'Why haven't they told you what you're accused of?' he asks.

'Well, they have, kind of. Everything, bar murder.'

He laughs. 'Can't they find the bodies?'

'No . . . Perhaps they want me to help find them.'

We take his two dogs up to the beach. We throw a ball or two and watch in silence as the tide rolls in. It has always been a slow process getting to know Pa, so many lost years, but here I feel at least something has begun between us that might eventually be a small positive. I do wonder, though, if my current status will somehow resurrect his shame, the roulette roustabout of the north. I know it fuels my own anguish.

Dogs exercised, the tide is on the turn as he loads them into the back of the car. His hand ruffles my hair, as if talking to the boy that was.

'It'll be right son, it'll be right.'

And off he goes, a nod and a few words asking me to let Stepmother know he will be home for tea. Where does he go every afternoon? I watch the car fade from view and hope he's not gambling again. The dogs seem to know, but they aren't talking.

As Year One drags on, I start to think that this situation might not be an aberration but a reality, and perhaps it is only the beginning if the Met are to scorch the earth as they focus on brand management and damage limitation, particularly as the Stephen Lawrence inquiry dominates the headlines.

'Fuck 'em. Fuck 'em all. Fuck Merseyside. Fuck the Met. Fuck SO10. Fuck all of them.'

I share his anger. My mistake was to think of the job as family – it isn't, but I cannot admit that yet, either to *him* or to myself. I will not use my knowledge to damage or compromise the organisation or the people I work with, because, despite it all, I know it will come good. This is what I believe. So shut it, I tell Marv. Just shut it.

Not that I am feeling any love from the job. Two commissioners' commendations for not only me but for the whole team, following the two successful covert operations, Kingcup and Rose, are blocked. The team are told it is to save embarrassment – it is nothing of the sort; it is the start of a premeditated process of softening me up, eradicating any positives in order to script fictions against me. Is this the beginning of a plan to mess with my head, make me more amenable to what is to come? The Bear later plays down his own part in having me vaporised, with my involvement in past covert operations completely disavowed. I am removed quietly, secretly, from evidential chains, silenced. I become a non-person. One that swims up and down, up and down, my reputation drowning.

Several months in, responding to a letter from Liz, who is worried sick, a commander writes to say she is disappointed that 'welfare contact has not been as she would have wanted'. Her honesty infuriates the DPS, but thereafter an infrequent, erratic form of welfare contact punctuates long days of non-activity. First up is the head of my divisional CID, the quiet, gently spoken Fruit Bat. On first sighting in a café he is clearly burdened by something, but I have no idea what. He intimates it, but says little, so we sit like two patients in a colonoscopy clinic, in stoic silence. Eventually, he flies off, never to be seen again, placed on long-term sick leave and then medically discharged.

I hear from Graham, my friend the racehorse trainer, who had been so good in assisting with my legend. He gets in touch to tell me he's had a visit from two officers from the DPS, describing them as 'slow foals', which isn't encouraging. Graham, not a man to mince words, offers his observations. 'Well, I said I'd speak to you, tell you they'd been, only fair. One of them didn't like that, bit full of himself I'd say.'

'Don't suppose he did,' I reply.

'No, I don't think he did. But still, it's only right. The other one was more . . . reasonable. Do you think it's a good cop, bad cop thing?'

'Maybe.'

'Said he thought you were probably a good man, but might have seen something untoward that could help them. I told them straight, I expect he saw summat untoward every time he walked out the door. Isn't that why he was good at his job?' I am grateful for the call, it lifts the spirits.

'Here, they never asked about the tons of horseshit your boss wanted delivered, mind,' he adds.

I burst into laughter – hope the probes picked that up. It's good to laugh. Graham's 'handsome is handsome does' outlook on life is a tonic; I've missed the company of him and his horses. He offers advice: I must keep busy.

'You can't take a horse out of training and just turn him out and leave – do him no good at all.' My bloodlines are far from thoroughbred, but I get the point.

In September, my pal the journalist meets a DPS superintendent at a social event, and my name comes up in conversation. The officer tells him that 'sadly some innocents may be sacrificed' and mentions the 'difficulty of finding reverse' in my case. In November, Liz's cycle is late, weeks late – good news, we hope. We have been trying for a family for a while, and maybe this is a sign that something good will come of this time after all.

Eleven months into my suspension, I get a surprise call from the Moth. He asks to meet urgently, saying he has 'good news' for me. He asks that I keep the meeting to myself, until we speak in person. I understand his meaning – the landscape is shifting. The Moth has a proposition he believes will be to my advantage. It follows a meeting with the officer heading up the Flying Squad inquiry – this is the Snipe, who I know by reputation, but not personally. The Moth helpfully refers to himself as the 'honest broker' in this mix, so I am the *commodity*, I assume.

We meet on 16 November, the date UNESCO was founded, my diary declares. I've no doubt the meeting will be educational. I do as he asks and tell no one after agreeing to meet. To ensure I don't miss any salient points, I decide to record the meeting, and it is a measure of the state our friendship that I feel the need to covertly record this in case the Met deny the meeting ever took place or the Moth disappears into the night. Recently passed over for promotion (he will soon make up for the disappointment), the Moth is stretching his wings to capitalise on the ongoing situation and manage his own position – I get why he flies toward the light. He is not an honest broker, and I am not a commodity – we are both bit players in a squalid narrative governed by false motives masquerading as 'non-negotiable integrity'. This is the start of my deployment into my own case, the army of one. What could possibly go wrong?

I meet the Moth in familiar terrain, a bar that seems to chime with the subject of our purpose, a grubby pub in a rundown area of King's Cross, still waiting to be remodelled. The Moth is excited with his news, of how the future might be rebooted. For him or me, I wonder, as Marv whispers, *'He is not your friend. Look at his face.'* He's probably right, but that's cops, and this is Copland. I am sure I have been followed to the meeting, but I don't check – I can't be bothered. The DPS exercising power and control over movement and mind is something I am getting used to, a totalitarian state insofar as my world is concerned.

We settle, and I hope Marv will be quiet; thank God the tape can't pick up his voice. It's like any other deployment, save it sickens me, the fact I need to record a meeting with a good friend because plausible deniability is increasingly the motto of this world. The Snipe has been recalibrating and has a message: the Moth is moving from best man to the man best placed to facilitate my return. Sniffing the air, his eyes bulge and twitch with strategy. First, we go through the protocols of the need to keep quiet about the approach as he takes delicate sips of his beer, sip, sip, sip. I think back to the wedding and Pa's comments – he'd certainly known duplicity in his life. In hindsight, this is not my best deployment, bound as I am by anger and a feeling of rejection by my surrogate family. I've broken my own rule: never bring emotion to a covert deployment, which is what this is. He takes another sip then places his palms down on the table and delivers the message, the plan, the strategy. I am 'a peripheral figure'. . . I don't feel like one . . . 'who could return to the fold'. . . a beast spared the bolt . . . 'with my integrity intact . . . if, and only if, I accept one of three proposals'.

It turns out integrity really is negotiable when you get down to it.

The three proposals are to be discussed at a secret meeting with the Snipe.

1. Give evidence against the main targets of his operation; they are not identified here but I guess will be at the meeting. *Main* targets, I note: the first meet *always* reveals more than you think.
2. Make a statement but not give evidence . . . *'Now we're getting warmer.'*
3. Give a running intelligence brief. *'Boom! Finally, we get there.'*

This third option must include rumour, gossip, tittle-tattle and my perceptions of my time on the Flying Squad. Nowhere else. Certainly not when we were compromised while working for the Dassie. Why muddy the water when being baptised? He tells me the Snipe's view was: 'Sifting through it, it looks like he's one we could recover back into the fold.' The Snipe has extended his bill. But sifting through what? I can't wait to hear the taped interviews. The justification for my treatment thus far, according to the Snipe, is that I have used my UC name to avoid paying a council-tax levy on my grandmother's old house – not something the DPS are really interested in, but it *could* be considered criminal.

They are so far off the mark it serves only to fuel my rage. Marv is already throwing punches in my head. Utter tosh: not only did I run a legend through the property, but so did an entire unit in another part of the country, with full authorisation. I tell him I am being treated like a terrorist. The Moth keeps to the agenda and tells me I have a couple of weeks to make a decision before a report is sent to counsel and the deputy commissioner, the officer in charge of discipline issues. What discipline issues? There is also one absolutely 'non-negotiable' element to the benefaction, if we are to go ahead. While I can select anywhere in the country for the meeting with the Snipe to take place and bring one unconnected friend – the Moth suggests himself, the honest broker warming to the task – I cannot have the Police Federation solicitor present nor any legal representative; in fact, there will be no deal if I inform my solicitor of the approach. *Deal?* I just want my job back, but given the first deal was solitary confinement, I suppose I ought to be feeling chipper. The gallows humour is not yet dead.

But I'm not feeling chipper – I am consumed with rage. As a result, I play a good hand badly. Of course I should meet with the Snipe. My skillset is such that, however complicated our choreographed dance would be, I am confident I would get 'product' on him. I'd get a taped record of the meeting and, in doing so, expose the squalid gaming of inconvenient truths. But I don't, stupidly. I think the proper thing to do is to report it to the Police Federation solicitors, for the benefit of all Federation members, and in doing so I prove myself to be a fool. This is not how the system works – it's rigged. If you rock the boat, more fool you – you don't understand the game.

Option three is the expected take, what they want me to go for, the part of the plan to allow me to 'return to the fold'. The Moth, I sense, sees this as an easy option, but it sticks in the craw, and a year of bile rises from deep inside me. From the outset, this was the plan: their intelligence needing a supplement in the shape of a good UC on a promise. You scratch our back, we'll plan your rehabilitation.

The reality of this 'intelligence brief' is as plain as day: remain suspended and report back to the DPS from inside meetings with the Federation solicitors, spying on legally privileged meetings and infiltrating conversations. Do this and I'll be back 'in the fold' in no time.

'*FUCK YOU!*' screams Marv as the train home rattles and shakes in the bowels of the city. At least we know now, Marv, at least we know.

When I was a kid in Trawler Town my trips to Grandma's were something special. Maybe it's the woman sat opposite, a new horse blanket on her knee, but I am suddenly reminded of her, and her musings on cinema, in particular of a scene from *The Charge of the Light Brigade*. Norman Rossington was a northern character actor and a firm favourite of Grandma's. In the film he plays Corbett, a drunk who makes good and rises through the ranks of the Light Brigade to become the regimental sergeant major. Lord Cardigan (Trevor Howard) takes a dislike to a particular young subaltern, wants him gone. He charges Corbett with spying on the officer, and in return for this the hapless NCO will simply keep his job. Pride, maybe honour, compels Corbett to tell Cardigan he can do it only if he reports the request to the subaltern. Cardigan tells him he has just committed career suicide and busts him back to private. As a boy, I couldn't understand why. 'Why has he done that to him, Grandma?'

'Because he's a deadeye, love. It's what they do.'

She offers no further explanation, and I watch on, strangely drawn to the charge into cannon fire. A deadeye, I will learn with age, has no soul.

Back home, I tell Liz the news, and she thinks it's positive, means I'll be back at work soon. 'Besides, some in the room already think you are a plant,' she says.

Which is true, and if they knew about the Merseyside operation, my role in investigating police corruption elsewhere, they'd be convinced of it, no doubt. It is fair to say I am isolated within the room – the biscuits have long gone soft – but who, I wonder, has told the Snipe I seem isolated? I arrange an urgent meeting with the lead solicitor, the Orangutan. He has an air of disappointed resignation. It has been a long year for him too.

'Can't say I'm surprised. I would strongly advise against the meeting,' he says before catching his words. 'I . . . You haven't met him, have you?' It's clear I have not from my expression. 'My concern is that they want you to be . . .' He stops, examines his desk, checks his notes as if looking for words that will make sense of it all before offering an analogy on cricket and then continuing. 'My concern is they simply want you to be . . .'

'A fuckin' mole on a chain,' Marv cuts in.

'A deniable UC?' I suggest.

'Yes, yes, sadly, very much so . . .' He changes tack. 'How are you?'

In over a year, no one has asked. 'Fine, getting fit. You know, all good.' It's not all good. Marv, more vociferous than ever before, is becoming problematic. The Orangutan nods slowly, as if it might lessen his load, and repeats his advice.

He's well aware of whispers in the room, having already been approached by some questioning my place and role in the hall of shame and biscuits. The good and gentle Orangutan tells me he has written to the DPS. I suggest he's more likely to get a meaningful reply if he writes to the MCC. He smiles, and so it proves.

He receives a reply in the Orwellian doublespeak that has become the norm, suggesting the question of cooperation is not something to be addressed at this moment in time. The Police Federation is now voicing concerns at my treatment and questioning the motivation for my suspension, and finally this prompts action.

One month after meeting the Moth, and two weeks before Christmas as the tree stands waiting to be dressed, there is another early morning knock at the door. Only three officers, this time. I'm told I'm to be arrested in connection with a Flying Squad operation that took place several years earlier, an op I have no recollection of when named. I ask for more information. There's an arrogance to them, aggression too. Probably nerves, given how ill-prepared they appear to be. When I launch into the real reasons I believe they are here – my recent offer to meet in secret with their boss and to discuss options for me to be rewarded and remoulded, action I consider certainly unethical and probably illegal – it's clear the hapless officers have not the faintest idea what I'm talking about. The arrest descends into farce.

A security gate outside the door to our basement flat is locked, so I ask them to wait while I get dressed. Again, I wire myself up, secreting a recording device on my person. I will likely be searched at the police station, so I choose a kit less likely to be discovered and again feel utter despair that it has come to this. Trying to retain some dignity with a covert recording device taped between the cheeks of my arse, I am arrested for 'failing to ethically investigate an offence'. What offence is not mentioned nor are answers given to my protests: this is a trumped-up wording for which no power of arrest exists. Liz witnesses the farce unfold. The officers finally resort to words lifted from the doctrine used by all police officers uncertain of the ground beneath them: it will all be sorted out at the station.

There is something else. Liz is late, and we hope she might be pregnant. We try not to get our hopes up, having endured many problems getting to this point. She suffers from endometriosis and is due to see her doctor later in the week. Yet again, I tell her not to worry.

The car takes us via a meandering, circuitous route through south London, the exact area where I had posed as a crooked businessman for nearly two years while working for the Dassie. This has all been carefully choreographed to intimidate me. At one point we stop outside the café I regularly used during Operation Kingcup. Eventually, we arrive at Fulham police station, a station new to me then, now memorable. The custody officer is as confused as I am as to the reason why I'm actually under arrest, which he duly notes in the custody record – not that it changes anything. After some discussion, the fudged wording is modified, now naming the corrupt former detective the Komodo as the informant and stating his allegation has been corroborated by three others. It's clear the custody officer is still unhappy with accepting me as a prisoner, while one of the arresting officers robotically repeats I am to be placed in a cell. It is as if nothing else matters, other than getting me locked away and hidden, presumably to reflect on my error of judgement in my reporting the offer to spy for the DPS to the Police Federation.

I have been arrested and placed in a cell a number of times before, when working as a UC. Perhaps I should tell them this, and avoid all the stress I am clearly causing, as by now the arresting officer is so nervous he searches me as if I am a radio-active isotope, which is probably a good thing, because all the while the recording device rolls underneath my scrotum. Not that I'm reassured any action I take will see the light of day. I am given a disclosure package of statements that mean nothing to me. I immediately hand it over to the custody sergeant, telling him I am confident if he reads it, it will confirm his initial thoughts. He wanders off to find the duty inspector, no doubt thinking *why me?* Not an uncommon occurrence in Copland. Two of the DPS detectives begin to bicker, arguing that the custody sergeant should not have been allowed to take the file as the third wanders in with a cup of tea, asking if anyone has seen his boating magazine, adding an absurd, Kafkaesque quality to the scene.

Protest is pointless. I know I will end up in the cells. When a course of action is predetermined in Copland, the merits of the decision are never the issue. It transpires that several other officers from the suspended group have also been arrested, two by appointment as they are more senior in rank – as I say, there's brass neck when it comes to the brass. The reason I was unable to recollect the operation becomes clear. My role within it was minimal to say the least, confined as it was to my last working day on the Flying Squad. It was a case that involved almost the entire office dealing with many arrests over 72 hours following a large-scale theft of cash from a Post Office.

The custody sergeant visits me in the cell block on the pretext of asking if I would like something to eat but really to tell me he has voiced concerns at my detention to the duty inspector, who displays the very best of career-minded front-foot leadership and advises him 'not to get involved'. I'm not surprised; this is the default position in policing when a situation arises that might impact on future prospects or career plans.

The custody officer is curious. He asks if it is a 'witch-hunt', given there are now so many rumours circulating about patterns of behaviour by the DPS. I suggest that if it were, I should have more rights. He wonders if it is 'convenient timing' for an under-siege Cabbage White, before promising a supply of hot tea however long the day lasts. The job runs on tea, remember. I am grateful. And it will be a long one: the Federation solicitors regard me as being so low down in the pecking order, my representative does not arrive until several hours later. He protests loudly at the lack of evidence and demands my immediate release, whereupon the DPS officer in charge disappears and returns with a hand-written statement, which he produces with a flourish that speaks more of hope than judgement. Highly unusual, because it wasn't included in the disclosure bundle they hoped would bamboozle anyone daring to raise questions. *'It's a fuckin' stitch-up. They're panicking.'* Marv may be right, but why?

Even more oddly, I am asked to believe they simply *forgot* they had the statement. A ridiculous suggestion but no surprise in the circumstances. It was taken from the custody officer involved in the administration of the prisoners arrested in the Post Office operation. I recognise the name – I know him, having worked with him in the past. The statement asserts that on the day in question, having booked out one of the suspects earlier in the day, it was *probably* me that was responsible for the information supplied regarding a later separate entry updating on events that took place while the prisoner was booked out, namely that no premises connected to the crime were identified by said prisoner.

The crux of the matter is that I have been arrested for my part in an operation involving dozens of officers and in which I had the briefest involvement. It took place on my last day with the Flying Squad before I left for a temporary secondment (Counter Terrorism), thereafter beginning a long-term covert deployment. I was neither one of the investigating officers in the case nor did I manage any element of intelligence regarding it. I had no involvement, other than this single day, yet I am supposed to have briefed a custody sergeant as to the state of play of the entire case and, having done so, now stand accused of 'not ethically investigating an offence'. Exactly what this means remained unclear.

The allegation against me has been made by the main police 'supergrass', the Komodo, though we have seen no evidence of that yet, statement or otherwise, and, we are told, it is corroborated by three men who were the actual thieves arrested. Again, no evidence of them naming or identifying me in any shape or form is produced. There follows a long pause, in which the Federation solicitor puts two fingers against his forehead and begins to tap – Morse code for God almighty, I wonder? The tap becomes a beat. 'And this . . . This is it?' The arresting officer nods unconvincingly, and the custody officer sits in silence, waiting for his shift to be over.

The duty inspector appears at the doorway, breaking the silence. All heads turn towards him, but any hope for sanity is short-lived as, upon seeing the tableau, he remembers his own advice and reverses with parade-ground precision. The Met is not ready for any inconvenient truths. The solicitor, perhaps to stop his relentless tapping forefinger, articulates his thoughts. He makes it clear how ridiculous this all sounds. Marv, meanwhile, makes it clear that come hell or high water I will be beaten down. The DPS officer seems fatigued, particularly when asked why there is no typed or signed copy of the custody officer's statement, or any statement indeed, making a direct allegation against me.

As the solicitor's fingers tap again, the officer states that he needs time to make further enquiries, thus allowing me to spend more time in the jug. Enclosed by quiet concrete walls, I wonder why they picked a sleepy part of Fulham? If they had wanted to keep the pressure on, surely they would have opted for a busy station with a howling cell block. I suspect there are two reasons: they have whipped management into line here – do not ask questions – or perhaps even now they still want me to re-plumb back into the group. When the custody officer brings me a cup of tea, he utters one word. 'Jesus!' I nod and say nothing, my arse cheeks still whirring, alive to the situation. He is on the button, I think to myself – if not Jesus, it's certainly God's work.

Alone in the cell, several hours pass. I worry about Liz, about what we hope the future will soon reveal for a couple struggling to breathe, and Marv is Marv, raging in the ginnel connecting hope to despair. I hear footsteps, voices in the corridor – the grey, heavily scratched cell door swings slowly open. The DPS arresting officer enters and pauses, his angular face uncertain how to begin – a Kinkajou, better known as a honey bear, I would say.

Liz has called the Federation solicitor's office with some news that is then passed on to me. Pa collapsed at home that morning and has been admitted to hospital. The Kinkajou doesn't look at me and says that matters will be expedited as soon as possible.

It will later be revealed that at some point on the day in

question, or thereabouts, other detectives conspired to steal some of the proceeds of the theft. So the implication is that I either conspired with those detectives or they used me as a patsy to mask their activities. Neither are true, but this is God's work, where truth is often the first casualty. Several officers are detained that day. All have a far greater involvement with the case – indeed, some will go on to be charged with offences – but of them all, I am detained the longest by far.

'Do you think that this was their intention?' asks the solicitor later, as I finally collect my things, on my way to call the hospital to enquire about Pa.

'You fuckin' think!'

'That's a very strong possibility,' I say.

It is night when I get back, and the flat is in darkness. I call out to Liz, but she doesn't answer. I find her in bed. I can see she has been crying – her green eyes are framed with livid red. I tell her it's okay, that I've called the hospital and the news is good. Pa is unaware of events and he is going to be fine. He needs stents, but the old scrapper is still standing. But her tears weren't for Pa, and she doesn't want to talk about it now. In the kitchen I find linen stained with menstrual blood on the floor and hear her begin to cry again. I don't know what to do. I stand at the door thinking, this is on me. I wash the linen of menstrual blood. I scrub and scrub and scrub in silence and rage. I make tea, in the dark, adrift, alone by choice. Sadness hangs over the flat, over me, over us. It won't ever leave.

Year Two begins as the last ended. I see Liz off to work, then I run or swim, work on my case. It gives me purpose, something to do, but it is not enough. A few days after Christmas, I meet with the Orangutan at his office to discuss the arrest.

'This is . . . ?' He trails off, takes a sip of coffee. 'There is tenuous and then . . . there is this.'

I make it clear to him that I know why I was arrested, because I didn't take up the offer and reported the approach.

He nods and goes on to explain there is concern among some in the group of suspended officers that I have been planted to spy on them. He needs to hear from me that I am not a plant. Decency compels him to ask, but he does so with a weariness. I've noticed it creeping into meetings, both the private and the tea-and-biscuit group affairs. He is a thoroughly decent and kind individual, but I wonder if he sees into the heart of this, the malevolence, the desire of the DPS to act with absolute impunity and, more importantly, to control the narrative. God forbid God's work should uncover corruption under the wrong stone.

Remember, this was a time when few people were inclined to believe that the police, and the Met in particular, would set out to destroy anyone perceived a threat. The perception is perhaps different today. Warning signs were ignored, such as when the editor of the Met's in-house fortnightly paper, the *Job* – a kind of in-house *Pravda* – found himself in conflict with his masters at the Yard. There was only going to be one winner. John Cleal resigned as a matter of principle when he was overruled by Scotland Yard and prevented from accurately presenting an article supporting their handling of a case involving a serious assault on youths in north London by police officers (who were later convicted of the crime). The Yard insisted that the piece expressly imply it was written by a serving officer, when it was in fact produced by the

Met's own PR department. An early example of what was to come, the new remit of Department of Professional Semantics, a new variant of God's work one might argue.

Over more tea and biscuits, I make clear my belief that the secret offer from the Snipe was always considered by them to be a win–win strategy. If I accepted, I would be tasked with infiltrating the group and reporting on anything considered legally privileged, but if I refused, there would be activity within the group anyway, conversations that I suspect they hoped to capture as 'product' (as covertly recorded conversations) from whomever they considered to be primary targets. My arrest also served to both exercise a greater degree of control over whom I could meet, given I would be on police bail throughout, and to bat away embarrassment at being challenged by Federation solicitors over my suspension. Gaslighted by any and all means available.

For now, it's just me, Marv and Richard Madeley. The Moth doesn't return my calls for several weeks – indeed, there is not much more welfare contact from the division, and nothing from SO10 after a few bizarre incidents in Year One when one of the supervisors, the Blister Beetle, would call from the office and ask to meet for coffee. He'd always be full of beans – 'Let's have a cuppa, mate,' – only to cancel hours before we were due to meet because of operational demands. On the fifth occasion, I asked him to stop calling me.

'Nah, come on, you know what it's like,' he protested.

I did, sadly, and I had no faith. I never heard from him again, which confirmed to me that it was another box-ticking exercise.

I had let my house to a housing association in east London years earlier, at a time when interest rates were going through the roof, and had moved into rented accommodation. As the market improved, Liz and I planned to sell her property, move back to mine and refurbish it. In February of Year Two, the DPS visit the tenant living in my house for no other apparent purpose than to cause distress, and they tell the occupant, who is unhappy the police are in the house, that I am an undercover detective. It is a gross act of reckless betrayal by idiots in a department out of control. We only discover this by chance when Liz calls the tenant and receives a torrent of abuse. The Federation solicitors write to the Snipe. The Snipe is a solitary, skulking wading bird, protected on the shores of the Met. After obfuscation and denial, he eventually claims to have left it up to the discretion of the individual officers attending as to whether they should disclose my status as a UC, which seems ludicrous. The Snipe is also a cautious bird, and he keeps his bill in the sand, not wanting to be drawn on the incident, but within days I have recorded the tenant disclosing the full extent of the utter disregard for the safety of a serving officer. An investigation follows, kept out of the reach of the DPS, and while SO10 fit a panic alarm in our flat for fear of reprisals now my cover is blown, little else changes. That the cascaded covert phone line that always bothered Liz has now been replaced by a panic button does nothing to ease her sense of despair.

In what turns out to be my last proper conversation with the Fruit Bat, just after the alarm is fitted, he articulates what I have been thinking and Marv shouting: *'The lunatics have taken over the asylum.'* I don't know how any of this will help us start our family, or even if this is the place to do so. Not that the controlling factions within the wilderness are concerned with such matters. It's well into Year Two of my suspension by now, and I cannot for the life of me understand why there has been no contact from Merseyside about their own corruption investigation. Aside from a coded message to SO10, I have not spoken to a soul about their operation, either within the Met or with the Federation solicitors. A few weeks after Fruit Bat's parting observation, I get a call from a detective who is to replace him as a welfare contact.

Enter the Flying Fox. Until recently he too was a level one UC. I'd worked with him briefly, years earlier, on a covert drugs importation case. He discloses that he too is under investigation by the DPS, accused of engineering a covert operation to claim overtime and expenses. It's a bizarre decision, appointing a welfare officer who is himself being investigated by the DPS.

From the moment the Flying Fox flies in to join me on the park bench, he rages at the length of time the investigation into him is taking. I do not believe there is anything sinister about his role, but you never know. I'm past caring. He's so aggrieved that he talks of little else, and while I get it, I'd appreciate a different topic of conversation from time to time. He discloses that his undercover partner is also under investigation and was approached and told that if she gave evidence against him, all allegations pertaining to her would disappear. Well, at least there is consistency in modus operandi, I think as we sip coffee and stare into the middle distance. Meetings with Flying Fox are more akin to an episode of *Mortimer and Whitehouse: Gone Fishing*, pondering life on the riverbank as he rages about the DPS and me wondering what to make for tea. Only the humour is missing.

Liz made a formal complaint after our safety was compromised and my UC background revealed, and she eventually receives a reply from a senior detective wheeled out of obscurity, who somewhat staggeringly suggests it's a civil matter, rather than one for the police, so there's nothing they can do. In August, I'm told favourable documents, commendations, letters of thanks have been removed from my personal file and that officers from my division have been warned against contacting me by the same individual responsible. Was that the Wombat, I wonder, who took over from me on division and whose best friend often seemed to me to be the bottom of a glass? Wombats, it is said, are not often seen but do leave plenty of evidence of their passage, treating any obstacle they encounter as a minor inconvenience.

When he is later promoted on to the DPS, a years' worth of my payslips are found in his desk. 'I guess they'll say they mislaid them,' suggests my solicitor. It won't end well for the Wombat, but by then I really am past caring. It is all part of the same egregious assault. A newspaper carries a front-page story of an illegal drugs factory shut down, resulting in multiple arrests. I was one of the first UCs who infiltrated the group, which led to this success, but I'm airbrushed from the case.

Another covert case I worked, a blackmail, due to go to trial at the Central Criminal Court, is dropped after pressure from the DPS that I assume relates to me. Victims are being denied justice, and the cord squeezes tighter. One commendation that isn't airbrushed is for a joint major crime initiative I was instrumental in planning and implementing. The commendation is handed to me in a supermarket carrier bag, again found under the Wombat's desk. It is the last act of the Fruit Bat, handing me a Tesco bag found by a civilian admin assistant who marched into his office and told him in no uncertain terms what she thought about an organisation that chose to hide it. To his credit, he told her he agreed, and I thank him, because right now, every little really does help.

Some weeks later, an anonymous package arrives in the post from central London, the sender unhappy at being 'brainwashed' against me. It is a small token of support – comfort and despair in the same envelope. It contains a highlighted report of the operation in the *Job*, in which another officer has assumed credit for my work. This package reminds me of the fact that not everyone buys into the endless diktats from the Ministry of Truth and it ought to lift my mood, but it doesn't. I know it was sent by one of my old team who knows the article was bullshit. Yet the fact they didn't simply pick up the phone, while understandable, is nevertheless debilitating. John Cleal's resignation changed bugger all.

All of this is compounded by my personal life: Pa's health is not great, and Liz, as she witnesses the impact on me, is struggling to understand how an organisation can treat a member of staff so viciously and with such impunity. The isolation, the abrupt transition from 16-hour working days to breakfast with Richard Madeley is enough to send anyone batshit mental. Though this, I guess, is part of the plan, and it's working. Not that I admit it. *'The fuck? What's wrong with you? Pull yourself together, you weak cunt!'*

Marv is relentless, but I'm just tired, obsessed with getting back to work, upping my training regime to keep myself going. They say it helps, right? Liz comes home from work one night to find me shadow boxing in the dark.

'You okay?'

'Yeah, fine. One-two. One-two. One-two.'

For the rest of Year Two, I am re-bailed time and time again, reappearing only to disappear. The DPS suddenly change tack, telling me there is no need to travel all the way into town just to be bailed again and again, and advise they will send a letter instead.

'They don't want a fuckin' record of this.' Marv's right, of course. I insist on attending each date in person in order to ensure there is an audit trail. The many custody sergeants I see get it, but I also see the look in their eyes. They know spite will be the response. And so it proves.

In November, keen to try again to start a family, Liz and I are exploring the idea of IVF treatment. Four weeks later, we receive a letter from the housing association from whom I rent the apartment. They have received information from an anonymous source that my circumstances have changed, that I'm no longer the partner of a former girlfriend who was the named tenant (who has long left) and am therefore a named occupant only, which is true. We never got round to changing the details when she departed. They wish to take possession of the flat. I walk the short distance to their offices and meet with a member of staff, and it's clear that she has had a visit from the DPS. She cannot disclose 'who advised the housing association' and, in reality, what's the point of contesting the action with everything else going on, and given the fact we are now looking to move back to the house I own? I thank her for her time and leave. A week later she contacts me again, far more sympathetic this time. I'm 'urged' to seek disclosure through my solicitor of 'the manner and form of the information disclosed by the third party'.

By now, as a direct result of the visit by the DPS, I'm forced to resort to threatening court action to gain possession of my own house from the tenant. It takes months, and when I do, it's uninhabitable. I later learn this latest poke by the DPS, contacting the housing association, caused a rift in the department. It is little comfort at the time, but it might explain subsequent mysterious offers of assistance.

Walking home one winter evening, I notice I am being followed, and not for the first time. Now begins the game of 'take out the surveillance team'. It's fun, I think in the moment, let's embrace it, but the reality is it signals the beginning of a rapid decline in my mental health. In the moment, however, for Marv and me, it is the glorious game: surveillance soccer. I burn three easily – they slink off the pitch as quickly as they can, exiting stage right pursued by Marv with a sore head. I lock on to a fourth surveillance officer, calling him out in the street, like a man or Marv demented. He stops, turns to face me and, as I square up to him, he puts a hand gently on my shoulder. Comforting, and with total sincerity, he says, 'Go home, mate . . . go home.' That's all. We both turn, go our separate ways, and I have never forgotten this small act of kindness. I wonder if we will meet again as I look back at the surveillance officer. I stop, realise I wasn't *going* home; I was walking *from* home, on my way to meet Liz, hours ago. She bears all this with extraordinary stoicism, but it is taking a toll.

That December I receive a letter ordering me not to attend Fulham police station, because after advice from counsel there will be no further action against me. Two years later, I will discover the Met was advised in unequivocal terms that there was no case to answer within six months of my arrest, but they instead chose to use police bail as a form of bondage. The true reason for this decision is still festering within its ranks, a secret known to only a few in Metland and which will take me more time, and tears, to fully understand.

So, still suspended, on we roll to Year Three. Constant challenges as to why I am still suspended are simply ignored; it is as if the impact, the grinding erosion of my mental health, is now an officially sanctioned action. I've lost weight, conditioning, have no real interest in food or appetite for anything other than being an army of one. The Lion visits. Back from his travels. I should be with him. He never talks shop, but he does listen, observes me, my rambling. I suggest a walk in the woods I used to go riding in. He doesn't bother to answer as he roles a ciggie with practised ease.

'You little fucker, don't let the bastards grind you down.'

'They're not. I'm fine.'

'What's with the fucking goatee?' he says, looking me up and down. 'You trying to look like a ponce?'

'Would it help?'

'Come,' he growls, grabbing his coat. 'We're going out.'

'To the barbers?' I ask. I've missed jousting with the Lion.

We arrive at a bar, tucked away in central London, a dimly lit watering hole favoured by the big beasts from the Yard. He quickly orders two Guinnesses.

'I'm not drinking . . . We're trying for a baby and . . .'

'Guinness is good for you, puts lead in the tank.'

'Pencil, the saying is pencil.'

'You're fucking quibbling now?'

The man of few words suddenly has a lot to say, and he wants to do so in a favoured off-grid police watering hole. Cops wander in, some peeling off to shake the Lion's hand, and though most have no idea who I am or why I am here, one does. A senior officer strides in with a few colleagues, full of laughter. He spots the Lion and walks over, hesitating when I'm introduced with a glowing report. The Lion, sensing anxiety, is not minded to back off.

'Don't worry about your pips,' he smiles. 'I put most of the fuckers on your shoulder.' The beat hangs in the air.

The Kookaburra arrives, having been invited – maybe made to come – by the Lion. In he bowls, with warm smiles and profuse apologies, claiming he was 'duped' by the Snipe into believing I was involved 'in the dark arts' but now feeling he was deceived. He is keen to make amends, offering to help in any way possible. 'You wanted to keep your fucking channels open,' says the Lion, never one to pull his punches, even with friends.

The Kookaburra fiddles with his tie. He was perhaps always better suited to the private sector, which he has recently joined. Once, in a covert operation with the Lion, he deviated so far from the plan he found himself trussed up half-naked in a hotel room and robbed of his 'buy money' – 'Duped again,' he tells me. They recount the story in graphic detail; as profanity peppers the Lion's sentences, the Kookaburra flushes like a naughty vicar. The story is fuelled by drink and designed to lift my spirits. While I have no doubt the Kookaburra was keen to ensure easy access to 'job' contacts, I bear him no malice, and he does lift the mood.

The Lion does not take no for an answer on any issue. Since arriving in the UK as a young refugee with a limited grasp of the English language, the F-Bomb has been the Lion's go-to noun, verb and adjective. Decades earlier, his wife, so used to hearing him drop it, assumed it was common parlance. One time she was asked what she thought of the food while seated at the top table of a divisional dinner early in his service and replied, 'Fucking lovely.'

The Lion and the Kookaburra spend the evening reminiscing and sharing tales, many of which I've heard before, but the sometime-double act is on good form. I half-listen as I let the Irish black silk embrace me. Both would be seen as dinosaurs or heroes, depending on the timing, agenda or the crime to be solved. When I get home, drunk as a sack, the first thing I do is shave off the goatee.

The following month, I'm still suspended and still challenging the reasons why. I'm arrested for a second time, this time by appointment, a letter inviting me to attend a police station at a specific time and date. I'm told there is now a further allegation against me; this is not made by the Komodo, but by one of the others arrested in the cannabis sting, the Slow Loris Monkey. As noted, the slow loris is known for its toxic bite, so perhaps I shouldn't be surprised that he is put forward late in the day to justify my continued isolation. It is falsely suggested that I was part of a group of officers of all ranks who stood in line to receive bags of low denomination coins (part of a large recovery again involving most of the office) as 'reward' for our hard work. And although on this occasion there is a typed statement bearing his name, after the hue and cry at Fulham, it isn't signed by him and is dated a few days after I reported the 'return to the fold' offer to the Police Federation. On it goes, an endless drip.

After three years, the Federation solicitor is not inclined to mince his words. He describes the allegation as a case of me seemingly 'being dropped into the scene'. The comment raises a chuckle from a new set of DPS officers, who imply the matter will be resolved quickly. I have no faith, but, true to their word, four weeks later I am told the matter will be subject to no further action. But I remain suspended.

Notwithstanding my growing sense I am simply spitting in the wind, with no hope of common sense or transparency, I continue to raise hell, demanding to have sight of the monthly reports outlining the reasons for my continued suspension. I am entitled to see them but am repeatedly denied access.

Responsibility for the monthly reviews, which must be formally documented, with detailed notes as to why I am suspended from duty, falls under the jurisdiction of two senior officers insofar as my case is concerned: the Carrion Beetle and the Egret. Egrets are known to avoid the coldest regions, though this particular Egret will come under intense heat when his own integrity is questioned. As for the Carrion Beetle, his activities and integrity will be exposed, causing intense public alarm. I'm met with flat refusals to explain why I cannot be reinstated. I make it clear that it is my belief they are either not completing the relevant documents or, worse, are falsifying them. I keep jabbing, not realising it is a fixed fight. I simply hope that one punch will connect, and that is the problem. They are connecting, and for that reason the policy of isolation continues. By now there is evidence there are other officers linked to matters under investigation, who are being treated very differently and are certainly not suspended. Not one of the alleged completed monthly reports, which would explain why I remain suspended, is ever released despite several requests.

As Liz and I prepare to start IVF, I inform the Yard. I don't know why I do this beyond the fact that our consultant suggests it. While not aware of exactly what is going on in our lives, she knows the pressures and suggests we should both endeavour to undergo this process in as calm a state of mind as possible. Our funds are limited, and we know the odds are tough. I don't know what I expected from the Met – certainly not what follows.

Because now a raft of unrelated disciplinary notices so preposterous as to be ridiculous cascade down from the coliseum of conjecture, falling like confetti. I play their game, informing the Met of my eagerness to be interviewed and making it clear that I intend to produce documents and call witnesses in response to the absurd disciplinary allegations, which range from having case files at home to not paying the correct council tax when I bought Grandma's house. We obtain statements from serving and retired officers up to the rank of commander that directly challenge and expose the false nature of the allegations, all made after I rejected the offer to become a deniable spy. While there is little doubt that offer became problematic, there are far darker secrets involving the behaviour of senior officers, which in my fatigue I do not fully see nor understand.

A junior colleague pitches up at our door, wanting me to know that the only reason he hasn't contacted me was because the Wombat, now promoted on to the DPS, had ordered him not to. Clearly upset, he now offers to make a statement in my defence.

'*Why the fuck now? Three years on?*' Marv suggests throwing him out. I wonder if there is something else he knows and opt to make tea. I offer him a biscuit, not that it worked for me.

In the August of Year Three, the senior consultant in charge of our IVF programme writes to the Met asking them to consider postponing the proposed disciplinary interviews for three months, but they refuse, a blunt rejection coming from the Snipe's second in command, the Pot-bellied Pig. It leads to the consultant wondering out aloud at our next appointment if the Metropolitan Police has a side the public rarely see. '*If only you knew.*' She has a calm, soothing demeanour – in one consultation, I feel as if my head is going to burst, and I wish I could talk to her about that. In any event, we all know the importance of not allowing the word *stress* to mix with what we're all here to discuss: IVF. She advises me to speak to my GP, and, back in the room, shutting out the noise, I say I'm fine. Liz suggests I should, and it is from here that, eventually, the first step towards some kind of repair is taken, but I have a nagging doubt that little else will come from these meetings. And I can't talk about that either. Not that we realise it yet, but it was the beginning of the end of our relationship. I feel ashamed, unable to articulate my feelings, mute, because no one can hear *him*, thank God, my secret sibling. Why would they? He's all in my head. And you never share that – first rule of being a UC. Besides, I'm not here to make myself better; I'm here to start a family. But I'm too busy thinking about my other police family, loyalty still bound with the bastard benefice of God's work.

I still cannot understand why Merseyside have not been in contact, or why SO10 are so inert – busy putting out fires elsewhere maybe, as a scandal threatens to engulf the department regarding the fraudulent purchase of land and assets using covert accounts by a crooked accountant. The ease at which he was able to mask the crime leads to a flurry of reputation management, a skillset the police will increasingly employ in order to keep the train running.

I change solicitors when it becomes clear there is a conflict of interest, as I am patently not involved in any of the cases that are now at the heart of the DPS's corruption inquiry. I should have done this in Year One. I move with the support of the Police Federation who, as my union, are funding my solicitors.

'Do you find you are masturbating more since this all began?'

This was not a question I was expecting when I sat down in front of my GP.

'Am I? . . . I, er . . . Well, I . . .'

'Fuckin' right.'

My GP, I suspect, finds me a difficult patient. I say little because I do not believe I am ill. I tell him very little about my work, beyond the fact I am prevented from doing it. But in time I begin to feel I'm talking to someone who wants nothing more than just for me to be well. For only the second time in my career I am signed off sick. It makes little difference to my situation beyond the DPS being able to prevent our IVF treatment going ahead without interference, not that Marv sees it that way. The first time I was signed off sick was after I went through a car windscreen when involved in a head-on collision. In comparison that was easier to deal with. I am diagnosed with depression linked to PTSD. Marv sees my certified sick as an overreaction by good people; I see it as chance to at least begin the IVF treatment with less pressure. Our life is conducted in a fog of uncertainty.

Medication for the depression doesn't really work, so my GP suggests a therapist, which also doesn't work, and I do not have the wherewithal to understand there is a real problem. My denial is compounded by Marv, who will have none of it.

'Get a fuckin' grip. What's wrong with you? You fuckin' disappoint me, you know that?'

'Leave me alone. I don't need you. I don't need *your* help.'

On one occasion, back at my GP's, an opportunity to change the subject arises. He is a gentle soul, but he seems troubled, and out of the blue I find myself asking why. It's a family issue, complicated, somebody not being honest about something or other – he too is seeing his doctor.

'Could I ask you . . . how would you gather evidence on something like that, you know, as a detective?'

'Sorry?' I haven't heard a word he said. This has been happening a lot: one minute I am in the room and then I'm not. Whoosh! I take a long look at him – he seems like a good man, burdened, and so it is that on my next appointment, after listening to what I think sounds like a legitimate issue, I arrive at my GP's with an assortment of easily purchased off-the-shelf kit and demonstrate how to build your own covert recording device. It feels good, to be working again in some way.

'How was the doctor?' asks Liz, when I get home.

'Wonderful,' I say, and this time I mean it.

I supplement this new, albeit brief, sense of purpose with a new regime, rising early two or three times a week, dressing smartly, telling Liz I have meetings and heading off to central London. It's all a lie. Sometimes there is a surveillance team I can play with on my way to the cinema, theatre or park bench. A smart-looking vagrant wandering around London, returning home to inject his wife with large doses of hormones. 'Had a good day, love?'

On one occasion, wandering along London's South Bank, I see the actor Mark Rylance, then artistic director of the Globe Theatre. He's walking along, deep in thought, when an idea comes to me, based on a recent chat with my GP. 'You need something to keep you busy,' my GP had suggested, as I'd built him a device the Stasi would have been proud of. But what area of study? I think about my drama lessons as a boy, the love of film created by Grandma. I'd read an interview with Rylance recently, and had seen him perform at the Globe, so why not ask him now what he thinks?

At the time, it makes perfect sense to me and Marv. I stride towards him, a strange, ragged bearded man in a suit (me, not him). He's moving quickly through the busy walkway. I'll nail him just before he turns in towards the Globe. Then, as I pick up pace, there he is, another man – the same man I'd seen a few streets earlier, and I know, I fucking know! All thoughts of Rylance-advice are binned as I realise another surveillance team is following me, just because they can, because money is no object. I'm not having it. Not today. It's a good team, running against directional flow, just like the spooks do, but I've fucking got you, mate, and if I've got you, I'll get the rest. Surveillance soccer, the game is back with a vengeance! Something about this particular game draws up my anger, because my shadow seems to be enjoying it. I thought they'd had enough of me kerbing them, embarrassing them, and had stopped this.

I lose it and run ahead, pinning the unlucky 'footy' surveillance officer against the wall.

'I am getting so fucking sick of this,' I say, spitting out the words. 'How much is this costing?' I demand, holding him firm against the wall.

'How much is *what* costing?'

'Fuck you! I'm just going to the fucking GLOBE THEATRE!' The last words are shouted, top of my voice, causing a ripple of concern to sweep along the busy footway, Londoners, as always, neatly sidestepping the scene – 'Whoops, there's another one.'

It's like the flick of a switch. I look at him and realise he is not a 'footy', and this is not surveillance soccer. I apologise to the tourist, explaining I mistook him for someone else, and luckily he laughs with me before being joined by his wife, who asks if I've ever been to Toronto. My true target, the artistic director, strides past oblivious. I watch him fade into the distance and wonder what the play is – can't really sit through one at the moment; can't seem to focus on anything. I go home and for the first time take the medication hitherto flushed down the toilet to join my career. Just another normal day. Move along there. Nothing to see here.

Summer draws to a close as our first course of IVF treatment is completed. Anyone who has ever experienced this last roll of the conception dice will understand the utter despair of it. The trauma, the waiting, hypodermic hope and prayers. Meanwhile, a new solicitor raises my case with parliamentarians and is shocked at the off-handed arrogance in the response. I tell Liz all will come good. Empty words. After so long I think the light is fading in both of us.

The first treatment fails, but on we go. I'm late for a meeting with our IVF consultant – yet another. On the way there, my divisional DCI calls and asks for an urgent meeting. I know and trust her – we worked together in the past.

'Where are you right now?' she asks.

'Out and about,' I say. What is the point of saying anything else. Our request to undergo the treatment without harassment was ignored, and I've no interest in discussing our IVF with the third senior detective through the revolving door, regardless of how much I trust her.

'I don't quite know what to say to you, after what has happened, why you are still suspended. It sounds like a crock of shit, if you'll pardon the language.' She chooses her next words carefully. 'You might not be able to answer this, but if you worked for SO10 in Merseyside, there may be a problem. Your security may have been compromised.'

I nod, as if we're standing in the same room, considering what exactly to say to her. Marv explodes. '*What fuckin' security!*' Surely my medication should be helping him too?

I arrange to meet with her as Liz and I carry on to our appointment.

'Everything okay?' she asks.

'Yeah, all good.'

It's not. In short, I discover the Capuchin and others have been told that the crooked businessman they thought they were dealing with is in fact an undercover detective and the subject of wide-ranging allegations. The Merseyside covert unit and the SIOs from

Operation Foxglove, Possum and Meerkat, hope that I'll agree to meet with them urgently. 'Agree' – what does she mean? Without revealing her source, she suggests it might be good news.

As this sinks in, a day later another former colleague in SO10 steps out from the shadows to reveal that the Bear and another malleable marauder in the covert unit, the Blister Beetle, had instructed him not to contact me. The Bear was just being a bear, and blister beetles are known for the defensive secretion of a blistering agent, a toxicity designed, I suppose, to avoid confrontation. 'Things going on. You have to think of your own career.' In drink he finds courage, though when I wonder aloud if he asked exactly what the 'things going on' were, he has no reply, and I haven't the energy to enquire further. We both stare into our drinks.

I find myself in a 'fast-moving landscape', as senior management are apt to say. It transpires that the head of the Foxglove corruption inquiry has been demanding to meet with me for two years. Eventually Merseyside, in their own words, 'give up on the Met'. When they discover that criminal proceedings have been quietly dropped or, as my solicitor puts it, the 'police bail used to keep me hostage' has ceased, they move to challenge the Met and make direct contact with my solicitor. This has never been done before in such circumstances, an outside agency dismissing information supplied from another service.

We meet in central London, drinks in hand in a surreal reunion. When I ask who said I would not speak with them, I'm told it was the officers reviewing my continued suspension: the Egret and the Carrion Beetle. I learn that the dialogue between the two parties became so heated it culminated in a request for a formal presentation of the reasons for my sustained suspension. It was granted only after the intervention of the chief constable of Merseyside following a request by the head of Foxglove. The head and the Possum are candid when meeting me and my solicitor in disclosing the hurdles the DPS put in their path. That throughout my suspension they were repeatedly told by DPS officers dealing with my case that I wished neither to speak nor to meet with them 'in any circumstances'. This was a complete fabrication.

At the subsequent presentation, the DPS trot out the same tired allegations of alleged disciplinary offences: work files at home, the fantastical notion I'd used my UC status to secretly pay less council tax on my Grandma's old house. The Possum, as head of a large undercover department, rises to the challenge. Possums are well known as nocturnal marsupials, but here the head of the covert unit is determined to bring a bit of light to proceedings, not to mention Scouse grit. He makes it clear he regards it as nonsense regarding the house – his own officers had made use of it – and wonders aloud how they square the fact I had a cascaded phone line in my house, notebooks regarding the most secret covert operations, and indeed a secret and confidential training manual against their so-called 'disciplinary concerns'. At the conclusion of the briefing, the first time my case has been *independently* audited, they inform the Met they have no issues with my integrity, regard me 'as a witness of truth' and now intend to contact me directly.

In order to appear in control, DPS officers dealing with my case quickly instruct my divisional DCI to reach out to me quietly. I discover the Possum sent a statement to the DPS stating that my 'commitment, professionalism and conduct' during

Operation Foxglove were 'exemplary'. The DPS did not pass on the statement. Because it did not fit the narrative required, I suppose. They later claimed to have lost it.

Both sides find themselves in a fix. And Merseyside are keen for me to help them out of theirs. It was an officer from special branch, close to the Capuchin, who disclosed my identity, including the fact that I am an undercover officer currently suspended. They ask me to give evidence in Operation Foxglove, and I am trying to digest this when the Meerkat leans in and asks my solicitor, 'What have they done to him?' as if I am not there, but I am, and though strangely comforted by this, I say nothing, because at the same time, I am not there. I am trying to make sense of everything. You see, I am not saying the DPS officers were representative of the entire Met or, as things will transpire, all of the DPS, but 'they' were representative of a failed system (it is still failing) and of a group of self-absorbed individuals hell bent on protecting both it and certain people within it. I agree to give evidence in Operation Foxglove. I walk out from the meeting with Marv coating me in abuse.

'You fuckin' cunt! You should have fuckin' asked them what took them so long!'

'I did. They said why . . .'

'They are just fuckin' with you. They need you to help them. They don't give a fuck about you!'

'Shut it. Just fucking shut it!'

I walk through central London, Marv raging in my head. I turn off into an alleyway in Soho. I stop, face the wall and begin to headbutt it. To headbutt him. To make him stop.

'Shut up . . . Shut up . . . Shut up . . . Shut up.' I feel the blood trickle down my face. It's like childhood in Trawler Town.

A few weeks later, Liz and I begin our next course of IVF treatment. Every press of the hypodermic followed by a silent prayer – who to I couldn't say, because I lost my faith in the Bastard Borough, but I pray all the same. It's a game of ovary roulette, always with the nagging reminder that we win fuck-all in Trawler Town.

Liz and I get away from London for Christmas, up to the Yorkshire Dales to escape from everything. I find tranquillity in the landscape, though I'm not sure Liz does. When my own light, energy and motivation had begun to fade, Liz had suggested a dog for company. Into our life came a small West Highland terrier, Henry. He quickly became my best pal, because dogs never ever let you down, do they? Good listeners, dogs. He listens to Marv and me as we march across a hard-frosted dales landscape and Liz rests in the room. I wonder which of us Henry prefers, Marv or me?

Into Year Four now, with no change, no work, no purpose, no interest. Our IVF treatment is not successful. We can fund one more attempt. Depression grips tighter. In January of Year Four the Met's attempts to derail Merseyside's request to call me as a witness in their corruption case is in tatters. MPs Stephen Timms and Andy Burnham take a particular interest.

The Warbler is now heading up SO10. He seeks direction from the DPS. Four years have elapsed since my Merseyside deployment. Acknowledging all that has taken place and given my health, he perhaps realises I might need to prep for any hearing on Foxglove. Ever petty and truculent, the DPS inform him it is entirely his decision as to whether I have access to the secret undercover officers' NUTAC manual. He clearly has no issue with my integrity, as he bobs it in the post! I've worked cases in the past where free transit mail has been intercepted by criminals, but the head of the largest covert unit in the UK decides it is fine to trust the secret undercover policing manual to the post box. What could possibly go wrong? Fortunately for him, nothing, and it arrives. I stare at the pages of the NUTAC manual, reading words I no longer feel connection with.

On a bitter winter morning I head out of London towards Liverpool. It feels good to be leaving as sleet lathers the carriage windows. I hope I find a little winter sun in the north to brighten the mood. I am only making this journey because the officers from Merseyside did not buy the Met's façade, and I don't buy into Marv's *'too late, fuck them all'*. By now they are aware of the DPS's offer in Year One for me to be their inside man, and the Badger, my cover man on Foxglove, offers a suggestion: 'They had to box you off after that, lad.' He meant silence me. He was right, but why? The assumption can only be that it was to prevent me from being called as a witness in any trial, disciplinary hearing or anything else that might challenge the DPS, who by now are coming increasingly under external scrutiny. As I stare out of the train window, I am not thinking of the Machiavellian workings of the top brass but what awaits me in the north.

What should clearly have been a corruption trial for the Capuchin has now boiled down to a disciplinary board, but they still require me to attend and be present in the city, ready to give evidence. A game of brinkmanship is playing out between Merseyside's own corruption inquiry team and one of its principal targets. I sit in the middle, or rather in a hotel near the waterfront; there is no sunlight, only grey mist.

The Badger, who is with me throughout, looks to lift my mood by reminding me of what initiated their corruption probe, the threat to a serving officer's life, and how they'd harried the Met to speak to me, never giving up. I like him a lot, but is he worried I'm contemplating walking out of the door? I'm not. I'm simply staring out at the redundant docks. If I intended to burn their operation, I could have done so years earlier by shouting about it the moment I was suspended. I didn't because I always believed I was coming back – not once did I betray my office.

The well-intentioned pep talk lifts neither of us. I think we have both come to realise the true measure of Copland. He's counting down the years to retirement; I'm just counting the number of days of my liquefaction. The Merseyside covert unit arranges a meal, a social get-together with some of the people I've worked with, a show of solidarity, again supportive, but it does me no good – the reverse, in fact. Cops talking shop, and stories of how busy they are, is the last thing I need to hear.

The last thing the Capuchin wants to hear, though, is the news that I have arrived in Liverpool. When this is confirmed, he accepts all charges against him. It was all a play; the information he had been given and thought would assist him, supplied by someone who is never revealed nor explored beyond the initial disclosure, led to a belief I would not attend. The last thing he wanted was me giving evidence. I have a coffee with my cover man the following day before I leave.

'Fuckin' jungle down there, lad. Wouldn't trust them with the steam off my piss.' Many years have passed since Ron suggested the same during basic training, and by now I am on the floor mentally.

I arrive back home in London as sleet still colours the city grey. Almost immediately Liz and I trudge off to another hospital appointment. We failed the postcode lottery for NHS treatment – this is it: our last roll. Dice. Needle. Hope. Wait.

It is now a time of whispers at all the favoured watering holes in the Copland jungle. And from within this world of smoke and mirrors, a conversation finds its way to me. The Dassie, hearing of our unsuccessful IVF treatments, made a crass remark that puts me in a spin and finally I snap. No more, not from this organisation, and not from him. You want a reason to get rid of me, I'll give you one right here and now, on the button nose of the Dassie, in front of his petrified cronies hopefully. After four years of isolation, my mind is a disturbed slurry. I decide to confront this pathetic excuse of a senior officer, push his buttons. If he swings first, I'll beat the holy crap out of the God's-work bully.

It is a pathetic and ridiculous idea. Whisper, whisper, whisper, goes Marv, encouraging, a broken, rattled detective travelling on the underground rattler for a reckoning. It's a dreary, cold mizzle of a night, bleak. A four-year winter. The pub I'm told he will be at, supping at others' expense, seems welcoming and warm as I peer in. A few cops are huddled together in animated conversation. No sign of him, so I wait outside, walk around the block to keep warm. Should have worn gloves – my hands are freezing. I've been here before, I think. When I get back to the pub, he still hasn't turned up; the Dassie is busy balancing his spinning plates.

As I shelter in a doorway opposite the pub, a car approaches, a driver and two passengers in the back. It's a 'job' car, a commander's 'perk' that comes complete with driver. He's not yet a commander, but he could be inside, feeling the velour and dreaming – one day soon. There is no sense or rationale behind my plan. The car crawls to a halt outside the pub, lamplit with precision for the show about to start – please, *please* let it be him. If it's true, let him repeat his thoughts on our attempts to start a family to my face, and if it isn't, I don't care. I jog across the road, not pausing to check if it's clear. I hear the horn blast first then the angry shout from the driver.

'You blind? Dickhead!' The van ploughs on into the night as I cross.

I look up to see the bony outline of the Egret, a rare sighting in the jungle. *'He'll do, that fuckin' coward.'*

I'm in the right place. The Egret is still supposedly writing the detailed monthly reports required to justify my suspension. He glances right through me before striding keenly into the pub with his female companion. As Egret's car inches forward to re-join the traffic, I notice two underlined words scratched in winter grime on the vehicle's rear. Someone has scrawled 'Cunt inside'. All clearly not rosy within the ivory towers.

I stare again through the pub window, cold and wet; I should be home with Liz. What the fuck am I doing here? This is not me, a rudderless Trawler Town boy lost in the dark. Have I really travelled no distance at all? A blind dickhead *'and a cunt'*, according to Marv – it ought to raise a smile. It doesn't. I head home, cold to the bone.

The IVF prayer goes unanswered. I knew it would. The light in Liz fades further and I don't know how to fix it. A few days later she comes home from work to find me wandering around with my hand stuck to the top of my head. It is a strange tic that had started that same morning.

'I know it looks weird, but I can't stop it.' I can't explain why I'm becoming increasingly agitated. Shut up, Marv, just fucking STOP TALKING! It's too late to introduce Marv to Liz, I fear. I hope patting my head will shut him up him – it doesn't.

That evening I end up in A&E, babbling incoherently about the incident in Merseyside with the gun and about loyalty, family and life.

And so Year Four ends with admission to a psychiatric clinic near Windsor, even though I insist I just need some sleep. Sandwiched between the forgotten margins of Slough and the conspicuous riches of Eton, the geographic paradox of the clinic is matched by the reality inside. There is a mix of patients: working class, captains of industry, breakdowns and bust-ups, the battered (literally in some cases) and the washed up on the tide, all housed in relatively comfortable surroundings, despite the relentless vigour of the treatment. It is a good clinic, with a talent for 'mending mentals', as one patient later tells me, a factory worker who sees me as a potential ally.

I am shown to a room, given a sedative and instantly fall sleep. For days it seems, maybe even weeks. I've never known sleep like it, so deep that I can feel my body recalibrating, regaining equilibrium. When I come round properly, weeks later, I am certain of one thing only, which is that I should not be here. Not with these dribbling idiots – they clearly need help, but not me. I just needed rest. This flimsy contempt is simply masking my fear.

A repair of sorts takes place in an eclectic collective of wonderful humanity. The psychiatric nurse who works with me is always calm, telling me stories of the Caribbean and demonstrating the patience of a saint. My consultant, imprisoned by a dictator when he was a young man, has the wisdom of one who has seen much. He flips my love of film like a coin to begin our discussions, gaining my trust. The psychotherapist I work with has Welsh roots and a keen ear, the spit of Auntie Kath in looks and disposition. I expect her to rustle up an Oxo cube and tell me the soup will make me better. I feel guilty that I never said goodbye to Aunt Kath, a boy always on the move, never looking back. I'm fortunate to have such care in the clinic but still refuse to accept that I am ill, because if I do, I know I will never work as an undercover detective again. The Bear's words follow me like Marley's ghost: 'Don't tell them what's *really* in your head . . . not if you want to keep working.'

But sleep? That, at least, I do accept, even if I am otherwise feigning acceptance of the treatment. I avoid purgatory, as I call group therapy, scared I might catch whatever virus it reveals: Trawler Town-rooted embarrassment that this is who I have become. Only when I'm told it's unlikely I'll be discharged until I participate in group therapy do I attend the daily torture, sitting in silence, dead cod eyes, at a loss to comprehend why anybody would speak openly in such a forum. Not Marv – he fucking loves it.

'Are you serious! You can't cope with that? What's wrong with you? Shit happens then you die. I'll tell you a fuckin' secret: I've not had a boner in weeks. Sure as shit it's the medication that cow's giving me at night.'

My eyes dart over to the matron and back before she catches me – too late. I stare out of the window – that's real. What's out there? Focus on that. Brain brother's raging monologues continue while I sit on my hands. If they knew what went on inside on my head, I'd never get out. But they don't, they have no idea, and best it stays that way.

Despite their efforts, I make little progress. You have to engage and accept that you need the help. It's only a matter of time before I begin to tap at my head again.

After two months, I'm discharged. The private healthcare policy will not go further at this point but I feel rested, strong, an army of one again. I realise I wasn't in there as a patient – you see, it wasn't a psychiatric clinic, it was a training camp. Sound the bell, brother Marv, because I am good to go again. LET'S GET REEAADY TOOO RUMMMMMBLLLE! Marv is ecstatic, dancing on his toes – he loves a fight.

The deniable detective is off the stool quickly. Boy, does he mean business. Straight into the fray, centre of the ring, working the body of the monolithic Met. Trawler Town Boy lands early, the way he was taught, his jab banging away. This will surely not go the distance! He looks fresh, full of vim, up for a fight. Boom! He lands a tremendous right, several officers stepping forward to make statements exposing the sham behind the discipline case against him. Bang! A thunderous hook as he reveals a senior officer and key author behind his treatment is being investigated for domestic violence, fraud and deception. Boof! A crunching uppercut to the chin of the undisputed champion of brand management as he accuses two named senior officers of falsifying monthly suspension reports. This fight surely will not go all the way. He continues to dance, middle of the ring, as the independent psychiatric consultant appointed by the Met reveals he was the subject of pressure as the DPS sought to influence and mould his 'independent' report. Bang! A thunderous hook as he steps inside and speaks outside of the police family to journalists about a police scandal of their own making. A corporate cover-up. But no, the monolith fights back. Trawler Town Boy's punches

*are not connecting . . . Perhaps they really are all in his head . . . At least
that's what his opponent would have you believe. It doesn't matter. He doesn't
hear the bell, which has long since sounded, signalling the end of this fight . . .*

Is anybody listening? . . . I guess not. I begin to doubt my sanity. My worth. I stop punching. I stop everything – dressing, eating, sleeping, Liz. This is it, my lowest point. The following month, my consultant advises that I should be urgently readmitted to the clinic. Defeat: they have won. Liz is to take me there, but I persuade her to visit after work, telling her that I need to go in by myself, to avoid goodbyes, to get on with it. It's true to a degree, but I'm not going back, not there. I'm not admitting to the humiliation of not being able to cope. I set off towards the clinic but remember nothing of the journey, arriving 300 miles in the opposite direction, in the Lake District.

I have no idea why, in fading November light, wearing unsuitable clothing, I attempt to walk up to the summit of Skiddaw. When I give up and eventually head back down, I can't find the car and end up sleeping rough. I am completely off-grid. I find the car a few days later while walking, which is now my sole purpose. Endless walking, marching, all I am capable of. Mind spinning, drilling down deep, trying to find a way to expose the past four years of abuse for rejecting the chance to be another kind of spy. Working it out, me and *him*, as I march, in my ear goading, cajoling, whispering. Marv – brother, friend, enemy, nemesis – telling me in plain, dockside terms, what a useless cunt I am, how weak I am, that I should have found the Dassie and landed one on his duplicitous chin, but I bottled it. I have both argued against and agreed with Marv all my life, his dialogue the necessary antistatic to dissipate the sound of disappointment.

But not now. I can't reason with him or even respond. I can only listen as he subjects me to a relentless barrage that exposes my complete inadequacy. He should work for the DPS – perhaps he does.

When he's done, finally, I do have a plan, his plan. I decide to quit everything, to kill myself, because at least then someone will listen to me, and I won't have to listen to Marv any more. Just maybe, if I die, somebody will take a careful look at the big beasts through a small lens. This is a game of roulette, Pa, you can win.

When I get back behind the wheel of my car, having made my decision, I am both possessed and free. In the winding country roads, I floor the accelerator, hurtling through shadows and around Lakeland peaks, ridiculous speeds. The many driving courses the state sent me on are incapable of keeping the car on the road. I push the Mini beyond its limits and feel the back of it slip away.

So, this will do, I think, caressing the steering wheel in antici-pation, no care of consequences, no thought for others. Maybe it is the shock as the car goes into a full spin that jolts me back to reality, and maybe it is me, not Marv, who suddenly realises that this is not the way. This is how I later justify it to myself, but in reality I couldn't give a fuck, believing everyone is better off with-out me.

I restart the engine and drive to the nearest town, checking into a B&B. By breakfast the next morning, after another night of conversation, I have a better plan. Across the small, homely dining room, sitting opposite, is a police officer – I am sure of it. At the time, I don't recognise him, but he is in the job all right. I may have something, someone else, in my head, but I have it still, the skillset. I catch his eye, take out a pen. While staring at him, never taking my eyes off him, I write on my forearm the words *Police officer* with an arrow. I raise my forearm, and he returns to his breakfast. It could be fantasy, existing only in my head. Later, when the police disclose 'a sighting' when concerned for my safety, I decide that it wasn't. Not concerned enough to save me from myself. Still concerned for the reputation of others.

I leave the B&B immediately and cut across country to the Yorkshire Dales. I park up and begin to walk loops around Hubberholme. It's where Liz and I came to escape London. This is the place to do it, and I realise I know this is the best plan because it was all foretold – it is even, perhaps, a message from my past.

When huge swathes of London were still affordable to the many, I traded my first home, a small apartment, for a small house, the same house where years later the DPS informed my tenant I was an undercover detective. The house to which Liz and I had recently returned. I had lived there only a few months when I was called to an incident several doors along the street. I never forget what unfolded, and as I march around the dales, I realise I was never meant to. This is why I believe everything is linked, I say to Marv, who is now strangely silent, his job done. As a detective in the Bastard Borough, a colleague, a detective sergeant, was sent to a house in my street, called in by uniform. The Frilled Lizard is a good man but a terrible detective. He was certain it was foul play. The deceased, newly married to a doctor, had been found dead inside her car in the integral garage. I had recently passed the sergeant's promotion exam and as I sat at my desk, the DI wandered out from his office explaining the Frilled Lizard needed a hand.

'Sounds a load of bollocks, this. He's off on one. Go take a look, would you? There's bound to be a suicide note somewhere.'

The house was only a hundred metres from my own and was the same in every way save for the fact mine had a small spit of a garden, a place to sit and wave at the freight train drivers as they trundled past, to and from the vast Ford car plant in Dagenham. A one-bedroom town house, with all life taking place above the garage, but not today.

You get used to death in the police, of course – its presence, its proximity – but never the bodies, or rather the faces. They linger. Decades on, I still see the faces of those who passed. I suspect most cops do.

Earlier that morning, I had walked past the house on my way to work. A glorious blue sky over a new street, full of youth and hope. In the garage, lying across the front seats of a small saloon car, a woman. As if she was asleep. There were a few soft toys for company, all neat and tidy. Her face was flecked by the discordant discolouration of suicide. Carbon monoxide binding to haemoglobin to create a mask of mottled purples and blues.

Captain Chaos the Frilled Lizard stumbled into the garage, pointing to a vacuum cleaner hose running from the exhaust pipe to the cabin and expounding his theory while a uniformed officer of many years' experience rolled his eyes. It seemed to me a suicide, as plain as this warm spring day. But he was adamant there was no suicide note. I walked through the house, familiarity at odds with reality. I didn't know my neighbour – I didn't know any of my neighbours in all my time in the police. I found the suicide note secreted in her bedroom, more soft toys guarding, pointing to its location. I read the note before placing it in an exhibit bag as a loud knock at the door revealed news she was recently married – the best man had arrived with the wedding album.

Now, staring into a pint in a pub overlooking a Norman church, I can't stop thinking about this young woman. It occurs to me that the reason is clear. A short walk from the pub, along an access road, there is an old barn. I will hide the car there and finish it. I write a suicide note inside the pub, borrowing a pen. It's red ink. I don't think it should be written in red. I had a pen, I tell the barman but . . . He looks at the unshaven oddball oddly. I don't finish the sentence, realising for the first time in years I feel totally free, liberated from the tyranny of the Met and . . . Marv. I put the note inside a small road atlas in the seat lining of the car – the best place for the note to be, an atlas. I drive to Skipton market to buy a suitable hose. It's market day, and halfway along the market, on one of the stalls, a variety of suitable hoses that bob on the breeze. I select one and a roll of gaffer tape. When I go to pay, I have no wallet. I must have left it behind in the B&B. I stutter and try to copper up enough change as Marv gives it to me. I don't have enough money – I really am useless. I sit down in a nearby café, having at least enough shrapnel for a cup of tea. Utterly despondent, a tear forms. I clamp my jaw, suck it back into my skull. *'You will not fuckin' embarrass yourself!'*

I don't how long I have been sitting there, talking with Marv – well, listening to him – when an older woman, laden with shopping, gets up, moves across the café and sits across from me. Eventually she picks up my mug of stone-cold tea, takes it to the counter and returns with a fresh one, pushing it gently towards me. She sits quietly, occasionally smiling, and stays until a younger woman appears outside the café. She leans across and squeezes my arm, smiles, and leaves with the girl outside. Not one word passes between us. Is it the kindness of this stranger that changes my direction? Probably. There was not a peep from Marv as she sat quietly beside me.

I leave the Yorkshire Dales and head south. At some point, I abandon the car, continuing south on foot, and arrive in sight of HMS *Dolphin*, the base where I did my basic submariner training. I do not know why I am here, so I keep moving on. Eventually, several days later, the police are called by a worried cashier in a building society. I went in to keep warm. I have now been missing for over two weeks. In this time the DPS have sent a letter suggesting that if I am unwell, I might consider resigning. When it becomes clear that I am missing, senior officers, I later learn, engage in a frenetic blame game, concerned how things might play out.

Back at the building society, police arrive, and I spend a few hours with a local sergeant. I don't recall what we speak about, but my solicitor tells me later that they had offered to drive me back to London and the clinic, but the Met had asked them not to. A car is sent from London by the Met to take me to the clinic. When I leave, the sergeant makes a point of telling me in front of the collecting officers that he has made a full record of our discussion and asks my solicitor to make a formal request for a copy of his notes. The notes were lost, it is later claimed. I sit in the car back to London, empty, exhausted. When I arrive at the clinic, Liz, who is waiting for me, bursts into tears, at my appearance I think, but that's not the reason. I don't realise the scale of the toll the last four years have taken on her. We are damaged. We will never be the same.

Nursed and Ratcheted

When I wake up, after sleeping for most of the first week, it is as a different man. I accept I need to be here in the clinic. A slow process of learning to trust the staff and clinicians begins. This time I listen to other patients with respect, empathy. This time I take my medication willingly, answer questions, take on board suggestions, attempt to implement the changes suggested. I demonstrate a willingness to speak about my childhood, my relationship with Ma and Pa and the two families, one blood, one blue, both united in betrayal. I exercise with the other patients, not to better become an army of one but to become whole again. I'm curious as to what brought others here, and I listen without prejudice to their stories and, occasionally, try to explain insofar as I understand myself why it is I find myself here. It is not easy – there are setbacks, resistance and, of course, Marv, who visits with ideas that would likely set me back not free if I listened to them. But there are breakthroughs, progress, small steps that move me towards the gates and home.

Several weeks in, I finally attend 'group' and, surprisingly, feel *present*, though at times it feels like swimming in the dry salt of tears. It's a different kind of pain. I still sit mute, unable to share personal insight as to why I am in such a forum, but neither do I sit in judgement and, over time, nor does *he*. *We* listen, absorb the process, the experiences detectives routinely push away for fear they may be contagious. Over the weeks my psychiatrist nudges me towards more personal participation, though it is not something I embrace easily.

The key for me is still to focus on the space outside the windows, using the world outside to protect the world inside. Reality is out there, and one day it seeps into the room. Something said in the circle strikes a chord, and I hear words emerge from me. I have no idea from where, or why now, but out they tumble, unfettered, all prompted by another person struggling to stay afloat. I talk about my sense of failure as a man, a husband and a detective. The acute sense of loss and failure in the gruelling IVF process, never truly believing it would work out for us, never able to share this. Then come memories that haunt me: the death of an officer whose family was extraordinarily kind to the naive Trawler Town boy in his first year in London. It was the Llama, the sergeant who bamboozled the Jogger, convincing him of my 'Turrets syndrome'. I'd bumped into him years later at Crown Court, and he asked if I had time for a beer. I said no, rushing off to prepare for a deployment and a meeting with an informant.

I promised to call him as he pushed his number into my hand. And I saw the look behind the smile and the jokes – I saw it and I ignored it. I didn't call him. Too busy being a failure, just another tired detective chasing rainbows, because in reality all this was nothing more than lip service. The informant didn't show. The job was under-resourced and overhyped. This was the future. A month later, I heard of his suicide. A few weeks afterwards, I attended his funeral in shame. Because what I saw that day was pain. It was plain enough to see, but still I headed for the door, chasing glory and afraid of something I didn't understand.

In the coming months, with the help of the medical staff, I do begin to slowly understand and engage with the narrative of the past. As Year Four comes to a close, I have at least made some progress, no longer spinning alone in a vortex of darkness, even if I'm not exactly filled with enthusiasm for what the intermittent shards of light reveal. One day, walking in the grounds, nearing the end of my treatment, a patient tells me another cop has bounded into the clinic as if on a 'weekend jolly', announcing to all he is a senior police officer. Good luck to him, I think. You're in the right place, mate. But I don't speak to him – I avoid him. I've come too far to fall back. I am discharged after four months in the clinic and become a day patient.

A new welfare officer is assigned to me by my old division, a newly promoted chief inspector, the fourth DCI to take over the division and whom I soon discover is mentored by the Dassie. His connection to the Dassie surely ought to disqualify him from acting as my welfare officer, given I have by now named the Dassie as one of the four key facilitators of my unlawful continued suspension, not only in reports to the Police Federation but also to solicitors and others. Yet I'm feeling more positive. Maybe it is just another coincidence, and he strikes me as not being entirely happy with the situation himself.

Since leaving the clinic I have been told off the record, by two sources from the Met and Merseyside, that I will soon be reinstated and promoted. I'm digesting all of this while walking through central London, having been called to a meeting with my solicitor, when I am surprised to bump into the police officer who a few weeks earlier I had been keen to avoid in the clinic. Small world, Copland, and a big jungle. And while I think it 'a bit odd', I know recovery is dependent on not hiding from emotions but confronting them, and I'm still on strong medication, so I shake the hand of my clinic alumni, the Salamander.

I feel I ought to explain that I too am a police officer. What I don't know at the time is that the Salamander is a Met superintendent. We speak at length, and I later realise that while I did not ask him about his job, he seemed particularly interested in me and my suspension. I gave him a précised history. Two incapacitated individuals sharing war stories? Not really – it was more one-sided. During our conversation I mentioned that it seemed clear to me that at least two senior officers involved in my case were guilty of disciplinary, if not criminal, offences. He asked me their names, which I volunteered, and we parted company, but not before giving me two contact numbers should I wish to talk further.

Perhaps it's the medication, perhaps it's the grapevine gossip indicating that I will be reinstated, but as I compute all this and this 'chance' meeting, I hear faint whispers as I walk through Green Park. Marv may be anaesthetised, but he's not dead.

A few days later, all disciplinary matters are withdrawn with immediate effect. I am reinstated and finally get my warrant card back. I am still signed off sick after my time in the clinic, so it might not be the moment for celebration just yet, but I feel that one day soon it will be. I accept I'm not 100 per cent fit and well, but I believe I will be one day.

The following month, I'm surprised to be told I am required

to undergo a further examination with a consultant psychiatrist employed by the Met. He'd first examined me during my initial admission to the clinic. Liz accompanies me, and at the second examination he reveals attempts to influence his original findings, that he was pressured to 'tailor his report' and was 'told off' for some of the comments he made in it. As the consultation progresses, following a casual observation from Liz about my reinstatement, he stops abruptly, stating that he feels in danger of being professionally embarrassed and that he has been misled by those instructing him. He immediately calls a halt to the consultation, and in our presence calls the senior clinician in the Met's occupational health department. With his full agreement, Liz makes a contemporaneous record of the subsequent conversation. And that's when I realise it really is over, I am never going back. I'm out, out of the back door, being medically retired, even with all action against me having been dropped.

'He's not well, you know. Best get rid of the fucker . . . before he returns an internal terrorist and fucks us all in the arse!' Hello, Marv, my old friend.

The next month I'm told I'm to be awarded a medal at a ceremony conducted by the new commissioner, the Hercules Moth. The medal is for 'long service and good conduct'. The letter drops as I am heading out the door with Henry the Westie to the meadows. I recognise the postmark, already know what it contains.

Maybe I'll read it a few miles in, by the river, or maybe over a coffee in town, contemplating what to do with the rest of my life. Our Kid is due to arrive today, and he wants a bath. He doesn't have one in his rented flat, so I've told him to come and soak for as long as he wants. Maybe I'll wait until he arrives.

'You will not fucking believe this, fella,' says a former colleague who has heard the news and calls before the letter arrives. The thing is, actually, I would. See, I'd believe anything by now, and maybe that's the best thing to do. Accept everything with a smile. As Henry carpet bombs the meadow with Westie pee, I sit by the river and open the letter. A starburst of joy and glad tidings leaps off the page.

'The Commissioner cordially invites you to a special ceremony where you can be presented with your prestigious award and where we can thank you for the service you have given the Metropolitan Police and the people of London.'

It may be over, I may feel numb, but I'm not dumb, and even the medication cannot fully stifle *his* whispers.

'A superintendent just rocks up to the clinic you happen to be in, not a police-affiliated facility, no other cop has ever been admitted there, but here he is!'

'Don't! I don't fucking care!'

'You fuckin' do, because you fuckin' know what lengths they will go to shut you down.'

'You shut up. Shut Up!' Sometimes, with me and Marv, I feel I'm the child and he's the man. And I hate him for it.

'You're nothing to them. Just another cunt to fuck over before a different narrative sees the light of day . . . And . . . You . . . Let . . . Them . . . Do . . . It!'

'They're quite strong, the tablets I'm giving you. We will need to adjust them in time,' said my psychiatrist when I'd asked about the medication I was taking. I couldn't bring myself to explain why I was asking, that I hoped they might in time silence Marv, for good. The inner bruv that now seems to only torment. But then again, I really ought to have listened to him, to Marv. The coincidences become just a little too convenient. I learn that the Salamander stayed only briefly in the clinic before heading back to his job, which is staff officer to the deputy commissioner, the Peacock Butterfly.

The Peacock Butterfly will in time take over the crown from the Hercules Moth, who in turn took over from the Cabbage White, his wings having taken him to the House of Lords, long the favoured habitat that our moths and butterflies colonise when leaving the jungle. A reward, one might argue. But for now, the Peacock's wings cover the overall charge of the DPS and, indeed, all disciplinary matters. Funny old world. Funny old business. And of course nor is this is the whole picture. There are other salient factors at play. Because to some degree, I am now guilty as charged – that is to say, an internal terrorist. You see, my whistleblowing was not limited to informing the Federation solicitors of my offer to become a UC for the DPS. But before any of this can be understood – medal, retirement, God's work – I am called back to Trawler Town.

Funerals

I'm going to invite Pa to the medal ceremony, but his heart finally throws in the towel, having gone into hospital for another round of surgery. The old fighter hoped he would be good to go again, aiming for at least another decade – he could always take a punch – but this time, the count is final. His death, as with much of his life, comes with little warning. One minute here, filling the room, laughing with the medical team, then gone. But was he ever really here?

At 5.15 in the morning, five days after surgery for a second coronary bypass, a nurse finds Pa slumped down in his chair beside his bed, as if waiting for a visitor. I hear the news as I cross London en route to the hospital. I listen in silence, Stepmother's eldest daughter the messenger. I ask to have time alone with him. I don't know why, but I need to be alone with him.

He lies in an austere side room, a thin sheet over him. No warmth in that, I think, as I close the door behind me. I have no words, or tears, but seeing him I let out a primeval roar, a torrent of sound that bounces off the walls, fills the room, every decibel a lament to lost opportunity and crushing reality. To this day, I have no explanation for it. It was simply a reflex action, as if I had no choice.

I place my hand on his. Other than the trip to the fishing widow's house, I don't remember ever holding his hand as a child. We sit together in silence, as we had done for the most part. It's all too much to take in. After a while, I rise to leave and kiss him on the forehead – it's still warm, his hand ice-cold. 'Goodbye, Popsicle,' I say. 'Safe journey'. No time for more words, no time to start again. In the aftermath of his death, there will be more surprises: the discovery of the true extent of his affair with a family friend and a final parting.

When his will was made, Our Kid and Bruv were both on periodic walkabouts, estranged from the family, it being our way. Thus both were excluded, along with two of Stepmother's daughters, for reasons unclear in a family that doesn't do clarity. Pa and Stepmother had awkwardly and solemnly declared that my youngest stepsister and I would be 'executives, love'. It was the only conversation I ever had regarding formal family matters. The reality was that only one son would ever likely need financial help, however small: Our Kid. The silent one. For years, he had been slipping slowly under the glassy surface of depression. A proud, working-class man, lost in a new age of austerity. I believed that Pa would in time be persuaded to remove me as a beneficiary in place of Our Kid, but that time never came.

Stepmother has no interest in rectifying the error now. The morning after his funeral, I arrive at the house with the intention of having that conversation, but it becomes clear that Stepmother is determined to punish Pa for his frailties and infidelity. There is a new will, I'm told, and a new purpose: she plans to sell up and move in with her favourite daughter.

As I digest everything, a weathered supermarket bag is thrust forward.

'I thought you might like these, a few of his things.'

It contains an odd selection: Grandpa's old penknife, which Pa always kept in his pocket, two pairs of rusting cufflinks that might have also been Grandpa's a pair of photographs of him in Malta with Grandma and Grandpa, the order of service and a receipt showing that the last time the bag was used purposely it was to carry two Frey Bentos steak and kidney pies, half-a-dozen eggs, milk, a jar of pickled gherkins and a tube of haemorrhoid cream. He would have chuckled at that and denied any knowledge of the cream. No sight nor mention of the garish pinky ring he said many times with pride would be mine, as I nodded awkwardly, knowing I'd never wear it, but still. The next time I see the ring will be years later, on an episode of *The X Factor*. It will come as no surprise. Perfectly normal in the abnormal family. And none of this matters, because all I really want to do is go up to his room and spend a bit of time looking in his wardrobe.

For 30 years, I had bought him a tie at Christmas, birthdays, celebrations. It became our thing. He kept them all, hung on tie racks I'd also bought him when Stepmother had complained he had too many, a conspiratorial wink to say, 'Keep them coming, son.' Whatever it was, it was *our* thing. Each tie spoke in a way of our relationship at the precise time of purchase. A few ties from his life, such as it was, would have been nice – shared moments from our past – but Stepmother is keen to kick on quickly. So I do the same. I walk out of the house and never go back. It was the right thing to do. No regrets.

I suggest to Our Kid he should not do the same, not cut off

contact, because by now, though he won't admit to it, it's clear he suffered some form of breakdown too. I hope Stepmother will eventually understand his vulnerability, but she is out of the blocks quickly, planning her new life and consumed by rage and grief, altogether a different kettle of fish in Trawler Town. Within months, he too leaves for good. 'Don't feel welcome, our kid. I'm not bothered. It's all over now anyway.' And so it was.

A month later, a few weeks from retirement, I am at Hendon Police College for the medal ceremony. Liz and I have by now moved away from London to an old stone town in the Midlands – peaceful, slow in pace. A suitable place to rest and mend, we hope, though only half of the plan will be achieved. Pa's ashes still warm, Our Kid slipping slowly down a hole, and Liz and I deluding ourselves we have survived intact, papering over cracks that begin to appear in our relationship, convinced all will be well, but it won't. Our scars burn rather than heal.

Marv sees the cordial invitation as an opportunity to toss a match into the rags that oil the machine and, for a few days, I agree with him. My thought process erratic, the moment the Hercules Moth pins the medal on my chest I will remove it and throw it into the auditorium, or skim it across the hall like the pebbles I threw across the sea as a child, unable to think of any better way to express my anger and frustration. Three skims and everything will be better. Back then, sometimes it was. But I am an adult now, and I don't want to have someone's eye out, so perhaps I'll simply refuse it and tell the audience why. I sit by the river and consider the most appropriate way to tell the commissioner of the

Metropolitan Police to shove his medal up whatever the arse of a Hercules moth is called. Do they have one?

Back and forth, the nonsense in my head begins again, because for all my treatment, nothing is more guaranteed to set me back than contact with the Met – even if it is to present me with a medal. On the morning of the ceremony, I'm still in two minds whether to attend. As those two minds bicker, I decide I will go, and Marv decides if we do, he will 'stick one on' the commissioner – get his attention, like. The sort of thing Pa would have said in any given situation: 'Keep up that behaviour and I'll stick one on you.'

LET'S GET REEEEAAAAADY TO RUUUUMM-MBBLLLLE!

'You sure you want to do this?'

'What's that?' Missing Liz's question entirely.

'London?'

'Yes, yes I do.' I don't say that I'm not sure which part of me will prevail – I simply don't know. But by the time I arrive at Hendon, I am certain I won't demean myself or the occasion, even though in my head either option makes perfect sense, all things considered. Perhaps with that in mind, and perhaps finally with the intention to speak with my own voice, the morning we are due to leave for London I sit down and write a letter addressed to the commissioner. It seems to me the Hercules Moth is cut from an entirely different cloth to that of his predecessor, the Cabbage White. The letter is raw, filled with pain and emotion. It begins, *'Whilst fully aware of why I am entitled to this award, the pride I ought to feel is replaced by an acute sense of despair . . .'* I write about the length of my suspension, and the brutality of it, stating that I believe the action of a few within the DPS constituted disciplinary if not criminal offences.

'You have blocked every attempt to bring this small group to account and allowed my career to be needlessly destroyed. I weep at the memory of the suffering you allowed my family to endure and the damage you inflicted on a service I was proud to serve.'

The ceremony is a strictly choreographed affair, and frankly just as well, given the mad debate that took place in my head in the run-up – at one point I considered stripping off and walking on stage naked, or wearing a wetsuit, mask, snorkel and flippers. *'But then where would you keep the letter, you cunt?'* Marv points out helpfully. In the end, I opt for a jacket and tie.

I sip tea with Liz and watch the crowd. There are a lot of people in attendance – the good and the not so. I see them all, smiling, glad to be somewhere else for the day. For the most part, I too wish I was somewhere else. But as I take my seat, something strange happens – an officer I do not recognise, or at least cannot recall, taps me on the shoulder. He clearly knows me, but I'm flustered, not remembering his name or where we met. What is wrong with me?

'I'm glad you made it. You deserve this. Fuck 'em.' 'Fuck 'em,' he repeats. I smile back at him. 'A lot of people know what happened to you. Least you're back . . . They're here, you know?'

'No . . . I'm not back. I'm retired, I . . . They?' His wife and Liz smile. I suspect they are both thinking, this job, *the job*, it really isn't worth it.

He was talking about the DPS. I can't see them. I'm not looking. I don't know what to say. I feel lost. Why don't I recognise him? The noise in the room from those assembled is a form of painful static, scratching at my brain. I used to be so good at this, listening, filtering several conversations at once, a kind of reverse ventriloquism, a skill that the very best have.

'You weren't the very best.'

'No, no . . . but I could have been.' Marv doesn't answer. I always hated that.

Yes! I fucking could have been, I was, I was . . . FUCKING ANSWER ME!

'You okay?' whispers Liz, seeing the strain on my face.

'He wouldn't have recognised you in a wetsuit, you cunt . . .'

'Yes, I'm fine.' I smile. *He* is here. It's only right – we've come a long way together. Not all bad, eh? The officer checks I'm okay too. I suddenly remember we worked together. Perhaps everything is going to be okay. The slick PR exercise begins and before long I am being ushered towards the stage.

Ahead of me, a stiff Hercules Moth goes through the motions. I'm up next. Maybe I'm hyped up, but as I walk towards him, I sense a ripple in the room – if not unease, anticipation perhaps. I look him straight in the eye as I stand waiting to go on stage. What could I now do, this close, after all the needless suffering? I'm completely present. I hear Pa in my ears: 'You're a big man but you're in bad shape . . .' How many times did we watch *Get Carter* together, each time a different reading. He would have . . . I hear my name called.

'Go on, stick one on him and tell everyone why . . .'

'Shake the commissioner's hand and then smile towards the camera,' says a minion, interrupting Marv. I feel anger rising from the pit of my stomach, hatred even. In a few years' time, the minion's boss will be forced to resign as head of the Met's multimillion-pound communications department, following an inquiry by the Independent Police Complaints Commission (IPCC), rather than face a case of gross misconduct over the award of a PR contract. The Hercules Moth smiles and shapes to pin the medal to my lapel. I keep my eyes fixed eyes on him. A stillness settles across the vast hall, at odds with the moment. I feel it.

Hercules's smile broadens. He calls me by my first name as his arm rests on my suit lapel, my own coming up quickly across his arm, locking it across my chest.

The eyes always give it away: when you disturb the environment, the person in the mix knows something is off. His eyes now widen with uncertainty. As his arm is momentarily pinned to my chest, I reach inside my jacket pocket withdraw the envelope and offer it to him.

'How are you? Is this a Christmas card?'

'Please read the letter. It's more important than this.'

He takes it and slips it effortlessly into his tunic.

'I will . . . Would you like a cup of tea together, and a chat?' he asks. And at that, all the rage and anger dissipate. There is genuine warmth in his voice – briefly, I believe him. Maybe my judgement was right. I re-join Liz and tell her what is about to happen.

An officer I have not seen since my time at West End Central taps me on the shoulder. 'Well done, Captain. That got everybody's attention.'

Him simply taking the letter, cracking a joke, doesn't feel like something to celebrate, but I'll take the offer of tea and a chance to talk. The Hercules Moth is due to mingle with all the recipients. Liz and I wait for our private meeting. We wait, and we wait. It never comes.

'God no, commissioner, please do not speak with him. He'll probably be wired' was, I imagine, the line of conversation. And while I had indeed 'wired' many conversations, I was not there to compromise or catch out the Hercules Moth. I really did just want to have that cup of tea and a talk. But the Hercules is not seen again. He takes to the wing, in this instance by summoning the Met's helicopter. Liz and I watch it soar up and away, and I recall the prophetic words said to a spotty young constable in the training ground a few hundred metres from the landing strip by the Scottish philosopher, who warned me it was a jungle. Police chiefs don't start the day wanting to make a difference – they start it hoping to make sure no one makes them look bad. I get that now. And as for Marv? Well, he was always on the button.

When my retirement papers come through, they do not include the 'exemplary' service certificate that was promised and should have accompanied it. After the medal ceremony, the DPS had immediately called the relevant department, speaking to the man who would issue it. He was then visited by the DPS, who ordered him not to. I recorded the subsequent conversation I had with him: 'It doesn't make any sense. It has never been done before. You should have it.' He tells me he has made a note of the incident. Good luck with that, I think, but it's all too late.

Trawler towns have always done a good funeral, seasoned, you might say, over many years. Plenty of practice. After burying Pa came the death of my best friend. Bud. A brain tumour. I'd known he was unwell for some time, but the end was swift. Too quick to comprehend. A few weeks earlier, I'd received a call from his fiancée. He had found love late and had big plans, but, like many Trawler Town dreams, they would never be realised. She'd suggested it might be a good time to travel north and visit. I'd arrived the next day and was shocked at his decline – the loss of mental acuity was stark. Bud was already leaving. I wanted to shout *don't*.

'A bastard tumour, mate!' It had taken residence inside his brain, forcing him to repeat nonsensical statements, but he greeted me as warmly as ever.

'Na'then! Good to see you, mate.'

'You too, mate.'

'Bit rum, all this.' I hesitated until he nodded at the television, and I realised he was referring to the TV. A decade earlier, in London, we'd laughed at his adventures as a gun-for-hire senior detective on a Commonwealth contract – it too had been described as a 'rum' adventure. That night, we drank too much, reminisced on a childhood in sight of water and made plans to one day ride coast to coast across American sunsets on a pair of Harley-Davidson Fat Boys. 'The Cod Head Tour'.

More for my benefit, I convinced myself the Bud of old was still in there, fighting. After all, he'd fought this with all his considerable might. We shared an awkward, gentle embrace before parting. I wondered if he knew this was goodbye. He smiled. 'Sail well, mate,' which made little sense at the time, but means so much more now. For a moment, I think the twinkle had returned, that we would sit down in the dunes with a beer once again, and roar at the world. He died ten days later.

I'm sitting in a modernist church, numb – not from cold but

from sorrow – and next to me is an old trawler skipper I first met as a teenager. A salt-scarred fisherman as tough as the decks he stood upon. He nods and shakes my hand – a proper handshake. 'Some day, mate, eh?' His gnarled hands, knuckles like mashed walnuts, grip the pew in front. Fishermen do not care for funerals, normally waiting until the last minute to enter the church. He sits quietly with his wife. Trawler Town, any trawler town, could be distilled through this one man. There's a story, I think to myself, my eyes desperately avoiding Bud's coffin, while my mind avoids all of the memories.

When the service ends, I help carry him out of the church into the morning air, spared the smell of processed fishmeal. That unique aroma long since vanished with all the other industries linked to fishing, withered on the vine of coastal 'progress' the length and breadth of the country. Roads are closed, police outriders escorting the large cortège as we walk to Trawler Town's one cemetery that stands a stone's throw from the dunes where in our youth we made plans and shared cans. We walk through streets once densely populated by fishermen and their kin, past Bud's childhood home on 'Skippers' Row', where his grandfather, father and uncles laughed with family members between voyages, plotting the next 'trip of fish'. In our Oxford bags and penny round collars, we planned different futures up in his loft. 'Your bedroom is in the roof, mate!' I didn't know anyone who slept in a loft conversion – it was less a sign of prosperity, and more a sign of the strength of his community. You stay in your street, with your kin. You make your house bigger.

Is it my imagination or do the curtains twitch as we pass? His pa did not share our enthusiasm for northern soul and Motown, often bellowing up the stairs, 'Turn it down! They can hear it at sea!'

Stepmother had by now realised her plans, pooling resources with her favourite daughter to buy Bud's childhood home. I focus on the coffin. It was a fine send-off, worthy of any feted skipper. His wake was epic, and he would have led from the front had he been able to join us.

Anatomy of the Ring

In those early days in the police, when it was all in front of me, the Mountain Goat warned that Copland was like a jungle, a unique wilderness. He was right, but it might also be described as a boxing ring, even a ring within a ring. Its promoters – who never step into the ring themselves – are Home Office mandarins and 'board-level' senior management – when was that term coined? – hoping to engage or distract the public with a never-ending display of pugilistic policing. In the ring within the ring are an increasingly disheartened rank and file, and it is here that constables and sergeants do battle. The exhibition is promoted by a bloated, top-heavy structure of overpaid management. Four supervisory ranks above inspector could easily be removed with no negative impact on leadership while creating huge fiscal opportunity for reform and enhancement to the role, numbers, and terms and conditions of front-line rank and file. At least remove the rank of *chief* inspector and *chief* superintendent– way too many chiefs, not enough constables. It would save north of £175 million a year, which could be better spent on more front-line officers. Nor do we need 43 police services for such a small landmass. But the ring within a ring does not want reform, transparency or even progress – status quo is the stated aim. Time and time again, the police are found wanting.

To understand the now, the chaos, the absolute despair in public opinion as time and time again the police are found wanting you must look back decades. The relentless march towards a set culture of failing upwards. A dynamic shift in style of management engineered to produce careers not capability. I remember hearing a commodore's rousing speech while in the navy, at the end of which all present would have walked through walls, never mind seawater. A level of inspiring leadership echoed to the same young man in a submarine sinking off the Barra Fan but never once witnessed in Copland.

I am at a loss to understand why a commodore – one rank below admiral – who will regularly command a carrier battle group of ten warships or more, is rewarded with a salary half that of a deputy commissioner, whose station became famous for witnessing the brutal murder of a police officer on the parliamentary estate. The constable in question did not hesitate to run towards danger and died because of it, while the then head of the organisation in which he served chose to lock the doors of his vehicle and observe the tragedy. A defining moment.

In the military he would have been shunned. In Copland 'board level' colleagues rushed to bolster his reputation with puffery. Birds of a feather. For the colleagues of the stricken officer I suspect a different kind of plumage came to mind. A white feather. One tragedy summing up years of disconnect. It will only change with the wholesale reform of top-tier leadership and geography placing rank-and-file officers front and centre.

I didn't beat the Met, and I was never going to. There's an old saying in boxing: size matters. One factor that supports this adage is a fighter's reach, and one might argue as an institution the police have such a long reach that it makes them untouchable. They survive largely unchanged, the undisputed champion of the world in self-preservation.

I believed the reason for my long suspension was my whistle-blowing the DPS's plan to use me as their inside man against those they considered their actual targets, then taint me after I reported the offer. The Dassie's inertia in revisiting the long-term covert operations in which south London police corruption clearly comprised personal safety and operational outcomes, was rooted in a fear of what, and who, would be exposed if the lid was lifted. I was the 'sacrifice' that they were happy to live with. But it was more than that – much more. Several officers directly concerned with my case and treatment later faced allegations of dishonesty and impropriety.

The two officers charged with justifying my continued suspension both faced serious questions regarding their integrity. The Egret was judged to have misled the public and the commissioner in a report by the IPCC into the shooting dead of an innocent man, Jean Charles de Menezes, and was openly criticised by a deputy assistant commissioner in his memoirs for his cavalier attitude to protocols, and labelled 'a dodgy geezer' when questioned by a senior parliamentary committee regarding his selective memory. The Carrion Beetle was suspended from duty, facing allegations of predatory sexual behaviour by a senior Home Office civil servant, with the Met settling the case out of court for a substantial six-figure sum. He retired before he could face a disciplinary hearing, taking up a job with a transport company to which he had rather fortuitously, some might argue, awarded a lucrative contract before retiring.

The Snipe figured prominently in two high-profile murder convictions that were overturned in light of concerns about surprisingly similar issues regarding the integrity of evidential exhibits. The Wombat was arrested for threatening police officers in a drunken fracas, and later faced allegations of threats to kill and was served with a harassment order by the courts in relation to a former girlfriend.

Rumbling along in the background were dozens of complaints from police officers and civilians working for the Dassie, which eventually exploded and led to him being removed from his command. All of the allegations, which are in the public domain, were unrelated, nor prompted by the Flying Squad inquiry. I could go on, but there are far more precise accounts regarding the integrity of those I challenged.

I discovered that not only did the Komodo – the only corrupt officer ultimately deemed reliable enough to be used in court – not make a single allegation against me, he wasn't even questioned to see if we had any relationship – because we didn't. It would have been far easier for me to challenge the allegations, and certainly more transparent, if all the interviews with the two corrupt officers had been recorded, as protocols required, but they weren't – not one single interview.

But in the midst of all the darkness, I had done something that I believe more than anything put an end to any chance I had of returning to my job. I stumbled upon another big beast in Copland's jungle behaving badly, and this more than anything decided my future. And it all started in Trawler Town.

After the late Bud's call, asking when I would next be heading north, we met up. We sat at the rugby club with a beer. He saw the nature of my suspension was having a huge impact on my health, and as a senior detective himself he knew enough of the ways of this world to suspect that God's work was at play. In fact, the age-old practice had recently upset the equilibrium in his own patch, and he'd felt compelled to share the incident. I understood why.

One evening a 999 call was made by a child regarding an assault by his father on his mother. 'Please come quickly. Daddy is hitting mummy *again*.' The call ended abruptly, but the operator traced it, and a car was dispatched. The address was a police property, the grace-and-favour home of a very senior officer. The victim, bloodied; the children, upset; the 'management board-level' senior officer, smiling. All a misunderstanding, an accident – but not to the constables. They, however, were talked out of pursuing it further, doing what should have been done, by the duty officer who pitched up. He had been recently promoted and could see problems ahead – God's work. Think of your career, he told the two constables, for everyone must think about their future when God's at work. So they left the scene. But this wasn't the end of the story.

The next day, the very same senior officer who was involved in the violent domestic walked into the communication room of the force HQ. All emergency calls are recorded. He was there to wipe the tape, to bury the truth, to ensure he remained travelling in the first-class carriage on the blue gravy train.

But the dissent grew louder, others joined the 'debate' about whether this was right. In the end, the very senior officer was advised to move, quickly, to pastures new. So he headed off to where the streets are paved with gold braid, and here the Clouded Yellow was welcomed with open arms into Metland by all the moths and butterflies simply too busy to be concerned with such . . . distractions.

And decades on, doing God's work and not the right thing means the repercussions still land, like punches in the night, for the women and girls subjected to violence from police partners, or like Sarah Everard, a killer rapist with a warrant card. All of which is never simply a case of a few rotten apples in the barrel, but an indictment against those who seed, plant and maintain the entire orchard.

Before Bud had even finished telling me his story, as his words pierce and sting, I felt *him* wake, rise and walk towards the ring – Marv. There was a number of ways I might have reacted to the story of the abusive senior officer, but in my state of mind, full of pain and rage, I whistleblew the incident, to journalists. Sickened by the utter fucking hypocrisy. Only later did I realise I was outed as the source by one of the reporters I briefed. Unwittingly in all probability, but that was that. That was me. Finished. 'You should never get into the ring angry, son, you never win.' Pa.

My suspension had, up to that point, continued primarily to prevent me from ever being considered a witness of truth, the mistaken belief that wider knowledge of the offer to become an informant would somehow be used to undermine not only the investigation into the Flying Squad but others too, I suspect. From there, as I became more vociferous, it became more about reputational management, protecting the further advancement of those officers who were increasingly aware of the concerns that were being voiced about an emerging pattern of behaviour. The Dassie, the Carrion Beetle, the Egret and the Clouded Yellow, who fled to the protection of pastures new only to discover that questions were now being asked of the 999 incident, and why that was. Factoring in the Machiavellian web, the line spun to Merseyside that I did not wish to speak with them, it is little wonder I thought suicide would make things a whole lot easier.

Bud's information came while at a point when the DPS could so easily have found reverse, that gear shift the DPS superintendent claimed was difficult to find. I was still suspended, but could have been reinstated, and my mental health would not have deteriorated to the extent it did. But sharing knowledge that I was aware of a cover-up involving a board-level cop ensured that I would remain so. When the assistant commissioner's staff officer bowled into the clinic, had I missed the real reason he was there? Was it linked as much to the Clouded Yellow as anything else?

'He's an internal terrorist, that cunt, he has to go.' Marv's assessment was probably on the money. It was certainly shared by others. There have been times in my life when I have wished I was more like him, Marv, more confrontational – in this instance I suspect it would have all been over a lot sooner had I been. You can think *too* much in the ring, Pa.

New Beginnings

I am officially retired on my birthday – a strange gift . . . What to do now? Nothing for a while, fix up an old house, try to fix myself. Eventually I get a job with the local council, running street markets, the banter with market traders often no different than the banter of a long-term sting, except that there's nothing in the tail. It helps a little.

Even while I was suspended, I was thinking about my life after the police, at one time finding myself in a nervous interview with a wonderful lady called Biddy Peppin, artist and senior lecturer at the University of East London. Twice I'd attempted and failed to pluck up enough courage to attend the interview, to see if a mature student with just a couple of old-money O levels, who might be capable of infiltrating a sink estate or a gilded enclave but little else, could undertake an honours degree programme. Given I was now in the main a mumbling, monosyllabic wreck, his confidence shot, it didn't look promising, but on the third attempt I made it to her office and, surprisingly, she offered me a place on her course, Film History, to which I was attracted for a host of reasons.

'Film, you cock! What about fuckin' carpentry?'

'Not very practical, son. What are going do with it?'

It's a complicated road, not least because of my psychiatric treatment, but I get there in the end. Had I not submitted my thesis, on police representation within British cinema, unsupervised to avoid further delays, a first was within my grasp, but I didn't care. It was utterly transformative.

I join a theatre group, a semi-professional Shakespeare company that continues my self-exploration.

'What the flying fuck are we doing here?'

'Oh shut up, Marv. Listen to yourself for once.'

Twice he wins and I drive out of the car park without leaving my vehicle, but after two years, I get in through the door, spending two seasons in this idyllic amphitheatre, cast in *Macbeth* and *Coriolanus*. Given the past, my casting feels accurate.

Meanwhile, at the suggestion of my solicitor, I submit evidence to an independent inquiry into professional standards and employment matters, even though being critical of the Met is a futile exercise, only serving to irritate old wounds and poke vengeful beasts. Nevertheless, when I am sent a copy of the report at its conclusion, in it I find ample evidence of God's work. The inquiry commissioned two senior former detectives to review policy files.

'They comment on poor practice in relation to policy files. The files they saw did not record all the important decisions.' Which was the plan, I suppose. There was *'a failure to adhere to the level of professionalism that would apply to criminal investigations involving the public, disproportionality and failure to use policy files effectively'*. *'Not pursuing lines of enquiry quickly, which would have resolved the case quickly'* – that was

the last thing the key individuals wanted to do. It was, as suggested in the report, *'all part of a picture of DPS officers operating outside the constraints imposed on ordinary investigations. We see no compelling reason for this to be tolerated and, once again, this indicates a need for proper supervision and oversight.'* Oversight was very much in play when it came to reputational management and, of course, the report changed little going forward. I went and listened to some of the hearings, watched as senior officers huddled and whispered, and realised I need to be a thousand miles away from the jungle.

A TV producer tries to recruit me to work undercover in a prison for a major documentary. I turn it down. Mentally, I know I am in no condition though I pretend otherwise. I also know I need light not dark. Instead, I audition for a drama school in London, focusing on a course that will still allow me to work. I'm offered a place and encouraged to accept it by the offer of a bursary following my audition. I don't know what to do.

'Well, fuckin' accept it, you cunt.' That's the thing with Marv and me – joined at the hip but polar opposites at times.

Somehow, I completed the film studies course, with the help and encouragement of wonderful lecturers, not least of all Raymond Durgnat, a hugely talented film historian, writer and academic whose encyclopaedic knowledge of many of the films Grandma introduced me to allowed me to reach into my past with different eyes and escape to far-off worlds. I lack confidence, yet my conversations with him are always encouraging. He tutors a screenwriting module and suggests a life lived offers a rich archive of opportunity to tap when the time is right. If nothing else, he recommends I invest in a pencil and notebook. 'Haven't you got one lying around from your former life? What was it again?' There is a twinkle in his eye. After I tell him I have always been interested in drama school, he suggests I bugger off and do it rather than 'dither'.

I bugger off and join the circus that rolls into town in the form of a major film shoot: Joe Wright's *Pride & Prejudice*. This, it turns out, is the final nudge in the direction of happy. I spot an ad offering work as an extra on the film and I get three weeks. I spend every day when not involved watching the principal actors and crew, fascinated, keen to understand the medium from a different perspective than a lecture hall or screen.

In the second week I'm given couple of walk-ons.

'Do you think you could improvise something for us if I give you an outline, Liam?' asks an assistant director.

'The fuck we can, mate, just point where!'

'Yes, I'd love to,' I say, toning Marv down. I may not be trained, or know which way the wind blows, but this? This I can do. On one take, a smartly dressed soldier (a re-enactment player) feels so aggrieved at the realism of my improvised invective, he tells me to 'Fuck right off and do one!'

My improvisation does not end up in the film, perhaps preparing me for the life ahead. I also realise that as a johnny-come-lately my best roles might be behind me. But it feels right.

Joe Wright is staying at an inn in the heart of the town where I often meet a pal for an ale and which is a hub for the actors and extras. Later, I'm in the bar with my pal, and he spots someone approaching me. 'That's the director. He just waved at you. He's walking over,' he says.

Before I can reply, Joe has threaded his way over. 'That was really good, man, what you did this afternoon. You got it straight away,' he says to a dumbstruck eejit who can only whisper a mumbled response.

'Tanks, peally enjibbled dooding it.'

'Stop gibbering, you soppy cunt. He says that to all the extras. He's just squeezing the flesh.' I think Marv's squeezing my larynx. Thankfully, my friend pitches in with his mellow public-school tones: 'Actually, he wants to be an actor. He has a good offer from a drama school, but he's hesitating – thinks it's too late.'

'You should, man. It's never too late. You've got an interesting face – do it.'

I had deferred the offer for 18 months, but they now need an answer or the bursary will have to go to someone else.

'Why the fuck would that work out, you utter knob?'

'Because it's now or never, Marv.'

The Script's in the Post

Moving back to London to train with the Actors Company marks the very end of my marriage to Liz. In one terrible hopeless argument, she accuses me of never really wanting her, that all I ever really wanted was stability, a home. This cuts like a knife. I can't respond. Liz and I have stumbled on, but the marriage is damaged beyond any kind of repair, unable to find ground on which to heal. We have both been through too much. Liz battles her own demons, and I am helpless, unable to understand. I will never regret meeting Liz, or the comfort and love she offered that I struggled to accept, or even comprehend, and I will always regret the impact my job had on her life.

Marv too is silent, listening in sadness, just he did as a child. What hurt most is that Liz was right, but I can't accept it. Because I of all people know that the notion of *home* is a falsehood. And I'm too tired to try again. As for *him*, he too is weary. For years it was his bark that kept me going, often when I had nothing left; if he were a dog, he'd be on the floor now, breathless panting, unable to stand. Still there, watching, and listening, faithful to the end. Always a wild spirit. A street dog.

You see, though Marv started out as my imaginary friend, he became so much more. He calms my thoughts when I'm too frightened to speak, silenced by uncertainty and sometimes violence. If I can't find the words, any words, he does. He was never a threat, not really. Marv came in peace, and I was grateful. Nevertheless, it takes me decades to understand that it is okay to say that Marv was, is, my friend. Because he hasn't left. He just kind of sits in his chair now, a tired old dog. He's seen a lot. I imagine he's grey around the muzzle. Still as potty-mouthed as ever.

Our final reckoning came over a painting I bought when coming to the end of my degree. In my final year, having taken time out when my mental health wasn't too good, I joined the class from the previous year in order to complete an art elective. I was partnered with three other students for a joint presentation. One gentle, quietly spoken Finnish student, Suvi, said hello, introducing herself almost in a whisper but illuminating the room the moment our presentation began. It ended the day on a high. Afterwards, we all went our separate ways. It was unseasonably warm, and because of this Suvi took a different route home and a few hours later was dead, murdered as she walked while talking with her mother on the phone. It was a shocking act of brutality. The killer was stopped earlier in the day by police in relation to an unrelated assault but allowed to go on his way.

Marv opened up a can of corrosive guilt: I am, *was*, a good detective. I should be doing my job in *'the job'*, protecting students, not sat on my arse with them pretending to be somebody else.

I raged at the machine, asking myself who I was trying to kid in my useless inertia. It lasted for months, years, and became focused on a painting. I had bought *Fragments* by another lecturer at the university, the artist Teresa Witz, who would go on to become the official artist of the London Olympics. Drawn hypnotically to it, inspired by the Vanitas theme, it held my gaze, but after the news of Suvi's death, whatever beauty I had originally seen in its form, I now couldn't look at it. Yet I forced myself, and it began to haunt me.

'It's that painting, you fuckin' idiot.'

Fragments?

'What's wrong with you? It's a nightmare.'

'Fuck you. It's not what I see.'

'The fuck you do. You're full of shit, always have been. Someone is murdered and you, you buy a painting? Cunt!'

'That wasn't the timeline . . . I—'

'Timeline! You're not a cunting detective any more, get it?'

And then the line I had feared for years, thrown as ferociously as Ma ever whipcracked her tongue or Pa threw a fist: *'Who the fuck are you?'*

I didn't, couldn't, reply.

I travelled a distance leaving Trawler Town, all manner of water all manner of weather. No map. One compass. All kinds of water under the bridge. Ivan the Terrible once shouted down from the wheelhouse that if the going was hard, the arrival was sweeter. I didn't understand then, and anyway he was pissed at the time. I did realise that my education was incomplete, though, and in that there was hope.

And yet still death visited, making my quest for . . . well, whatever it was, it was complicated. I am cut in half by the death of my brother, Our Kid. Suicide. He put himself into an angry sea, knowing I would understand why. When Ma died suddenly, six weeks later, I found myself standing in an empty house on the Welsh coast, feeling more like a detective than a son. Desperately searching for one solid clue that might make some kind of sense of it all.

For a time, the painting Marv so objected to hung in an unused room before I eventually bubble-wrapped it and stowed it away for over a decade. I tried to loan it to a friend, 'I haven't got the space.' In reality, I meant head space. Because whatever beauty I thought I saw in it, all I could now see was my past, shattered fragments reflected in glorious colour, and I couldn't bear it. A vow never to unwrap it again, until I found whatever it was I searched for.

That peace finally came when I began to write about my experiences. I was told on day one of my UC training that our only limit was imagination, and I believe this even more now. I count myself blessed for a series of brief encounters, passing acquaintances and chance meetings imbued with kindness and wisdom, which, even in the darkness, set me on a new trajectory. But there's one person, more than any other, who has made all this possible. Someone who looked beyond my emotional scars and, to my utter amazement, loved me in equal measure. Her wisdom restored not only my confidence but my belief in humanity and, in that, there remains a tenuous connection with the past.

There is an old term for a UC, now redundant, based on the simple fact that detectives were individuals who sought to expose criminal networks by purchasing friendship, trust, with an illusion. They were known as 'Buyers', accumulating the wealth of intelligence. Becoming part of that small exclusive band, I mistakenly thought it would lead to the one commodity I had pursued my entire life: peace. But I was wrong. What I sought was not to be found in the fraternity of shadows. It is built on very different foundations. And if you believe the inner voice is capable of tears, I can tell you Marv cried tears of joy for the first time in his life in the early hours of an autumnal morning in a Yorkshire maternity ward, 13 years ago. And I finally found exactly what it was I searched for. Family. And that you cannot buy. Trust me, I tried.

As for *Fragments*, it now hangs prominently on a wall in a house full of love. It is my daughter's favourite. Why, I ask? 'The explosion of colours, it's like there was a . . . glitch! But it's all right, Dada.' She takes my hand. 'Because it all worked out . . .'

Funny thing is, *he* likes it too.

Acknowledgements

The whole cast:
Robyn
Richard
Editors one and all
Anna
Ebury
Conville & Walsh

Friendship above all:
Michael
Paul
Liz
Duncan1
Duncan2
Lee

Kindness and inspiration:
Adam
Andrew

ACKNOWLEDGEMENTS

Francis
Ray
Keeley
And a docklands campus in all weather.

The kindness of a stranger in Cumbrian cafe whose hand led
from wilderness to humanity.

Pa. So much more was possible.

Our Kid.

And finally. Nothing but nothing without and the reason why:

Julia Christian Meredith.